'Dr Majumdar's edition of the letters between Rabindranath Tagore and James Cousins illuminates a little-known friendship of the great Bengali writer and thinker with the Irish writer, teacher and Theosophist who made India his second home. Majumdar's meticulous annotation of the correspondence and his wide-reaching introduction to the book make this an important contribution to the study of Tagore and the connections between Indian and Irish culture.'

Nicholas Grene, *Emeritus Professor of English Literature, Trinity College Dublin, Ireland*

'Sirshendu Majumdar has brought to light a correspondence by two minds who fostered art, literature, and education in a time of upheaval and transnational change. Dr. Majumdar's insights and impeccable scholarship reveals a friendship that was both more intimate and earnest than many literary friendships, including that of W.B. Yeats and Tagore. These letters are remarkable for their honesty, humor, and professional hopes—they veer in tone from reverential to professional to jocular. Majumdar's expert overview helpfully puts their words in their cultural and historical contexts. By editing the letters of these two remarkable friends, educators, and cultural leaders, Majumdar has done a great service to students and scholars of Indian and Irish revivalism, as well as postcolonial studies. In reading these exchanges, we witness a rare exception to colonialist dynamics: Tagore's and Cousins's shared, and enviable, vision for a universal humanism.'

Joseph Lennon, Associate Dean, International and Interdisciplinary Initiatives; Emily C. Riley Director of Irish Studies; Professor, Department of English, Villanova University, USA, and author of *Irish Orientalism: A Literary and Intellectual History*

'As James Cousins wrote to Rabindranath Tagore, 'Poets get put to queer jobs'. A quarter century of correspondence between these poets, carefully edited and contextualised by Sirshendu Majumdar, demonstrates a close ideological affinity between Irish cultural nationalism and Indian cultural self-assertion. Both poets proposed an alternative modernity, challenging the modes of metropolitan modernity in Britain and Europe, because each worked in the context of decolonisation. Practical educators and organisers of education, their shared pedagogical ideals and project — a humanist and counter-imperialist universalism — integrated arts and crafts, music and dance, poetry and philosophy into a holistic approach to the revival of the nation and world reform.'

Seán Golden, *Former Professor, Universitat Autònoma de Barcelona, Spain*

RABINDRANATH TAGORE AND JAMES HENRY COUSINS

This book presents a set of original letters exchanged between Rabindranath Tagore, the first Asian to win the Nobel Prize for Literature, and the eminent Irish poet and theosophist, James Henry Cousins. Through these letters, the volume explores their shared ideas of culture, art, aesthetics, and education in India; aspects of Irish Orientalism; Irish literary revival; theosophy, eastern knowledge, and spiritualism; cross-cultural dialogue and friendship; Renaissance in India; anti-imperialism; nationalism; internationalism; and cosmopolitanism. The book reveals a hitherto unexplored facet concerning two leading thinkers in the history of ideas in a transnational context.

With its lucid style, extensive annotations and a comprehensive Introduction, this book will be an essential read for scholars and researchers of Indian literature, Bengali literature, comparative literature, South Asian studies, Tagore studies, modern Indian history, philosophy, cultural studies, education, political studies, postcolonial studies, India studies, Irish history, and Irish literature. It will also interest general readers and the Bengali diaspora.

Sirshendu Majumdar is Associate Professor of English, Bolpur College, West Bengal, India. He is the author of *Yeats and Tagore: A Comparative Study of Cross-Cultural Poetry, Nationalist Politics, Hyphenated Margins and the Ascendancy of the Mind* (2013) and co-editor of *Rabindranath Tagore: Humanity and Cultural Affinity* (2016). His areas of interest are Irish studies, WB Yeats, Rabindranath Tagore, modern European literature, nineteenth- and early-twentieth-century Bengal, print culture and translation. He was a Trinity Long Room Hub Visiting Fellow at Trinity College Dublin, 2018–2019.

RABINDRANATH TAGORE AND JAMES HENRY COUSINS

A Conversation in Letters, 1915–1940

Edited with an Introduction, Notes, and Appendices by Sirshendu Majumdar

LONDON AND NEW YORK

First published 2022
By Routledge
2 Park Square, Milton Park, Abingdon, Oxon OX14 4RN

and by Routledge
605 Third Avenue, New York, NY 10158

Routledge is an imprint of the Taylor & Francis Group, an informa business

British Library Cataloguing-in-Publication Data
A catalogue record for this book is available from the British Library

Library of Congress Cataloging-in-Publication Data
A catalog record has been requested for this book

ISBN: 978-0-367-67650-6 (hbk)
ISBN: 978-0-367-71114-6 (pbk)
ISBN: 978-1-003-14935-4 (ebk)

DOI: 10.4324/9781003149354

Typeset in Bembo
By Deanta Global Publishing Services, Chennai, India

In memory of
Bikash Chakravarty

CONTENTS

FIGURES

PREFACE

Rabindranath Tagore (Thākur, in Bengali; 1861–1941) was a poet, dramatist, novelist, short story writer, music composer and writer of songs, essayist, painter, founder of a school and a university, educationist, and thinker. He is the first non-Western recipient of the Nobel Prize for Literature (1913) and is modern India's cultural icon. During his long eighty years of life, he produced an astounding amount of writing and more than two thousand five hundred drawings and paintings; he also wrote thousands of letters to his relatives and associates, and also to friends, Indian as well as western.

James Henry Cousins (1873–1956) was an Irish poet, dramatist, journalist, and teacher, and, later on, an art critic; he was also a theosophist. He made a significant contribution to the early phase of the Irish Revival. He migrated to India along with his wife, Margaret Cousins, in 1915, to serve as the literary sub-editor of the paper *New India*, started by Annie Besant of the Theosophical Society in Adyar, in Madras (now Chennai). Both James and Margaret Cousins were active in the suffrage movement before they arrived in India. Margaret Cousins was accomplished in music, and wrote books on music and also on Asian and Indian womanhood.

I have added brief chronologies at the beginning to give a preliminary idea of the diverse nature of Tagore's and Cousins's literary works and activities. A detailed chronology of Tagore, prepared by Kshitish Roy, can be found in *Rabindranath Tagore 1861–1941: A Centenary Volume* (1961). Alan Denson's painstaking work *James H. Cousins and Margaret E. Cousins: A Bio-Bibliographical Survey* (1967) provides a detailed chronology of James and Margaret Cousins.

In the Introduction, I have attempted to draw the broader historical and cultural contexts of the letters – India's and Ireland's cross-cultural relationship and their decolonising process; the world shattered by World Wars; racial, political, economic, and other conflicts among the nations, and how these two seminal minds, from the margins of the empire, emerged as cosmopolitan thinkers who not only thought of their respective nations, but also strove to create an alternative world, more humane and unified, through their creative, intellectual, and educational efforts. The broader issues on which Tagore and Cousins converse in the letters are art, literature, nationalism, and internationalism; their respective institutions and their ideas of education occupy a large space; but, as a whole, the world of these letters is variegated and extensive. As such, I have added notes on many of the points. The list of works consulted in a volume of this kind may be helpful as a reference guide. In the Appendix, I have included representative letters, lectures, essays and interviews of both Tagore and Cousins which are difficult to obtain, and which have direct and indirect bearing on the letters. There is also an Index at the end.

ACKNOWLEDGEMENTS

The letters of Rabindranath Tagore and James Henry Cousins are in the holding of the Rabindra-Bhavana Archive, Visva-Bharati, Santiniketan, West Bengal, India. The letters are not continuous, as most exchanges of this kind are not; some of the letters may have been lost, or there may not have been responses from either end. Still, they help us to construct the story of a remarkable friendship.

I am grateful to the authorities of Rabindra-Bhavana, Visva-Bharati, particularly to Professor Amal Pal, the Director (officiating) of Rabindra-Bhavana, for granting me permission to bring out the letters, two drafts of a Tagore poem, Tagore's letter to the Nobel Committee and to include the photographs and facsimiles of letters in this volume.

I am also indebted to Nilanjan Bandyopadhyay, Special Officer at Rabindra-Bhavana, who extended immense support and help all along.

I am particularly grateful to Joseph Lennon for sharing with me some rare writings of James Cousins.

Sukanta Chaudhuri, Emeritus Professor at Jadavpur University, my teacher, suggested the new title of the book. I am grateful to him, as always. Professor R Shiv Kumar and Sushovan Adhikari gave generous help; my thanks are due to them.

I must acknowledge my indebtedness to a few others who gave me immense help and support.

Utpal Mitra, and at a later stage, Shovan Ruj, at the Rabindra-Bhavana Archive, gave unstinting assistance. Supriya Roy corrected some errors and provided me with materials to which I did not have access. Asish Hazra, former librarian at Rabindra-Bhavana, has also been helpful in many ways. Sanjib Mukhopadhyay gave the much-needed technical support and some editorial advice, even while convalescing from his illness. Bairam Khan, my colleague, and Nemai Chand Saha of Visva-Bharati Library gave help at crucial moments. I am grateful to them all.

My visiting fellowship at Trinity Long Room Hub, though on a different project, enabled me to have access to some materials relevant to this volume in Trinity College Dublin Library and the National Library of Ireland. I thank the members of the staff of the Hub and the two libraries.

I remain immensely indebted to my first reviewer whose excellent suggestions encouraged me to substantially extend the scope of the Introduction. However, I alone am responsible for any of the volume's shortcomings and errors.

Antara Ray Chaudhury and Rimina Mohapatra at Routledge India deserve special thanks for their immense patience, advice, and support.

Basudhara, my wife, and Snigdhadipta, my daughter, remain the unacknowledged collaborators of this work.

CHRONOLOGY

Rabindranath Tagore's creative output both in Bengali and in English (original and in translation) was monumental; moreover, he was engaged in manifold activities as an artist, playwright, composer of music, and song writer, as a landlord and promoter of rural welfare and agricultural co-operatives, as the founder of a school and a university, as a thinker and a public intellectual. Coupled with all this were his incessant travels and innumerable lectures, at home and abroad. The following brief chronology mentions Tagore's works in Bengali and English and his travels, lecture tours, educational and other activities to offer an impression of this remarkable life.

James Cousins was involved in the suffrage movement and was a major figure in the early phase of the Irish Literary Revival. He was a poet, playwright, journalist, art and literary critic, a schoolteacher, and a theosophist. In India he continued with his creative activities, while devoting himself to promoting education under the aegis of the Theosophical Society and indigenous art and culture. He was visiting professor in Japan and the USA and also went on lecture tours to many European countries and America, where he put up exhibitions of Indian paintings and spoke mostly on Indian art and culture. The subsequent chronology highlights Cousins's major works and activities.

Rabindranath Tagore: A Brief Chronology

1861: Born on Tuesday, 7 May at Jorasanko, Calcutta, India.
1878: *Kabi-kāhini*, a verse narrative is published; travels to England.
1881: First verse play *Vālmiki Pratibhā* is staged in the family house; begins composing his first novel, *Bouthākuranir Hāt.*
1883: Married to Mrinalini Devi on 9 December.

1884: *Chhobi o Gān, Prakritir Pratishodh, Saisab Sangit* – poems and songs.

1886–1887: *Kodi o Komol* – poems; *Rājashri* – novel.

1888–1895: *Māyarkhelā* – verse drama; *Rājā o Rāni* – play; makes an attempt to read Goethe's *Faust* in original German; travels to England for the second time; major plays *Visarjan* (Sacrifice) and *Chitrāngadā* (Chitrā); *Sonār tari* (The Golden Boat) – poems; short stories; *Yuropyātrir diary* (Traveller to Europe) – accounts of his travels to England; sets up *swadeshi* (indigenous) stores jointly with his nephews.

1896–1900: Takes over the editorship of the journal *Bharati*; *Kanikā, Kshanikā* – poems; *Galpaguccha* – short stories.

1901–1905: *Brahmacharyashrama* (the Santiniketan School) founded on 22 December 1901; *Naivedya* – poems; *Chokher Bāli* (A Grain of Sand) – novel; *Rabindra Granthābali* – collected poems, plays, and stories; takes active part in the anti-partition (of Bengal) movement and introduces the ceremony of Rākhibandhan (tying a thread on the hand as symbol of fraternity among different communities); *Ātmashakti* – book of essays and lectures.

1906–1911: *Bhāratvarsha*– essays on Indian history and society; *Kheyā* – poems; *Naukādubi* – novel; several volumes of essays, including those on literature and literary theory; book of sermons entitled *Santiniketan*; *Sikshā* – essays on education; *Gorā* – novel; *Gitānjali* – poems.

1912: Third visit to England; meets Yeats and other poets and intellectuals; starts revising the draft poems of *Gitanjali: Song Offerings* with Yeats's assistance; *Gitanjali: Song Offerings* published with an introduction by WB Yeats on 1(?) November by the India Society; buys Surul Kuthi, which later becomes the centre of Rural Reconstruction Institute of Visva-Bharati; delivers lectures in America; *Dākghar* (The Post Office) – play; *Jivansmriti* (reminiscences); *Achalāyatan* – play.

1913: Awarded the Nobel Prize for Literature; *The Gardener*; *The Crescent Moon*; *Chitra* – play; *Glimpses of Bengal Life* (short stories in translation); *The Post Office* staged at the Abbey Theatre; conferred D Litt (*Honoris Causa*) by Calcutta University.

1914: *The King of the Dark Chamber* – play; *The Post Office* published by Cuala Press and then by Macmillan; *Sadhana: The Realization of Life* – lectures delivered in America in 1912; *One Hundred Poems of Kabir* (translation); Charles Freer Andrews joins the Santiniketan school; commencement of translation of his English works into several European languages; 20 students of Gandhi's South Africa Phoenix Farm take up residence at Santiniketan school; *Gitimālya, Gitāli, Utsarga* – poems.

1915: *The Maharani of Arakan*; a self-help programme is taken up on 10 March at Gandhi's instance – the day is still observed at Visva-Bharati; conferred Knighthood on 3 June, the King's birthday; contributes a sonnet on Shakespeare to the *Shakespeare Tercentenary Commemoration Volume* at the request of the Shakespeare Society of England.

1916: *Fruit Gathering*; *Hungry Stones and Other Stories*; *Stray Birds*; two lectures in Japan 'The Nation' and 'The Spirit of Japan'; resentment among a section of the Japanese; meets Paul and Mirra Richard in Japan; lectures on nationalism at several places across America; lectures criticised at many places; *Phālguni* – play; *Balāka* – poems; *Chaturanga* (Quartet) – novel; *Ghare Bāire* – novel.

1917: *My Reminiscences*; *Sacrifice and Other Plays*; *The Cycle of Spring* – play; *Personality*: essays – lectures delivered in America; *Nationalism* – collection of lectures delivered in Japan and America in 1916; protests against the arrest of Annie Besant, advocate of Home Rule for India.

1918: Foundation of Visva-Bharati on 22 December 1918; *Gitanjali and Fruit-Gathering*; *Lover's Gift and Crossing*; *Māshi and other Stories*; *Stories from Tagore*; *The Parrot's Training*; invited to Australia; *Palatakā* – stories in verse.

1919: *The Centre of Indian Culture*; *Home and the World* (translation of the novel, *Ghare Bāire*, 1916); visits Theosophical Society at Adyar, Madras, as the Chancellor of the National University founded by Annie Besant in 1917; translates 'Janaganamana' into English as the 'Morning Song of India' at the request of James Cousins; visits Madanapalle; relinquishes knighthood in protest against the Jallianwalabagh Massacre; signs the Declaration of the Spirit of Independence on 26 June at the request of Romain Rolland; Kala-Bhavana, the department of Fine Arts, established in Santiniketan.

1920: Travels to Europe and America to propagate his idea of Visva-Bharati and raise funds for it; meets Sir Horace Plunkett in London; meets, among others, Sylvain Levi in Paris.

1921: *Greater India* – essays; *The Wreck* (translation of the novel *Naukādubi*, 1906); *The Fugitive* – poems; *Poems from Tagore*; *Glimpses of Bengal* – (translation of selected letters written 1885–1895); *Thought Relics*; lectures at Harvard University; meets Leonard K Elmhirst, an agriculture student at Cornell; meets Romain Rolland and Patrick Geddes in Paris; in Germany, meets Count Keyserling, Gerhart Hauptmann, and Thomas Mann; lectures at the Swedish Academy; critical of Gandhi's Non-Co-operation movement in lectures such as 'Sikshār Milan' (Union of Cultures) and 'Satyer Āhbhān' (The Call of Truth'); Sylvain Levi arrives at Visva-Bharati as the first visiting professor.

1922: *Creative Unity* – essays and lectures; on 6 February, the Rural Reconstruction Institute at Sriniketan under the direction of Elmhirst is formally inaugurated; tours and lectures in South India; visits Cousins at his home in Adyar and gives the lecture entitled 'A Vision of India's History' before proceeding to visit Ceylon; several western scholars such as Moritz Winternitz, V Lesney, Stella Kramrisch, and others arrive at Visva-Bharati.

1923: Commencement of the publication of the journal *The Visva-Bharati Quarterly*; William Pearson dies in a train accident in Italy.

1924: *Gorā* (translation of the novel *Gorā* 1910); *The Curse at Farewell* – play; visits and lectures in China and then in Japan; sails for Peru; offered hospitality by

Victoria Ocampo in her garden-house near Buenos Aires – develops deep friendship with her; poems composed during this trip collected in the volume *Purabi* (of the East) shows first notable signs of doodles, many resembling prehistoric animal shapes.

1925: *Poems*; *Talks in China*; *Red Oleaneders* – play; *Broken Ties and other Stories*; Gandhi visits Santiniketan and holds discussion on the idea of *khadi* as symbol of India's struggle to assert her self-identity; writes an essay explaining the reasons for his opposition to the idea of *charka* (spinning-wheel) as a means of attaining self-reliance; *Puravi* – poems.

1926: Visits Italy; meets Mussolini; meets Benedetto Croce; proceeds to Villeneuve in Switzerland and meets Romain Rolland and is upset with the misinterpretation of his statements in Italy; meets Sir James Frazer, George Duhamel, and others; proceeds to Vienna; writes the famous letter to the *Manchester Guardian* denouncing Fascism; proceeds to England and visits Dartington Hall, Elmhirst's school; visits Norway, Sweden, and Germany; holds a long discussion with Albert Einstein in Berlin; lectures in Prague and in Budapest; visits Greece and Egypt.

1927: Visits South-Asian countries – the Malay Peninsula, including Java, and lectures, appealing for funds for Visva-Bharati.

1928: *Fireflies*; *Letters from a Friend*; *The Birthday Book*, ed. CF Andrews; *Lectures and Addresses*, ed. Anthony X Soares; visits Sri Aurobindo at Pondicherry on the way to Ceylon.

1929: *Thoughts from Tagore*, ed. CF Andrews; *On Oriental Culture and Japan's Mission* – lecture; visits Japan on way to Canada on invitation to attend the Triennial conference of the National Council of Education, Canada; visits several American universities, including Columbia, Washington, and Harvard, on invitation; on the way back, visits Indo-China on invitation; *Yātri* (traveller) – travelogue; *Yogājog* – novel; *Sheser Kabitā* (Farewell, My Friend) – novel.

1930: Exhibition of nearly 125 paintings at Galerie Pigalle, Paris; Hibbert Lectures at Oxford; a lecture at the Quaker Society – the first non-Quaker to be accorded that honour; exhibition of paintings at Birmingham; revisits Dartington Hall; in Berlin, meets Einstein; exhibition of paintings at Gallery Casperi; visits Russia; an exhibition of paintings in Moscow.

1931: *The Child*; *The Religion of Man* – the Hibbert Lectures; *Gitabitān* – collected songs; *Sanchayitā* – selected poems; *Dui Bon* – novel; *Chandālikā* – drama.

1932: *The Golden Boat*; *Mahatmaji and the Depressed Humanity*; *Sheaves* (poems and songs); visits Persia; accepts University Chair of Bengali at Calcutta University.

1933: Delivers Kamala lectures at Calcutta University entitled *Mānusher Dharma* (Religion of Man); plays performed and paintings exhibited in Bombay.

1934: Goes on the third tour of Ceylon with students of Santiniketan for cultural performance; meets Tan Yun-Shan and proposes the establishment of Sino-Indian Cultural Society at Santiniketan; exhibition of paintings in Madras; *Mālancha, Chār Adhāya* (Four Chapters) – both novels.

1935: *East and West* – letter exchanged with Gilbert Murray; conferred D Litt by Benaras Hindu University; *Shessaptak* – prose poems; *Bithikā* – poems.

1936: *Education Naturalised* – lecture; *The Collected Poems and Plays of Rabindranath Tagore* – selections from earlier volumes in English translation; Dacca University confers D Litt (*Honoris causa*).

1937: *Man* – lectures at Andhra University; *Visvaparichaya*, an introduction to science in Bengali; *Chitāngadā* – dance-drama; *Patraput* – prose poems; *Shyamali* – prose poems.

1938: Osmania University confers D Litt (*Honoris causa in absentia*); exhibition of paintings opened in Calmann Gallery, London; *Prāntik* – poems; *Senjuti* – poems.

1939: Hindi-Bhavana inaugurated at Visva-Bharati; Subhas Chandra Bose visits Santiniketan; the first volume of the Visva-Bharati edition of his collected works published; *Ākāshpradip* – poems; *Shyamā* – dance-drama.

1940: *My Boyhood Days* – translation of childhood memories, *Chelebelā*; Oxford University holds a special convocation at Santiniketan to confer D Litt (*Honoris causa*); *Nabajātak* – poems; *Sānāi* – poems; *Chelebelā* (memoir of childhood days).

1941: *Ārogya* – poems; *Janmadine* (poems mainly on the theme of his birthday); birth anniversary observed on the Bengali New Year's Day on 14 April; delivers the famous message 'Sabhyatārsankat' (*Crisis in Civilization*); the Maharaja of Tripura confers the title Bharat-Bhaskar (The Sun of India); dies on 7 August at Jorasanko, the house where he was born.

James Henry Sproull Cousins: A Brief Chronology

1873: Born on 22 July at 18 Canour Street, Belfast, Ireland.

1883–1885: Educated at the National High School at Belfast.

1889–1891: Works as office-boy, filing clerk, and correspondence clerk in a coal-importer's office.

1891–1894: Works as a secretary to a Belfast businessman.

1894: *Ben Madighan and other Poems.*

1895: Becomes a member of the Gaelic League in Belfast.

1897: Reads George Russell's (AE's) volume of poems *Homeward: Songs by the Way*, is deeply touched by their spiritual power and decides to move to Dublin; arrives in Dublin in May; meets George Russell, WB Yeats, and the Fay brothers; *The Legend of the Blemished King and other Poems* published.

1900: *The Voice of One.*

1902: In April, acts in AE's play *Deirdre*, first publicly performed with Yeats's *Cathleen ni Houlihan*; in October, his plays *The Sleep of the King* and *The Racing Lug* are performed by The Irish National Dramatic Company; attends Annie Besant's lecture 'Theosophy and Ireland' and is deeply influenced.

1903: Marries Margaret Gillespie on 9 April at the Sandymount Methodist Church; *The Sword of Dermot* performed for the first time the same month; both James and Margaret Cousins become actively involved in the Irish women's suffrage movement.

1905: Begins teaching in The High School, Dublin; teaches English literature, and subsequently, Geography.

1906: *The Quest.*

1907: *The Awakening.*

1908: On 16 May, joins the Theosophical Society in London and assists in the formation of the Dublin Branch of the Society; James and Margaret Cousins along with Francis Sheehy-Skeffington, the Easter 1916 martyr, found the Irish Women's Franchise League; begins editing *The Irish Citizen*, the journal of the Gaelic League; involvement with the League continues till 1914; *The Bell Branch.*

1910: Composes the 'Suffrage Sonnets' during 1908–1910; 'To One in Prison' is written with Margaret's month-long incarceration for participating in the suffragette movement in the background.

1912: Demonstrator in Geography to Professor A J Herbertson at the Royal College of Science, Dublin; *Etain the Beloved and other Poems*; trip to Normandy where at Maud-Gonne's house first listens to Yeats reciting from Tagore's *Gitanjali* manuscript and is overwhelmed; *The Wisdom of the West: An Introduction to the Interpretative Study of Irish Mythology.*

1913: *The Bases of Theosophy*; moves to Liverpool in June to work for a vegetarian food company; meets Edward Carpenter, the English socialist and poet who was interested in Indian philosophy and spiritual ideas; gives an account of Carpenter in the book *New Ways in English Literature.*

1914: *War: A Theosophical View.*

1915: *Straight and the Crooked*; sails for India in October to work for the Theosophical Society at its international headquarters at Adyar, Madras, as literary sub-editor of the paper *New India* started by Annie Besant.

1916: Begins working as a lecturer in English at the Theosophical College at Madanapalle, in July.

1917: *New Ways of English Literature* (with a dedicatory verse to Rabindranath Tagore); appointed Vice-Principal of Theosophical College at Madanapalle; *The Kingdom of Youth: Essays towards National Education*; *The Garland of Life: Poems of West and East.*

1918: *The Renaissance in India*; appointed Principal of Theosophical College at Madanapalle.

1919: Tagore visits the Theosophical Society for the first time in February; Cousins pays a return visit to Santiniketan – his first visit; *Ode to Truth*; *The King's Wife*; *Moulted Feathers*; *Footsteps of Freedom: Essays.*

1919–1920: Guest Professor of Modern English Poetry at Keiogijuku University, Japan. Lectures subsequently published as *Modern English Poetry: Its Characteristics and Tendencies*; was awarded an Honorary Doctorate by the same university in 1923.

1920: *Sea Change*; resumes the responsibility of the Principal of Theosophical College at Madanapalle.

1921: *The Play of Brahma: An Essay on Drama in National Revival*; tours Sind; James and Margaret Cousins visit Santiniketan from 4 to 18 October.

1922: *Surya-Gita* (Sun Songs), poems for Rabindranath Tagore; *Work and Worship: Essays on Culture and Creative Art*; *The Cultural Unity of Asia*; becomes Director of studies at Brahmavidya Ashram (School of Universal Study) at Adyar, Madras; is nominated member of the Court, the highest body, of Visva-Bharati.

1923: *The New Japan: Impressions and Reflections*; *Modern Indian Artists*; Keio University confers Honorary D Litt; pays a short visit to Santiniketan.

1924: Paintings collected by him at the Jagan Mohan Palace, Mysore, are declared open to the public; writes an introduction to the catalogue of paintings.

1925: Both James and Margaret Cousins tour Europe from March to August; visit Nice, Genoa, Rome, Florence, Venice, Milan, Paris (lectures on Indian paintings), Rotterdam, London, Wales and Dublin; meets Irish leaders William T Cosgrave and Eamon de Valera; visits Sligo, Yeats' native place; founding of the Theosophical World University announced in Holland; *The Social Value of Arts and Crafts*; *Samadarsana (Synthetic Vision): A Study in Indian Psychology*; *The Philosophy of Beauty: A Western Survey and an Indian Contribution*; *Forest Meditation and other Poems*; *Heathen Essays.*

1926: *The Rainbow and other Poems*; *A Tibetan Banner.*

1927: *The Sword of Dermot*; *Geosophy: The Philosophy of Geography*; *Two Ways to Wisdom: Lectures on Chinese Philosophy.*

1928: Both James and Margaret Cousins tour Europe and America from April to October; James Cousins gives one lecture on Indian architecture and sculpture and another entitled 'Oriental Ideas in Education' in Geneva; visits Belgium, England, and Ireland; exhibits Indian paintings in London in October; visits New York, Philadelphia, Boston; at Boston Museum of Fine Arts gives talk on 'Life and Scenery in India'; lectures at Harvard University on Hindu architecture and sculpture; gives lecture entitled 'The Art Revival in India' at Columbia University; gives talks entitled 'Hindu Conceptions of Beauty' and 'The Influence of India in Asian Culture' at Northwestern University, Evanston; at Iowa State University gives lectures entitled 'The Historical background of Indian Painting' and 'The University of the Future' (convocation address); puts up exhibition of Indian paintings at Chicago and lectures on Indian art and 'The Spirit of Indian Culture'; on the way back visits Tokyo, Kyoto, and gives a talk entitled 'The Religious Life of India' at Otani University; visits Shanghai, Hong Kong, and Singapore; *The Shrine and other Poems*; *The Path to Peace: Essays.*

1929: *The Girdle: Poems.*

1930: Leaves in April for lectures in Europe and America; exhibits Indian paintings at Geneva; gives lecture entitled 'Art in Education' in Switzerland; a professor who knows Tagore, persuades him on board the ship to America to exhibit Indian paintings in the ship's lounge; gives talks at several colleges and universities in America; at Iowa, gives two lectures entitled 'The Synthetical View of Life' and 'Poetry as Intuitive Scripture'; lectures on Indian culture, philosophy, literature, and art at several other universities; gives a lecture entitled 'The Early Days of the Irish Dramatic Revival' at the University of California, Santa Barbara; *The University and the Future* visits Santiniketan in late February; probably last visit to Santiniketan.

1931–1932: Guest lecturer in Modern English Poetry at the College of the City of New York.

1932: *A Wandering Harp: Selected Poems*; inaugurates with Joseph Campbell The Irish Foundation in New York; Spends 'Literary Year' from July to March 1933 on Capri; Margaret Cousins stays back in India.

1933: On returning to India appointed Principal of Besant Theosophical College at Madanapalle; lectures on education in Karachi; *The Work Promethean: Interpretations and Applications of Shelley's Poetry*; *A Bardic Pilgrimage: Second Selection of Poetry of James Henry Cousins.*

1934: Appointed part-time art adviser to the Government of Travancore; *A Study in Synthesis.*

1935: Sri Chitralayam, the art gallery of the state of Travancore, opened to the public by the Maharaja of Travancore; the Maharaja confers Veera Srinkhala (Bracelet of Prowess) and the scholar's shawl in recognition of distinguished service to the state in the field of art and culture; the Madras Provincial Educational Conference confers the ancient Sanskrit title of Kulapati (educator of multitudes); *Three Lectures on Educational Principles and Practices.*

1936: The Adyar Academy of Arts (later called Kalakshetra) is inaugurated.

1937: On 14 January, ceremonially admitted into Hindu worship and christened Jayaram; travels to Bali and Java as part of the royal entourage; put in charge of the Government Museum, Trivandrum.

1938: *The Oracle and other Poems*; resigns as Principal of Besant College; appointed full-time art adviser to the Government of Travancore.

1940: *Collected Poems.*

1941: Gives two lectures on art – one, entitled 'Art in Education' at the All-India Education Conference, and another, entitled 'Art and reconstruction' at the Theosophical Society; *The Faith of the Artist.*

1942: *The Hound of Uladh: Two Plays in Verse*; pays tribute to Tagore in an article entitled 'Last Words of Poets' (Especially Rabindranath Tagore) in the periodical *The Young Citizen* in August.

1944: *The Aesthetical Necessity of Life* – three lectures.

1946: *Reflections Before Sunset: Poems.*

1947: Compiles a handbook of Travancore; edits *The Annie Besant Centenary Book.*

1948: Tenure as art adviser to the Government of Travancore abruptly terminated; takes up the position of the Vice-President of Kalakshetra at Adyar.

1949: *Twenty Four Sonnets.*

1950: *We Two Together* – duo-autobiography of James and Margaret Cousins.

1954: Margaret Cousins dies on 11 March.

1956: Dies on 20 February at Madanapalle; remains cremated.

INTRODUCTION

This introductory chapter locates the hitherto largely unexplored friendship between Tagore and Cousins in larger historical, cultural, and intellectual contexts: of Indo-Irish cross-cultural relationship when both nations were undergoing decolonisation; of a world ravaged by the World Wars, and racial, political, and economic hostilities among the nations, and brutalities perpetrated by tyrannical regimes. It foregrounds how Tagore and Cousins, as colonial writers and intellectuals, were thinking not only of their respective nations but also of a world that could be humanised and threaded together by repudiating the very idea of the 'nation' – particularly through Tagore's strong critique of nationalism – and by espousing internationalism as the alternative. It shows how their shared ideas of internationalism and universal humanism, largely informed by Tagore's Brahmo heterodoxy and Cousins's theosophical belief, can be read in the larger frame of contemporary transnational, anti-imperial and cosmopolitan networks. As many of the letters are about their thoughts on education, the Introduction examines their key educational ideas and how the institutions they built – Tagore, his Visva-Bharati, and Cousins, his Brahmavidya Ashrama – could translate their ideas into practice with the fundamental importance accorded to art, creativity, and freedom.

DOI: 10.4324/9781003149354-101

Tagore's letters: a footpath in his life history?

On 14 November 1915, Rabindranath Tagore wrote his first letter[1] to James Henry Cousins, 'the Irish poet from India',[2] in response to a letter that Cousins had written to him, enclosing a copy of the newspaper *New India*; that particular issue of *New India* included Cousins's review of the Eighth Exhibition of the School of Oriental Art in Calcutta (now Kolkata). Thus began their twenty five-year-long friendship.

As Tagore and Cousins speak to each other, we are led into the world of their shared ideas on poetry, art, education, and also on questions of nationalism and internationalism. In one sense, Tagore's friendship with Cousins, more than his friendship with William Butler Yeats (1865–1939), would seem to have brought into closer proximity the cultural and intellectual affinities between India and Ireland and extended the horizon of cross-colonial dialogue at a moment when both nations were undergoing the process of decolonisation. But Tagore and Cousins thought much beyond the peripheries of their respective nations. During the first few decades of the twentieth century, as the world was being shattered by the two World Wars, racial, political, economic, and other forms of antagonisms and hostilities among the nations and by brutalities inflicted by tyrannical regimes, Tagore and Cousins emerged from their colonial margins as global, cosmopolitan thinkers. The letters eminently demonstrate how these two seminal minds, through their creative, intellectual, and practical efforts, were striving to thread together the fragmented world on the principles of universalist humanism. For us then, the letters are not merely a living testimony to the hitherto little explored story of Tagore's friendship with a European poet and intellectual; they also shed new light on the cultural politics of the times.

Cousins gives us an account in his duo-autobiography, *We Two Together*, of his first meeting with Tagore. The possibility of the meeting emerged after he had written 'a leading article … a Report of the young Indian Society of Oriental Art in Calcutta'. The article, published on 17 November 1915, not only introduced the 'East' to the otherwise West-oriented Arts League of the Theosophical Society formed in December 1915 but also had 'history-making consequences'. Sir John Woodroffe (1865–1936),[3] who read the article, was impressed and

1 See Letter No. 1 in this volume. Cousins's letter could not be traced.

2 The appellation was first applied by William Rose Benet in *The Saturday Review of Literature*, 8 (4 June 1932), p. 772.

3 John Woodroffe's family was of Irish Protestant descent, but his father converted to Roman Catholicism; on his mother's side, he was related to Allan Octavian Hume, a British civil servant and theosophist, who had helped found the Indian National Congress in 1885. Woodroffe was in the colonial judicial service and was raised to the position of the Chief Justice of Calcutta High Court. He was a noted orientalist who translated several texts on Tantra (under the pseudonym, Arthur Avalon) attempting to reclaim Tantra's status from the 'negative reputation' into which it had fallen because of its misinterpretation by western orientalist scholars. He was also a connoisseur of art; a moving spirit behind the foundation of the Indian Society of

invited Cousins to the exhibition of Oriental Art in Calcutta.[4] The annual exhibitions of the Indian Society of Oriental Art, Rathindranath Tagore observes, 'were a great feature of the winter season in Calcutta and served a most useful purpose as a cultural and social occasion, not only for that city but for the whole country, since people from all over India used to flock to the then capital during the "season"'.[5] To Cousins, who had freshly arrived in India, an invitation to Calcutta to see the exhibition was naturally a welcome opportunity.

The Bengal School of Art was a movement which attempted to recreate Indian art on nationalist lines. The main impulse to the movement came from Ernest Binfield Havell (1861–1934), who became the head of the Calcutta Art School in 1896, and Ananda Kentish Coomaraswamy (1877–1947), a noted theorist of Indian art and culture; both Havell and Coomaraswamy were of the view that India's culture was anti-materialistic and essentially spiritual and her art embodied that spirit. Havell recruited to his cause Abanindranath Tagore (1871–1951) and Gaganendranath Tagore (1867–1938), Rabindranath's nephews; Abanindranath was in search of a native style in consonance with the upsurge in the nationalist sentiment of the times, as an alternative to the contemporary 'academic' style of painting derived from the West.

The School gained additional momentum from Okakura Kakuzo (also known as Okakura Tenshin, 1863–1913), the Japanese art critic, who arrived in Calcutta around 1900 and met Abanindranath. Okakura advocated the idea of pan-Asianism chiefly through art and was resisting the impact of the western style on Japanese art.[6] He brought a few Japanese artists to work with Abanindranath; these artists influenced Abanindranath's style in certain ways. These 'oriental' artists exhibited their works in London, Berlin, and Paris in the early decades of the twentieth century and were highly appreciated.[7]

Cousins had arrived in Madras (now Chennai) in November 1915 from Ireland via Liverpool to serve as the literary sub-editor of the theosophical newspaper

Oriental Art (1907), he lent support to Abanindranath Tagore's new Bengal School of Art. See, for a detailed study, Kathleen Taylor, *Sir John Woodroffe, Tantra and Bengal: 'An Indian Soul in a European Body?'* (London and New York: Routledge Curzon, 2001).

4 For Cousins's account of the invitation and his visit to the Exhibition of the Society of Oriental Art see James H. Cousins and Margaret E. Cousins, *We Two Together* (Madras: Ganesh & Co., 1950), pp. 259–264.

5 Rathindranath Tagore, *On the Edges of Time* (Calcutta: Visva-Bharati, 1962), p. 78.

6 Okakura, it may be mentioned, was a student of Ernest Fenollosa, the American orientalist, when the latter taught at the Tokyo Imperial University towards the end of the nineteenth century. Okakura assisted Fenollosa in translating Japanese Noh plays into English. These plays made a deep impact on Yeats's drama.Okakura's idea of Asianism, particularly as elaborated in his book, *The Ideals of the East* (1903), has been brilliantly critiqued by Rustom Bharucha in his *Another Asia: Rabindranath Tagore and Okakura Tenshin* (New Delhi: Oxford University Press, 2006), pp. 16–20.

7 See Partha Mitter, *Indian Art* (Oxford: Oxford University Press, 2000), pp. 169–179. See also Tapati Guha-Thakurta, *The Making of a New 'Indian' Art: Artists, Aesthetics and Nationalism, c.1850–1920* (Cambridge: Cambridge University Press, South Asian Edn., 2007).

New India; he had introduced himself in his first letter to Tagore as a friend of Yeats. Tagore had very warmly replied to Cousins that 'I am glad to have this opportunity of knowing you who are a friend of Mr. Yeats, for whom I have a deep love and respect.'[8] Cousins reached Calcutta from Adyar on 14 January 1916 to attend the exhibition, and the 'next morning' Sir Woodroffe took him to the Tagore family home at Jorasanko in Calcutta where he met Rabindranath Tagore for the first time.[9]

Tagore had met Yeats for the first time in London in 1912. Yeats was the leader of the Irish Literary Revival[10] and founder of the Abbey Theatre in Dublin in 1904. Tagore's play *The Post Office* was staged for the first time at the Abbey Theatre in 1913 at Yeats's initiative. Yeats collaborated with Tagore in revising the translations of the latter's Bengali poems for the English *Gitanjali* (1912) and wrote a memorable introduction to the volume. Yeats found Tagore's poetry, as he famously wrote in his introduction, not only the 'work of a supreme culture' but almost a mirror-image of Irish literature: 'A whole people, a whole civilization, immeasurably strange to us', Yeats continues, 'seems to have been taken up into this imagination; and yet we are not moved because of its strangeness, but because we have met our own image, … or heard, … for the first time in literature, our voice as in a dream.' Yeats assumed that Tagore had the privilege of uninhibited creativity unlike Irish poets who had to confront 'propagandist writing'.[11] Earlier in the year, Yeats had announced Tagore to a small audience of poets, artists, and intellectuals in London proclaiming, 'I know of no man in my time who has done anything in the English language to equal these lyrics.'[12] Tagore eventually won the Nobel Prize for Literature in 1913, the first non-western to be accorded this honour. The English *Gitanjali* with Yeats's introduction and the Nobel Prize can be said to have laid the foundation of Tagore's reputation in the western world. Ten years later, in 1923, Yeats also received the Nobel Prize for Literature; his friendship with Tagore continued till his death in 1939.

8 See Letter No. 1 in this volume.

9 See Cousins and Cousins, *We Two Together*, pp. 261–264.

10 The Irish Literary Revival was a modern literary movement in Ireland that began after the fall of Charles Stewart Parnell, leader of the Irish Parliamentary Party, in 1891 and lasted upto 1922, when the Irish Republic was created following the Anglo-Irish Treaty in 1921. It drew upon the efforts of earlier scholars and writers to revive Ireland's Celtic heritage. The fall of Parnell created a political vacuum, and Yeats thought that it was time to replace the political movement with a cultural movement focused on Ireland's lost tradition. With this in view, he immersed himself in ancient Irish myths, legends, folklore, and recycled these in his writings. Cuchulain the legendary figure came to symbolise heroic nationalism and became a central figure in many of Yeats's poems and plays. Other prominent members of the Revival were Lady Gregory, J M Synge, George Russell, Douglas Hyde, James Cousins, Edward Martyn, and George Moore, many of whom made invaluable contributions to Anglophone literary modernism.

11 W. B. Yeats, *The Collected Works of W.B. Yeats, Vol. V, Later Essays*, ed. William H.O'Donnell (New York: Charles Scribner's Son, 1994), pp. 167–168.

12 Reported in *The Times*, 13 July 1912.

In a lecture in Dublin shortly before *The Post Office* was staged at the Abbey Theatre, Yeats is reported to have said that '[t]here was a curious resemblance between the condition of India today and the condition of Ireland, and he thought the movement in India, controlled by its intellectual spirits, should point a moral for Ireland.'[13] Yeats's enlistment of Tagore for the cause of Ireland and the Irish Revival gave Tagore a permanent place in Irish cultural imagination. George Russell (pseudonym, AE; 1867–1935),[14] Yeats's contemporary and another leading Revivalist, also found in Tagore lessons for Ireland. For instance, in reviewing *Letters from Abroad*, Russell underlines Tagore's views on 'crowds' and comments: 'There is something for us, who have also many political lunatics in our national household.' Taking a cue from Tagore's condemnation of the dehumanising effect of nationalism, Russell, in the same review, almost self-reproachfully asks: 'How often in Ireland have we not been asked to sacrifice our complete humanity … to patriotism?'[15] In another review essay he celebrates the

13 Reported in *The Irish Times*, 24 March 1913.

14 George William Russell was an Anglo-Irish poet, critic, painter, and editor. He was a mystic and theosophist, and later, at Yeats's suggestion, undertook organising co-operative societies in rural Ireland under the auspices of Sir Horace Plunkett. AE was editor of the paper *The Irish Homestead*, the organ of IAOS, in which he wrote extensively on the value of co-operatives for rural Ireland. The paper merged with *The Irish Statesman*, which he also edited. Among his more important works are *Co-operation and Nationality* (1912) and *The National Being* (1916), in both of which he visualises a new social, economic, and political order for Ireland based on co-operative principles. Tagore's attention was drawn to *The National Being* by Andrews; Tagore's own copy is in the holding of the Rabindra-Bhavana Library at Santiniketan. Tagore got further inspiration from it for his rural development schemes, and wrote to Nagendranath Ganguli thus: 'I read your paper *Karmi*. It is good. If you disseminate to the readers the value of AE's *The National Being* then it would be appreciable. We have to understand, that those who cannot strike a balance with the drift of time and want to return to the past against the current of time, are killed by time. … The medicines and diet discussed in AE's book do not follow any blind tradition — it speaks of the compromise of the present with the present.' Rabindranath Tagore, *Palli Prakriti* [The Nature of the Village] (Calcutta: Visva-Bharati, 1962), pp. 234–235 (My translation). Further, in 'The Cult of the Charka', Tagore wrote: 'It was while some of us were thinking of the ways and means of adopting this principle [co-operative] in our institution that I came across the book called "The National Being" written by the Irish idealist AE, who has a rare combination in himself of poetry and practical wisdom. There I could see a great concrete realization of the co-operative living of my dreams.' *The English Writings of Rabindranath Tagore*, Vol. III, ed. Sisir Kumar Das (1996; New Delhi: Sahitya Akademi, 2002), p. 545. AE contributed the poem 'First Love' to *The Golden Book of Tagore*. There was considerable interest in Russell, particularly, in view of his affinity with Tagore. Some important essays comparing Tagore and AE were also written in leading contemporary periodicals. Two of such essays are G. Ramchandran's 'A.E., Poet and Seer' in *The Modern Review*, Vol. LXII, July–December 1927, pp. 23–26 and Ajit Kumar Chakravarty's 'The National Ideals of Tagore and AE' in *The Modern Review*, Vol. LIV, July–December 1933, pp. 403–405. But whether the two poets met each other could not be determined.

15 AE, 'Literature and Life: The Wisdom of the East' in *The Irish Statesman*, Vol. V, August 23, 1924, p. 758.

Indian poet by claiming that '[i]t is Tagore who more than any other maintains in our Iron Age the dignity of poetry[16]

Even now, Tagore occupies an enviable position in Irish cultural writing. For instance, Edwina Keown and Carol Taffee, editors of the volume entitled *Irish Modernism*, in their introduction, club Tagore with Pound and Yeats as the trend-setters of an early international modernism, poets who saw the 'need to open their cultures to otherness'.[17] For Declan Kiberd and P J Mathews, '[t]he Irish were the first English-speaking people in the twentieth century to decolonise'; during the Revival, Ireland 'decided to become metropolitan' and '[i]ntellectuals overseas began to read into Ireland a version of their own ideal aspiration'. They further contend that the Irish supported not only India's cause for freedom; writers and scholars from the days of the Revival have strengthened Ireland's reciprocal relationship with India.[18] Kiberd and Mathews have corroborated their argument by including a part of *The Post Office* in the recently published *Handbook of the Irish Revival* – a collection of some of the best writings from the Revival era – they have edited, making Tagore thereby an inalienable part of Irish culture. Few writers have indeed been given such a pre-eminent position in the literary canon of other nations. Cousins, we must add, carried with him a part of the Revivalist cultural baggage when he arrived in India.

Tagore, apart from being was a literary, artistic, and musical genius, was also a marvellous letter writer. The frank outpourings of his thoughts, ideas, and feelings in his letters reveal to us a world that often remains disguised in his literary works; hence, his letters occupy a special place in his oeuvre. In the introduction to *Patradhārā* (Stream of Letters, 1938), Tagore distinguishes between literary writings which are meant for a wide range of public beyond the borders of personal life, and letters, especially personal letters, which reflect the diverse shades of the writer's day-to-day world, 'its echoes and their reverberations', and the conversation of daily life.[19]

The first volume of Tagore's English letters is *Glimpses of Bengal: Selected from the Letters of Sir Rabindranath Tagore 1885–1895* (1921). It is a translation of selected Bengali letters written to Indira Devi, his niece, portraying his experiences of the natural beauty and peasant life of riverine Bengal, and his thoughts and feelings, during his sojourn in Eastern Bengal managing his family estates as a young landlord. These letters are 'like a footpath in my life history, unconsciously laid

16 AE, Review of Tagore's *Talks in India* in *The Irish Statesman*, Vol. VI, August 29, 1925, p. 794.

17 Edwina Keown and Carol Taaffe, eds. 'Introduction' in *Irish Modernism: Origins, Contexts, Publics* (Oxford and New York: Peter Lang, 2010), p. 29.

18 Declan Kiberd and P.J. Mathews, eds. *Handbook of the Irish Revival: An Anthology of Cultural and Political Writings, 1891–1922* (Dublin: Abbey Theatre Press, 2015), pp. 239–240.

19 See Rabindranath Tagore's 'Bhumikā' (Introduction) to *Patradhārā*, Vols I–III (Santiniketan: Santiniketan Press, 1938), p.i.

by the treading of my own thoughts' Tagore wrote to Yeats, at whose instance he had them translated.[20]

Tagore's English letters to his western friends are, however, of a different nature; in them, we do notice occasional streaks of the personal, but they are mostly intellectual exchanges and are about his public life. On one occasion, he bemoaned to Charles Freer Andrews (1871–1940), one of his closest English friends, that though he wanted to write 'simple letters', he could not, as 'the worldwide agony of pain fills my mind with thoughts that obstruct natural communication of personal life!'[21] The overwhelming preoccupation in these letters, broadly, are his joys and agonies over his standing as a poet of world repute, his ideas of nationalism, internationalism, and humanism, his concern for India, his responses to issues of racial and East–West conflict, his struggles with the founding of his university, Visva-Bharati, and the ideals enshrined in it. The burden of these preoccupations, nonetheless, does not obscure Tagore's affective side.

Many of the letters Tagore wrote, for instance, to Andrews, over several years, bear testimony to all this; they were first published as *Letters from Abroad* in 1924; the volume was expanded and reissued with prefatory essays by Andrews as *Letters to a Friend* in 1928. While the letters reveal a disguised mood of 'deepening depression and fatigue',[22] there are also moments of happiness enjoyed in the recipient's friendship.

Imperfect Encounter: Letters of Rabindranath Tagore and William Rothenstein 1911–1941 (1972), edited by Mary Lago, is the first volume in which the letters of both the poet and their recipient are brought together. Rothenstein valued his friendship with the poet and even thought of him to be 'the interpreter of India's soul', who had borne 'upon his single shoulders the genius & honour of India!'[23]

A Difficult Friendship: Letters of Edward Thompson and Rabindranath Tagore 1913–1940 (2003), edited by Uma Dasgupta, unfolds 'their instant intimate friendship,

20 Tagore to Yeats, 17 June 1918. Rabindra Bhavana Archive (hereafter RBA), File No. 442.

21 Rabindranath Tagore, *Letters from Abroad* (Madras: S. Ganesan, 1924), p. 24. Charles Freer Andrews (1871–1940) was a Cambridge-educated Anglican clergyman who came to India in 1904 as part of the Cambridge Mission. He became enthusiastic about Tagore after he heard about the poet from Sushil Rudra at St Stephen's College in Delhi. Andrews met Tagore for the first time at William Rothenstein's home in London in 1912, and was overwhelmed. His accounts of his first meeting with Tagore were published in *The Modern Review* in 1912. In 1914, he left St Stephen's and joined Tagore in Santiniketan to become the poet's life-long associate and friend. He accompanied Tagore in many of his travels abroad. Andrews wrote poems, essays, and books on a variety of subjects. For accounts of Andrews's life and activities see Benarasidas Chaturvedi and Marjorie Sykes's, *Charles Freer Andrews: A Narrative* (New York: Harper and Brothers, 1950) and Hugh Tinker's, *The Ordeal of Love: C.F. Andrews and India* (New Delhi: Oxford University Press, 1979, reprint 2015). A selection of Andrews's writings can be found in Marjorie Sykes, ed. *C. F. Andrews: Representative Writings* (New Delhi: National Book Trust, 1973).

22 See *Imperfect Encounter: The Letters of William Rothenstein and Rabindranath Tagore 1911–1941*, ed. Mary Lago (Cambridge, MA: Harvard University Press, 1972), p. 271.

23 Ibid., p. 25.

the stressful turn it took, and the reconciliation it reached'.[24] Dasgupta's recently edited volume, *Friendships of 'Largeness and Freedom': Andrews, Tagore, and Gandhi: An Epistolary Account 1912–1940* (2018), focuses on 'their friendship and their principles for pursuing the freedom of India'.[25] *The Tagore-Geddes Correspondence* (2004), the letters of Tagore and Patrick Geddes, a Scottish sociologist, biologist, town-planner, and educator, compiled and edited by Bashabi Fraser, has brought to light the shared ideas of the correspondents.[26] *Bridging East and West: Rabindranath Tagore and Romain Rolland Correspondence 1919–1940* (2018), edited and French letters translated by Chinmoy Guha, shows how Tagore and Rolland attempted to 'break the frontier' and 'build bridges between the East and the West at a crucial point of time in history'. Guha observes in his introduction to the letters that 'in spite of their mutual respect and admiration [they] occasionally collided with each other, and yet never gave up'.[27]

In this respect, Tagore's friendship with James Cousins appears to be rather tranquil and devoid of conflicts and collisions. Their relationship is marked by mutual respect and affection and even an undertone of reverence on Cousins's part. Charles Freer Andrews, William Winstanley Pearson,[28] Leonard Knight

24 *A Difficult Friendship: Letters of Edward Thompson and Rabindranath Tagore 1913–1940*, ed. Uma Dasgupta (Delhi: Oxford University Press, 2003), p. 11.

25 *Friendships of 'Largeness and Freedom': Andrews, Tagore, and Gandhi: An Epistolary Account 1912–1940*, ed. Uma Dasgupta (Delhi: Oxford University Press, 2018), p. xv.

26 *The Tagore-Geddes Correspondence*, compiled and edited by Bashabi Fraser (Kolkata: Visva-Bharati, 2004).

27 *Bridging East and West: Rabindranath Tagore and Romain Rolland Correspondence (1919–1940)*, edited and French letters translated by Chinmoy Guha (New Delhi: Oxford University Press, 2018), p. xxii.

28 William Winstanley Pearson (1881–1923) was a Cambridge-educated Englishman who came to India in 1907 as a teacher of Botany at the London Mission Society, Calcutta. He met Tagore for the first time in London in 1912. He learned Bengali and helped Tagore in his translations. He joined Santiniketan as a teacher in 1914 and soon became very popular. He wrote his memoir, *Santiniketan: The Bolpur School of Rabindranath Tagore* in 1916. His other book, *For India* in which he supported India's aspirations for nationhood, was banned by the then British government, and he was arrested and sent back to England. He returned to Santiniketan in 1921. He had to return to Europe in 1923 to recover from ill-health and died the same year on 18 September in a train accident in Italy.

Elmhirst,[29] and Edward Thompson[30] were Englishmen; the first three were close associates of Tagore, and Andrews and Pearson sometimes collaborated in translating his works; Thompson wrote two books on Tagore and translated some of his works. But none of them can be said to have been deeply engaged with ancient Indian cultural and literary tradition.

With Cousins, things were different; to repeat, he was not English, but was of Irish descent; Ireland, it needs to be recalled, was in an 'anomalous state', because while it suffered under English colonial domination at home, Irishmen were recruited to serve in different capacities in England's overseas colonies. Before he migrated to India, Cousins had made his presence felt on the Irish literary and cultural scene. He was a well-known poet whose poetry received admirable reviews, a champion of the Gaelic movement and an active participant in the suffrage movement (he even wrote a number of 'suffrage sonnets'). He made valuable contributions to the early phase of the Irish Literary Revival: he wrote plays for the Irish stage and literary criticism, was associated with Yeats and George Russell (AE), among other notable poets and writers, and was drawn towards Celtic mythology and mysticism under the influence of AE; he was a theosophist which had given him an extensive idea of ancient Indian spiritual tradition.

In India, Cousins continued to write poetry and plays in which he sometimes fused Indian subjects and Irish myths and motifs. Austin Clarke, a distinguished

29 Leonard K. Elmhirst (1893–1970) studied history at Cambridge and came to India in 1915. He was distressed by the plight of Indian farmers, and in order to ameliorate their condition, he proceeded to Cornell to study agriculture. Elmhirst had become Tagore's admirer since he read the English *Gitanjali* in 1915. He met Tagore for the first time in America in 1921 while he was still at Cornell. On Tagore's invitation, he came to Santiniketan in November 1921 after completing his studies at Cornell, and soon took up the responsibility of the rural reconstruction work at the university. Elmhirst left Santiniketan in 1923, but he had made significant contribution within fourteen months of his stay at the university. He and his wife Dorothy, later on, set up Dartington Hall in Devonshire, England, in 1925, modelled on Tagore's Visva-Bharati. Some idea of Elmhirst's experience at Santiniketan can be gathered from his book *Poet and Plowman* (Calcutta: Visva-Bharati, 1975).

30 Edward John Thompson (1996–1946) was a Wesleyan Methodist missionary who taught English at the Wesleyan Mission High School and College in Bankura in Bengal from 1910 to 1922. He studied Bengali seriously, taking an examination in the language. In 1923, he returned to England on the ill-paid job of lecturer in Bengali at Oxford to teach Bengali to Indian Civil Service probationers who would serve in Bengal. Thompson came to know Tagore in 1913, and began to take deep interest in the poet and his work. He wrote two books on Tagore, *Rabindranath Tagore: His Life and Works* (1921) and *Rabindranath Tagore: Poet and Dramatist* (1926). Tagore was unhappy with Thompson's first book, but the second book greatly distressed him, and even created a rift in their relationship. Thompson also wrote poetry, fiction, biography, history and co-authored a book on the British rule in India. See Uma Dasgupta's beautiful introduction to the Tagore–Thompson relationship in *A Difficult Friendship*. Dasgupta has also listed most of Thomson's publications in her book. See also Harish Trivedi's essay '"That he is an English man and I a Bengali:" Tagore and Edward Thompson' in his *Colonial Transactions: English Literature and India* (Calcutta: Papyrus, 1993), pp. 126–144 and Michael Collins's 'Rabindranath Tagore and the Politics of Friendship' in *South Asia: Journal of South Asian Studies*, Vol. XXXXV, No. 1, March 2012, pp. 118–142.

younger contemporary poet of Yeats, has noted how in Cousins's writings from India there is a confluence of Irish and Indian elements. In a review of Cousins's *The House of Uladh: Two Plays in Verse*, Clarke notes that while one of the plays, *The King's Wife*, based on the life of Mirabai, is the result of Cousins's association with 'the new cultural movements of India', in *The House of Uladh* he returns 'to Irish mythology'. 'This', continues Clarke, 'reminds us of the active part which he [Cousins] played in the early days of our own literary revival.' The play is significant because 'in his symbolic recension the poet has developed the mythological figure of Cuchulain into the later phase of the saviour-hero' while it also 'blends eastern and western thought'. But more than this, Clarke deems Cousins fortunate, because, by leaving Ireland, he escaped the 'decreasing excitement of our revival to find in India a new cultural stirring'.[31] India thus provided Cousins a new space and a new ambience for his creativity. Alongside writing and publishing poetry and plays, Cousins also promoted Indian art in Europe and America through lectures and by putting up exhibitions of Indian painting in different cities across the world; he acquired a reputation as an art and literary critic, and published philosophical treatises, a book on the philosophy of beauty, collections of essays on culture, a duo-autobiography with his wife Margaret Cousins, and a large number of pamphlets on art, culture, and education. In fact, he was so immersed in Indian art and culture that he rarely spoke on Irish literature; and whenever he did, his subject was restricted to the Literary Revival of which he had been a part. He played a dominant role as an educationist for the Theosophical Society and founded an institution to which he gave an Indian (Sanskritic) name, Brahmavidya Ashrama (school of universal culture); but it was very unlike Tagore's Santiniketan school which was modelled on the ancient Indian hermitage, while Cousins chose to follow a European (the French Enlightenment) rather than the ancient Indian intellectual tradition. Admittedly then, Cousins's double identity as an Irishman who made India his home, coupled with his theosophical mooring and Celtic-mystical orientation, and finally, his embracing of Hinduism in later life, distinguish him from the Englishmen we have mentioned above.

Cousins had come across Tagore's name for the first time when he heard Yeats recite from the English *Gitanjali* at Maud Gonne's house in Normandy in 1912; he was deeply moved and he felt that the poems were 'in the purest of musical speech full of authenticity of creation … and glowing with a spirit of the seers of all time'.[32] Tagore, in fact, had made a deep and lasting impression on him. In a lecture in 1937, Cousins declared that ever since he had heard the *Gitanjali* poems in 1912, the fourth poem of the volume had become his ideal for education.[33]

31 Austin Clarke, 'An Irish Poet in India' in *The Irish Times*, 22 May 1943, p. 10.

32 James H. Cousins, 'First Impressions of Tagore in Europe' in *The Modern Review*, Vol. XIX, August 1916, p. 177. The full essay is reprinted in *New Ways in English Literature* (Madras: Ganesh & Co, 1917). See Appendix for the essay.

33 Reported in *The Modern Review*, Vol. LXII, July–December, 1937, p. 468.

When he first met Tagore in Calcutta, he was fascinated by the poet's personality and records his impression in *We Two Together* thus:

> It was Rabindranath, majestically refined and gentle, in a fawn cloak from neck to feet, his greying locks falling to his shoulders, his patriarchal beard adding yet unlived years to his toll of a little over fifty and obscuring nothing of his beauty and nobility of countenance. He had, he said, come specially from Santiniketan to greet a fellow-countryman of Yeats who had prefaced Gitanjali. He offered me the freedom of his home in a voice that surprised me with its high tone and exquisite modulations.[34]

The following year, he wrote a poem, 'To Rabindranath Tagore', as the dedicatory verse to his collection of literary criticism, *New Ways in English Literature* (1917):

> I thought for golden poesy
> In dedicated prose to pay,
> Veiling impossibility
> In that old kindly courteous way.
>
> But all your flowing tide of fame
> Went singing round my echoing shore
> When on page I put your name –
> And made my debt but tenfold and more!
>
> Yea, and the world that holds your praise
> Moves thus between two powers at feud:
> Speech that undoes what it essays,
> And silence like ingratitude.
>
> Yet since a sacramental hand
> May sanctify the humblest weed,
> I lift our love's transforming wand
> And give intention for the deed;
>
> With one deep wish that, till the set
> Of sun across your song's wide sea,
> Our backs may bend with growing debt
> For your pure golden poesy![35]

34 Cousins and Cousins, *We Two Together*, p. 264.

35 James H. Cousins, *New Ways in English Literature* (Madras: Ganesh & Co, 1917, revised edn., 1919).

By the time of Tagore's seventieth birth-anniversary, Cousins had grown in stature and intimacy with the poet, and was asked to contribute to *The Golden Book of Tagore* (1931); he sent the poem entitled 'The Choice' from Santa Barbara, California:

If choose I must a resting-place
What time my feet began to fail,
By God's most hospitable grace
I choose a brook-side in a vale.

I ask not ocean's trumpeting
Or hills that hearken to the skies;
For one is loud with questionings,
And one is silent with replies.

But by my brooklet's lyric leap
My heart may contemplate at ease,
Life's deep desiring for the deep
Mingled with mountain memories;

And my own rivulet of rhyme
May run from summit unto sea,
Singing between the banks of time
The music of Eternity.[36]

Cousins had migrated to India to join the Theosophical Society at Adyar, and he remained tied to the Society all his life; his growing friendship with Tagore brought him in direct association with Visva-Bharati. He was nominated to the Court, the governing body of Visva-Bharati, when it was being formed in 1922. It is true that his closer ties with Tagore or his nomination to the Court of Visva-Bharati did not make his association with Visva-Bharati as deep as was Andrews's or Pearson's or even Elmhirst's. Nor did he become a part of Tagore's inner circle. As a member of the Theosophical Society, Cousins had to carry out the educational responsibilities of the Society; he also had to run the new institution he had founded in 1922.[37] But Tagore invited him to teach a course in English literature at Visva-Bharati and also sought other kinds of help from him; he offered Cousins the responsibility of editing the journal, *The Visva-Bharati Quarterly*, which Cousins declined. Incidentally, it was Cousins who had initiated the idea of 'the necessity of a magazine, at least quarterly, to disseminate

36 James H. Cousins, 'The Choice' in *The Golden Book of Tagore*, ed. Ramananda Chatterjee (Calcutta: The Golden Book Committee, 1931), p. 61.

37 On this issue see the Letter Nos. 22–26 in this volume

the ideas of the International University … and as a result of our conversation, "The Visva-Bharati Quarterly" arose', Cousins recalls.[38] Cousins contributed a number of essays to *The Modern Review* and *The Visva-Bharati Quarterly* (beginning with its inaugural number in 1923), and is, presumably, the only writer of an insightful review of Tagore's *Creative Unity*, a copy of which Tagore had sent him immediately after the book's publication in 1922.[39]

Cousins's essays are replete with references to Tagore; in any case, it would not be an over-statement to say that Tagore was the lens through which Cousins saw much of Indian culture. For example, Cousins observes that India 'is repeating history by making her captor captive by the infusion of the magic of an ancient culture in such utterances of supreme spirituality as come through so perfect an instrument as Rabindranath Tagore'.[40] He also recalls that at the exhibition of Oriental Art in Calcutta, referred to in the opening part of this essay, Rabindranath Tagore 'was most helpful in my endeavours to absorb the significance of what was taking place'.[41] Many of his educational and aesthetic ideas have a strong affinity with Tagore's. At Adyar, he gave a weekly commentary on Tagore's *Gitanjali*, and even attempted to 'develop a Tagore philosophy from the Tagore poetry'.[42] To cap it all, Cousins was the only person whom Tagore had recommended for the Nobel Prize.

It is strange that after his death in 1956, Cousins gradually receded into oblivion.[43] But that he was highly esteemed and recognised for his contribution as a poet, art and literary critic, commentator on Indian poetics, and as an educationist is affirmed in the long obituary tribute written by Ordhendra Coomar Gangoly, the eminent art critic and scholar and one of the founders of the Indian Society for Oriental Art;[44] Cousins's close association with Tagore adds a different magnitude to his role in the intellectual and cultural world of

38 Cousins and Cousins, *We Two Together*, p. 396.
39 The review has been reproduced in Appendix of this volume.
40 James H. Cousins, *Renaissance in India* (Madras: Ganesh & Co, 1918), p. 6.
41 Cousins and Cousins, *We Two Together*, p. 265.
42 Ibid., p. 396.
43 Two book-length studies of Cousins are William A. Dumbleton's *James Cousins* (Boston, MA: Twayne Publishers, 1980) and Dilip K. Chatterjee's *James Henry Cousins: A Study of His Works in the Light of the Theosophical Movement in India and the West* (Delhi: Sarada Publishing House, 1994). See also Selina Guiness' 'James Cousins and His Nation of Free Slaves', pp. 68–80 and Joseph Lennon's '"Where the East and the West Are One": James Cousins and Postcolonial Aesthetics', pp. 81–96 in Tadhg Foley and Maureen O'Connor, eds. *Ireland and India: Colonies, Culture and Empire* (Dublin and Portland, OR: Irish Academic Press, 2006). Joseph Lennon has a chapter entitled 'James, Seamus, and Jayaram Cousins' in his *Irish Orientalism: A Literary and Cultural History* (Syracuse: Syracuse University Press, 2004), pp. 324–370. In addition to these see the section on Cousins in Sirshendu Majumdar, *Yeats and Tagore: A Comparative Study of Cross-Cultural Poetry, Nationalist Politics, Hyphenated Margins and the Ascendancy of the Mind* (Bethesda, Dublin, Palo Alto: Academica Press, 2013), pp. 133–137. Sachidananda Mohanty's *Cosmopolitan Modernity in the Early 20th Century India* (London and New York: Routledge, 2015) has chapters on Cousins and Tagore. I am indebted to all these works.
44 For the obituary note see *The Modern Review*, Vol. XCIV, March 1956, pp. 222–224.

India in the early decades of the twentieth century as the letters in this volume show. Apart from all this, he is also known to have devoted his 'energies' to the 'welfare of the poor and the oppressed' and had an interest in developing agricultural co-operative societies.[45] It is in view of Cousins's experience of developing agricultural co-operatives in Ireland in association with Sir Horace Plunkett (1845–1932) and George Russell that Tagore solicited his help in this matter. In one of his letters, Tagore desperately wrote to him:

> We specially want you to study Agricultural Co-operation in Ireland and let us know how far its methods can be adapted to our Indian condition. We shall be very thankful to you if you can persuade some experienced man who has worked with AE, to come and help us in our village work for about six months or longer if it is possible.

The letter shows that Tagore had sought Cousins's suggestion and that Cousins had advised Tagore to invite George Russell to Visva-Bharati, because, later in the letter, Tagore urges Cousins to 'exercise your influence on AE and try to send him to us'.[46] Tagore's interaction with Cousins, therefore, was not restricted to intellectual and cultural spheres; it spilled over to domains of practical necessity as well. Many of the letters in this volume demonstrate this.

Tagore's idea of friendship

The historian Peter Robb contends that while Europeans had business and social relations with Indians, they 'rarely joined with them in useful friendship', and that, Indo-European friendships were determined by 'mutual exclusion rather than dominance and subjection'. Robb's inference is based on the diary of Richard Blechynden (1759–1822), architect, surveyor, and Superintendent of Roads – a man of practical affairs, so to say.[47]

But contrary to Robb's view, we have several instances of friendship between Indians and Europeans which were not restricted to the sphere of business and commerce; in fact, the friendships of Tagore, Gandhi, and other eminent Indians with many Europeans were intellectual and affective in nature. William Rothenstein (1872–1945), the painter, is Tagore's earliest English friend with whom he developed a close relationship during his third visit to England in 1912. Rothenstein, on the death of Tagore, recalled that their letters are '[o]ne

45 Alan Denson, *James H. Cousins and Margaret E. Cousins: A Bio-Bibliographical Survey* (Kendal: Alan Denson, 1967), p. 15.

46 See Letter No.22 in this volume.

47 Peter Robb, *Useful Friendship: Europeans and Indians in Early Calcutta* (New Delhi: Oxford University Press, 2014), p. 42.

memorial of our close friendship'.[48] In a Bengali essay on Rothenstein, Tagore observes that:

> Just as the rose is a distinguished flower in the garden, a friend is also a person of a particular class. There are people in the world who are born as friends. They have the immense and natural power to give company. … Just as light flickers naturally from the jewel, the ability to give company also naturally emanates from the life of those endowed with special powers.[49]

Earlier, in a very short essay called 'Bandhutwa O Bhālobashā' (Friendship and Love), Tagore had distinguished between friendship and love in sartorial terms – friendship is like a homely dress while love is more ornamental.[50]

Martin Buber has observed that '[F]riendship is … [a] form of … dialogical relationship … based on a concrete and mutual experience of inclusion … the true inclusion of one another by human souls.'[51] Tagore's friendship with Andrews goes a long way to demonstrate this idea. In a short autobiographical account Andrews recounts:

> Personally, I have never in my whole life met any one so completely satisfying the needs of friendship and intellectual understanding and spiritual sympathy as Tagore. His very presence always acts as an inspiration. To be with him, to be at unison with him in some creative work, is a privilege which it is very difficult to state in words. Indeed, it has been by far the greatest privilege of my life. No one has been more fortunate than I have, in personal relationship.[52]

He also speaks in the same vein of his second friendship with Gandhi. On Tagore's side, the moving address that he gave at Santiniketan on Andrews's death on 5 April 1940 would similarly contradict Robb's thesis, as much as it would show how deeply Tagore valued his friendship. The following words from Tagore's address would prove our point:

48 *Imperfect Encounter*, p. 25.

49 Rabindranath Tagore, 'Bandhu' (Friend) in *Rabindra Rachanābali*, Vol. XIII, Collected Works: 125th Birth Anniversary Edition (Calcutta: Visva-Bharati, 1991), p. 668. (My translation). All subsequent citations from Tagore's Bengali writings are in my translation and from this multi-volume edition unless otherwise stated; abbreviated hereafter as *RR*.

50 In *RR*, Vol. XIV, p. 690.

51 Martin Buber, *Between Man and Man* (London: Routledge & Kegan Paul, 1947), p. 119.

52 C. F. Andrews, 'My Life Story' in *The Visva-Bharati Quarterly,* Vol. VI, Part I, NS, May-July 1940, p. 17. Hereafter *Visva-Bharati Quarterly* abbreviated as *VBQ*.

> When we are separated from a man with whom our relationship touched only the necessary businesses of life, nothing remains. ... But the relationship of love, infinite, mysterious, is not subject to the limitations of such material intercourse, nor cabined and confined in the life of the body. Such rare companionship of soul existed between Andrews and me.[53]

Admittedly, few friendships between two individuals from the two sides of the divide in a colonial context have struck such a deep chord. Such intimate and strong bonds of friendship at the individual level also worked towards mutual understanding of the respective cultures and helped in bringing the nations into closer ties transcending the asymmetries of political relationship.

Artists and writers such as the French Impressionists, the Blue Rider Group, the Bloomsbury Group, and others are known to have worked together in collaborative circles. Andrews, Pearson, and Elmhirst, along with others, can be said to have formed a similar 'collaborative circle'[54] working at Tagore's Santiniketan School, and later, at Visva-Bharati.

Postcolonial theorists generally explain the relationship between the English or Europeans and Indians in the imperial era as constituted of the binaries of dominance and subjection respectively, but many scholars have also shown the existence of alternative kinds of relationship. Ashis Nandy, for one, has argued that a small section of British intellectuals 'opted out of their colonizing society ... [and] search[ed] for a new utopia untouched by any Hobbesian dream'.[55] In her book, *Affective Communities*, Leela Gandhi has illustrated how certain individuals and groups belonging to the imperial culture 'have renounced the privileges of imperialism and elected affinity with victims of their own expansionist culture' and have thus produced narratives of participants in the 'cross-cultural collaboration between the oppressor and the oppressed'.[56]

Other scholars have also shown that literary, artistic, and intellectual activities opened up channels of communication that enabled recognition of mutual affinities and facilitated the exchange of ideas between India and Britain or Europe in colonial times. Drawing upon the history of art in colonial India, Partha Mitter, the eminent art historian, has remarked that in the encounter of colonialism and nationalism in Indian art between 1890s and 1920s, identities were constantly

53 Rabindranath Tagore, 'Charlie Andrews' in *VBQ*, Vol. VI, Part I, NS, May-July 1940, p. 1.

54 See Michael Farrell, *Collaborative Circles: Friendship Dynamics and Circles & Creative Work* (Chicago, IL and London: The University of Chicago Press, 2001) for a fine study of collaborative creativity.

55 Ashis Nandy, *The Intimate Enemy: Loss and Recovery of Self under Colonialism* (New Delhi: Oxford University Press, 1983), pp. 35–36.

56 Leela Gandhi, *Affective Communities: Anticolonial Thought and the Politics of Friendship* (Delhi: Permanent Black, 2006), pp. 1–6.

modifying the stereotyped dichotomy of the self and the other in their very moment of mutual encounter.[57]

Mitter has also demonstrated how Kandinsky was influenced by eastern ideas as they filtered through the writings of theosophists such as Helena Blavatsky and Rudolf Steiner while Swami Vivekananda's lectures on yoga impacted Malevich and his circle; on the other hand, Gaganendranath Tagore, Rabindranath's nephew, was one of the earliest artists of modern India to have imbibed cubist influences. 'In this fascinating "world upside-down",' Mitter observes, 'the Indian painters turned to the West while the European avant-garde headed East for inspiration.'[58]

Bob van der Linden, in his recent book, *Music and Empire in Britain and India* (2013), has studied how the relationship between India and Britain developed during the imperial era through the medium of music, a relationship that subverted the imperial ideology. Musicologists such as Arthur Fox Strangways and Arnold Bake, Maud MacCarthy and John Foulds, among others, not only believed in mutual respect for non-western music; some of them took great interest in Tagore's music as well.[59]

Therefore, in the early twentieth century, on the one hand, imperialism expanded its reach and nationalist sentiment acquired greater intensity; on the other hand, the flow of ideas and the formation of East–West networks of relationship that gained momentum through the efforts of liberal-minded writers, artists, and intellectuals on both sides, gave a fillip to the emerging spirit of cosmopolitanism and internationalism. While internationalism broadly implies the equality of all nations despite their respective differences, cosmopolitanism and universalism are comparatively complex ideas and difficult to pin down to broad consensual definitions.[60] Amanda Anderson, among others, has given a very cogent explanation of cosmopolitanism which may be helpful here:

> In general, cosmopolitanism endorses reflective distance from one's own cultural affiliations, a broad understanding of other cultures and customs, and a belief in universal humanity. … In the twentieth century, I think, we

57 Partha Mitter, 'Reflections on Modern Art and National Identity in Colonial India: An Interview', in *Cosmopolitan Modernisms*, ed. Kobena Mercer (Cambridge, MA and London: MIT Press, 2005), pp. 24–49.

58 Partha Mitter, *Art and Nationalism in Colonial India, 1890–1922: Occidental Orientations* (Cambridge: Cambridge University Press, 1998), p. 6.

59 See Bob van der Linden, *Music and Empire in Britain and India: Identity, Internationalism and Cross-Cultural Communication* (New York: Palgrave Macmillan, 2013).

60 See, for example, the debate in Joshua Cohen, ed. *For Love of Country?* Martha Nussbaum, et al. (Boston, MA: Beacon Press, 1996). Also, Carol L. Breckenridge, et al., eds. *Cosmopolitanism* (London and Durham, NC: Duke University Press, 2002) and Bruce Robbins and Paulo Lemos Horta, eds. *Cosmopolitanisms* (New York: New York University Press, 2017).

> can fairly say that it is defined against those parochialisms emanating from extreme allegiances to nation, race, and ethnos.[61]

She distinguishes between an 'exclusionary' and an 'inclusionary' form of cosmopolitanism. Exclusionary cosmopolitans, like the ancient Stoics with whom the idea of *kosmoupolites*, that is, citizen of the world originated, deny all forms of local affiliations and pursue an abstract universalism; for inclusionary cosmopolitans, 'universalism finds expression through sympathetic imagination and intercultural exchange'.[62]

Writers, artists, and intellectuals from both sides of the imperial divide, who formed transnational constellations, fraternities, or networks, were mostly 'inclusionary' cosmopolitans; many of them had the advantage of travelling across their national borders and developing closer relationships. Rabindranath Tagore, for example, despite his location in the colonial periphery, was a world-voyager and engaged in conversation and dialogue with some of the leading minds of his times. Cousins migrated to India from a European colony, but he travelled widely across Europe and America, lecturing and meeting many eminent personalities. Many internationalists and cosmopolitans were also strong opponents of imperialism, and championed the case for cultural and political freedom of the colonised nations. The Theosophical Society was one such globally active internationalist body with its network of lodges all across the world.

Cousins, Tagore and 'spiritual democracy'

The Theosophical Society was founded by Helena Petrovna Blavatsky (1831–1891) and Colonel Henry Steel Olcott (1832–1907) in New York in 1875, but its headquarters was shifted to Adyar, near Madras, in 1882. Theosophy means 'Divine Wisdom', and the broader aims of the Society, as laid down by its founders, were:

> a) To form a nucleus of the Universal Brotherhood of Humanity, without distinction of race, creed, sex, caste, or colour.
> b) To encourage the study of Comparative Religion, Philosophy, and Science.
> c) To investigate unexplained laws of Nature, and the powers latent in man.[63]

61 Amanda Anderson, *The Way We Argue Now: A Study in the Cultures of Theory* (Princeton, NJ and Oxford: Princeton University Press, 2006), p. 72.

62 Ibid., p. 73. One might also think here of Edward Said's idea of cosmopolitan orientalism as demonstrated in his book *Orientalism* which crosses the East–West 'barrier', leading towards a 'non-dominative and non-essentialist type of learning'. See Said's 1995 'Afterword' to *Orientalism* (1978; London: Penguin, 1995), pp. 336–337.

63 H. P. Blavatsky, *An Abridgement of The Secret Doctrine*, eds Elizabeth Preston and Christmas Humphreys (London: The Theosophical Publishing House, 1966), p. xv.

The cardinal ideas of the Society were derived from ancient eastern spiritual traditions or 'universal religion', as they called it.[64] The foundational texts of theosophy are *Isis Unveiled* (1877), and more significantly, *The Secret Doctrine* (1888), written by Blavatsky. While *Isis Unveiled* is based on occult and hermetic traditions, *The Secret Doctrine* draws chiefly on ancient Indian texts – the Vedas and the Upanishads. The predominance of ancient Indian ideas in *The Secret Doctrine* may be due to the fact that it was written after the headquarters of the Theosophical Society was relocated to India.[65] The central ideas of theosophy as may be gleaned from Blavatsky's writings are those of 'universal but impersonal oneness, a divine spark in each human being, measuring time in cycles rather than linearly, and the justification of ethical behavior based on karma and reincarnation'.[66] But theosophy also incorporates strains of occultism, neo-Platonism, Kabbalism (a term used by Blavatsky to include all kinds of esoteric knowledge), and other forms of spiritualistic practices such as the use of a medium and automatic writing. This explains the combined importance of *Isis Unveiled* and *The Secret Doctrine.*

While the Theosophical Society claimed its objectives to be religious and cultural, and professed to exclude politics altogether, it became one of the chief internationalist movements in the early twentieth century to challenge the imperialist ideology, especially in its espousal of the ideal of the brotherhood of man, while it facilitated an East–West cultural and intellectual communication. Janet Oppenheim has pointed out that in 'the closing decades of the nineteenth century and the opening years of the twentieth, it was possible to perceive Theosophy as part of the vast liberation movement designated to topple the materialistic, patriarchal, capitalistic, and utterly philistine culture of the Victorian Age'.[67] After Annie Besant took over as the president of the Society, she formed the All-India Home Rule League in 1915 that gave the Indian nationalist movement a more radical turn. The Society thus became overtly politically involved.

Theosophy considers ancient eastern philosophy and spirituality to be superior to Christianity and western culture. Cousins states that 'Indian culture is as alive today as it was millennia ago: and a live culture, especially if it be falsely regarded as a rival culture to that of its overlordship … is not likely to be regarded as sufficiently harmless' adding that, 'truth' as understood by the English is utilitarian and 'an entirely territorial and racial affair'.[68] Theosophy thus challenged

64 Mark Bevir, 'Theosophy as a Political Movement' in *Gurus and Their Followers: New Religious Reform Movements in Colonial India*, ed. Anthony Coupley (New Delhi: Oxford University Press, 2000), p. 160.

65 See David Weir, *American Orient: Imagining the East from the Colonial Era through the Twentieth Century* (Amherst and Boston, MA: University of Massachusetts Press, 2011), p. 187.

66 W. Michael Ashcraft, *The Dawn of a New Cycle: Point Loma Theosophists and American Culture* (Knoxville, TN: University of Tennessee Press, 2002), p. 17.

67 Janet Oppenheim, *The Other World: Spiritualism and Psychical Research in England 1850–1914* (Cambridge: Cambridge University Press, 1985), p. 183.

68 Cousins, *Renaissance in India*, p. 7.

the privilege of forming the fundamental spiritual and ethical notions for entire mankind which the imperial (Christian) culture had arrogated to itself on the basis of its political-economic dominance.

However, theosophy's belief in the hierarchy of races is one of its fundamental weaknesses. Its belief in the superiority of the Aryan race led many western theosophists, including Cousins, to embrace Hinduism. Annie Besant, herself of Irish descent, identified Celts and Indians as Aryans, thus establishing a racial identity between India and Ireland.[69] At the same time, theosophy's doctrine of 'universal humanity' and 'universal brotherhood' enabled it to form powerful networks and conglomerates of intellectual and cultural relationship between the metropolitan centre and the colonial peripheries.

For Cousins, as for many other Irish orientalists such as Yeats and AE, theosophy became a potential avenue through which an Irish-Asian cross-colonial identity could be forged. Joseph Lennon has shown how, because of Ireland's ambivalent location within the Empire, Irish writers sought cross-colonial identity, particularly with India, in their nationalist aspirations.[70] Yeats was profoundly aware of the impact of theosophy on the general western sensibility; as Tagore's English *Gitanjali* was taking shape, he assured Rothenstein that the Theosophical Society had already prepared the European mind for appreciating the spiritual poetry of Tagore's *Gitanjali*.[71]

Yeats's presumption was not merely based on his own encounter with theosophy;[72] he was, early on, trying to retrieve the ancient Irish mystical tradition. At the same time, he had acquired interest in Indian spiritualism and mysticism and was trying to mingle the Irish and Indian traditions together in his work. In 1906, long before he had met Tagore, he spoke of a 'spiritual democracy', arguing that '[i]f we had produced a political democracy we had lost the spiritual democracy to which the troubadours sang.'[73] His idea of 'spiritual democracy' was further buttressed by Tagore's advent on the western literary scene. Ronald Schuchard comments that 'the arrival of the Bengali poet Rabindranath Tagore in the Imagist complex invigorated Yeats's cultural imagination … [and]

69 This reportedly gave impetus to the caste and other forms of social stratification existent in India. This is also one of the reasons why theosophy appealed mostly to upper-caste Hindus.

70 Joseph Lennon, *Irish Orientalism: A Literary and Cultural History* (Syracuse, NY: Syracuse University Press, 2004), pp. xxvii–xxix.

71 Yeats to Rothenstein, 10 Aug 1912 in *The InteLex Electronic Edition of the Collected Letters of W.B. Yeats* (2002). Hereafter, the letters of this collection are cited by their *InteLex CL* code number. In this case, *InteLex CL* 1960.

72 In fact, he was critical of the Society in an article on Lucifer in the *Weekly Review* and had to resign from its inner circle, and had sharply 'told them they were turning a good philosophy into a bad religion.' See his letter to John O'Leary dated [c.8] Nov [1890] in *The Collected Letters of WB Yeats 1865–1895*: Vol. I, eds. John Kelly and Eric Domville (Oxford: Clarendon Press, 1986), p. 234. But the connection remained till the last years of his life.

73 Reported in *The Aberdeen Daily Journal*, January 13, 1906, p. 3. Cited in Ronald Schuchard, *The Last Minstrels: Yeats and the Revival of the Bardic Arts* (Oxford: Oxford University Press, 2008), p. 204.

enforced his belief that … a spiritual democracy was still possible in the West'.[74] In fact, despite Ireland's location in Europe, some of the leading Irish writers and intellectuals in the late nineteenth and early twentieth centuries (who were theosophists as well) had turned towards India as a potential source of cultural revival of their own tradition; their own revival, they believed, would also lead to Europe's revival as well. These revivalists saw the renaissances in Ireland and India as simultaneous, analogous, and even interconnected cultural phenomena. Therefore, cross-colonial empathic relationships between Ireland and India emerged through mutual cultural, literary, and intellectual transactions.

Theosophy, Brahmoism, and the Empire

Tagore's initial connection with theosophy was, at best, tenuous. In his short story 'Hungry Stone' he dismisses theosophy. Even the Brahmo Samaj, the most intellectually sophisticated heterodox sect in the nineteenth- and early-twentieth-century Bengal, of which the Tagore family was in the vanguard, was cautious in its response to theosophy. When the Theosophical Society asked the Brahmo Samaj for intellectual support, the Samaj responded mildly and remained noncommittal. Their journal, *Tattwabodhini Patrika*, declared:

> We have much pleasure in expressing our hearty sympathy with the second of the three objectives [To promote the study of Aryan and other eastern literatures, religions and sciences, and vindicate their importance]. … It is surely a source of great gratification to us that we have now our long-cherished opinions on the greatness of our forefathers and the high value of the store of knowledge they have bequeathed to us shared by such learned persons of the Western world as the Founder and the Corresponding Secretary of the Theosophical Society.

But the conclusion struck a note of caution: 'We do not share in all the opinions of the Theosophical Society!'[75] Tagore himself was cautious in his approach towards the Theosophical Society, probably because of Annie Besant's radical political stance. A letter he wrote to Andrews in 1918 makes this plain:

> I have many things to ask your advice about – about myself, our ashram and about Nagen. Nagen writes me a letter with a piteous appeal to you to help him in procuring for him some decent employment in Hyderabad or any other place. I had the idea of asking Cousins for a professorship; but to enter into any relationship of obligation with Mrs Besant and her crew

74 Schuchard, *The Last Minstrels*, p. xxiii.
75 Editorial in *Tattwabodhini Patrika*, No. 466, Saka1804, p. 40.

> may cost me my freedom, and that is why I hesitate, though the situation for Nagen is getting more and more cruel everyday.[76]

Cousins knew of Tagore's wariness about Mrs Besant; so, when Tagore sought his assistance for Visva-Bharati, he was forthright in his response:

> I wonder if you have thought of the probable effect of my association with Dr. Besant and the Theosophical Society on any work which I might undertake for Visva-Bharati ... Such experience and capacity as I have would, if circumstances so permitted, be bent to fulfilling your ideals, not pushing any notions of my own save as they were in affinity with yours.[77]

To this Tagore sincerely replied: 'I am in complete agreement with what you say regarding your relationship towards the Visva-Bharati and the Theosophical Society. There should not be the least cause for misunderstanding and differences of opinion.'[78] Tagore's reply shows that while he did not want anyone to exercise authority on his institution, he was open to those who understood, shared, and respected his ideals, in the true spirit of universalism that Visva-Bharati enshrined. Interestingly, Tagore, during his third visit to England in 1912, seems to have taken a fleeting interest in theosophy, presumably influenced by Yeats. In a letter, Yeats wrote to one, Miss Elizabeth Radcliffe, who worked as a medium for automatic writing, asking her if she would 'write' for Tagore who 'is a great saint & a great man so perhaps you could care to,' assuring her that ['y]our secret would be safe with him'.[79]

Around 1915, Tagore became closely associated with the Theosophical Society, which may have brought about a shift in his views about the Society and theosophy as well. We cannot determine if his friendship with Cousins since that time had brought about this change in him. But he was elected Chancellor of the National University formed under the aegis of the Theosophical Society on 30 December 1917. In 1919, he went to Bangalore where he read the paper 'The Centre of Indian Culture' in which he explained, for the first time in English, the ideals of Visva-Bharati, the university whose foundation stone had been laid in Santiniketan on 22 December 1918. The Centre for the Promotion of National Education, Adyar, published the lecture in the form of a booklet. From Bangalore, Tagore went to Madanapalle where he translated on 22 February 'Jana gana mana' into English as 'The Morning Song of India' and Margaret

76 *Selected Letters of Rabindranath Tagore*, eds. Krishna Dutta and Andrew Robinson (New Delhi: Cambridge University Press, South Asian Edition, 2005), p. 213. Nagen is Nagendranath Ganguli, Tagore's son-in-law. Later on, he became a professor of rural and agricultural economics at the University of Calcutta.

77 See Letter No. 24 in this volume.

78 See Letter No. 25 in this volume.

79 Yeats to Elizabeth Radcliffe, 16 August 1913. *InteLex CL* 2240.

Cousins set the notes for the song. Tagore, we might add here, did not support Besant's Home Rule League, but when Besant was incarcerated, he wrote publicly demanding her release as Besant's 'martyrdom' to him was 'for the cause of suffering humanity'.[80]

On the other hand, Tagore's visit to Madanapalle was for Cousins a historic event. But more eventful was Tagore's translation of 'Jana gana mana' into English, and Cousins effusively records this in his duo-autobiography:

> From the memory of a week of intense happy activity around the poet stands out the event that made literary history, and carried the name and thought of Tagore into the minds and hearts of millions of the young in schools and colleges and outside them and ultimately gave humanity the nearest approach to an ideal national anthem.[81]

That Cousins had a very strong attachment to the song is demonstrated by his later remarkable responses to it. He presented the song in America even before it was adopted as India's national anthem. He notes that the song was sung as a 'daily dedication' at Madanapalle College. He and Rukmini Devi Arundale had also sung the song as an 'Indo-Irish duet in Bengali words' at the World Congress of the Theosophical Society in Iowa in 1929, in response to Annie Besant's question of why India had no national anthem.[82] He again sang the first stanza of the song, first in Bengali, following it up with Tagore's English translation, in New York in 1930. Cousins recalls:

> The geographical recital of this introduction to the "Morning Song of India" did not obscure the declaration that the Will behind human thought was also behind the future of India and that victory for that Will meant victory of all and the defeat of none. Then flashed into my mind what must have been the earliest hint of "Jana gana mana" as the national anthem of India. … In the reverent silence that followed I ended my address: "I offer you the 'Morning Song of India' not as the national anthem of one nation as opposed to others, but as the international anthem of humanity."[83]

This magnificent observation powerfully demonstrates how the song's universal import was perceptible to Cousins but, unfortunately, not to Tagore's Indian detractors then. The question whether to accept 'Jana gana mana' over Bankimchandra's 'Vandemataram' as the national anthem was publicly debated in the 1930s. Even Tagore himself had to respond to bitter questions as to whether

80 *Selected Letters of Rabindranath Tagore*, p. 183.
81 Cousins and Cousins, *We Two Together*, p. 341.
82 Ibid., p. 499.
83 Ibid., pp. 519–520.

the song was addressed to King George the Fifth. In two letters, one in 1937 and the other in 1939, he clarified his intention. In the second letter, he indignantly replied:

> I should only insult myself if I cared to answer those who consider me capable of such unbounded stupidity as to sing in praise of George the Fourth or George the Fifth as Eternal Charioteer leading the pilgrims on their journey through countless ages of the timeless history of mankind.[84]

But it is worth noting that, much earlier, in a letter dated 1 June 1913, Yeats had written to Lady Gregory about the song:

> I had a farewell visit from one of Tagore's followers. … He told me a charming story about Tagore. I told him how Sarojini's brother was sad over a poem welcoming the King written by Tagore. The Indian's face was full of amusement. He said, 'The National Congress people asked Tagore for a poem of welcome. He tried to write it but could not. He got up very early in the morning and wrote a very beautiful poem – not one of his best but still beautiful. When he came down he [Tagore] said to one of us, 'There is a poem which I have written. It is addressed to God – but I give it to the Congress people. It will please them. They will think it is addressed to the King." He added that all Tagore's own followers knew it meant God but others did not.

This letter reveals that the real intent of the song was known even in England from the time it was written. However, Yeats concludes his letter quipping that he did not disclose the truth about the song so that Edmund Gosse, whom he was trying to convince at that time to have Tagore elected to the Academic Committee of the Royal Society of Literature, should find no pretext to disagree with the proposal.[85]

Cousins, however, played a more decisive role in the national anthem debate. In an open letter he called the song 'the Conjoint Voice of India' and strongly supported its significance for adoption as India's national anthem. Part of the letter that Cousins wrote, reads:

> Janagana specially recognizes the diversity of human life in India, and gives it its true unification, not an impossible uniformity of externals, but the real unity that comes of mutual aspirations towards the Universal life in which all share.

84 Cited in Probodhchandra Sen, *India's National Anthem* (Calcutta: Visva-Bharati, 1949), p. 7.
85 Yeats to Lady Gregory, 01 Jan 1913. *InteLex CL* 2050.

> In this all the faiths can join without reservation and in using only the first stanza, no mutilation is done to the others and no unspoken apology for omitted offence is needed. … Admittedly there is no laudation of one's own country over another in the anthem. But such laudation is only a nation-wide demonstration of the inferiority complex, and India should be beyond boastfulness.

He concludes the letter stating that the song expresses 'not the shifty sentiment of expedient tolerance, but the eternal law of unity in diversity'.[86]

We might surmise that Tagore's association with the Theosophical Society and his friendship with Cousins may have awakened his personal interest in theosophy in course of time. In the late 1920s, Tagore began to take interest in spirits and held planchette sessions through a young girl Uma, a student at Santiniketan. In the late 1930s, Tagore drew Maitreyi Devi's[87] attention to two 'strange stories' in a theosophical journal (presumably *The Theosophist*). When Maitreyi Devi asked Tagore if he believed in such things, the poet retorted:

> Just as there isn't enough evidence to prove it, neither is there enough to disprove it completely. When both sides are equal, why should we disbelieve it for nothing? [I]t is quite possible that there are things which can never be thoroughly established … they are meant to remain hidden. But it happens that at special moments and to some specific persons glimpses of them are revealed.[88]

Moreover, the Theosophical Society's ideal of the universal brotherhood of mankind may also have impressed Tagore. The Brahmo Samaj also espoused the ideal of universal humanism. So, this common universalist ideal might have drawn Tagore closer to the Society. Tagore's family, we have already noted, not only belonged to the Brahmo Samaj but were its leaders. Tagore describes the position of his family thus:

> We were ostracised because of our heterodox opinions about religion and therefore we enjoyed the freedom of the outcaste. We had to build our own world with our own thoughts and energy of mind. We had to build

86 James Henry Cousins, 'Vande Mataram Dispute' in *Madras Mail*, 3 November 1937, RBA, File No. 72.

87 Maitreyi Devi (1914–1989) was the daughter of the eminent Indian philosopher Surendranath Dasgupta. After her marriage in 1934, she went to live at Mongpu in Darjeeling with her husband; Tagore was her guest at Mongpu a number of times since then. She wrote a number of books on Tagore. In 1976, she received the Sahitya Akademi (Indian Academy of Letters) Award for her novel *Na Hanyate* (It does not Die).

88 Devi, *Tagore by Fireside* (Calcutta: Rupa, 1961), pp. 69–70.

> it from the foundation, and therefore had to seek the foundation that was firm.[89]

What Tagore says about his own family also applied to other Brahmos. The Brahmos derive their appellation from their belief in Brahmā as the Supreme reality. The movement was initiated by Raja Rammohun Roy (1772–1833), and after his death in 1833, Devendranath Tagore (1817–1905), Rabindranath's father, led the movement. Tagore observes that Rammohun Roy had re-introduced India's ancient tradition of the worship of Brahmā in the modern age. In his words: 'India had proclaimed her own truth through Rammohun Roy. This message was uttered at the moment when the foreign master had arrived to initiate India into a new faith.'[90] The 'new religious movement', Tagore explains, 'was a strict monotheism based upon the teachings of the Upanishads'; it was thus not merely 'revolutionary' but a 'truly modern' movement in its 'revelation of the spirit in man'; it also instituted in his family 'a faith in the loyalty to an inner ideal'.[91]

Between 1909 and 1912, Tagore wrote a number of seminal essays through which he extended the idea of universal humanism which he claimed to be foundational to the Brahmo movement.[92] Significantly enough, Tagore's delineation of universalism from the platform of the Brahmo Samaj is based on his reinterpretation of the essential characteristics of the Hindu tradition. As a heterodox sect, the Brahmos had to face the hostility of orthodox Hindus who refused to consider Brahmos as Hindus; on the other hand, some 'progressive' Brahmos were of the view that they were not Hindus. With powerful intellectual arguments, Tagore attempted to convince the members of his sect that Brahmos were essentially Hindus. In defending his point, he invoked and virtually redefined Hinduism by fleshing out its inclusivity and universality. In a less known but significant essay, 'Hindu Brahmo', he draws upon the Hindu tradition and argues that:

> A great power which is exerting itself enormously in India among Hindus despite the presence of several divisive forces, has blended the blood of the Aryan with that of the non-Aryan; that power has appropriated the Saka, the Hun and the Greek colonies; that power has given place to hundreds of

89 Rabindranath Tagore, *Talks in China* (Calcutta: Visva-Bharati, 1925), p. 29

90 Rabindranath Tagore, 'Brāhmosamājer sārthakatā' (The Significance of the BrahmoSamaj), in *RR*, Vol. VIII, 1988, p. 610. See, for an excellent study of Brahmo intellectual thought, David Kopf's *The Brahmo Samaj and the Shaping of the Modern Indian Mind* (New Delhi: Archives Publishers, 1988).

91 Tagore, *Talks in China*, p. 33.

92 On this point I am indebted to Bikash Chakravarty's 'Introduction' to his *Poets to a Poet 1912-1940* (Calcutta: Visva Bharati, 1998), pp. 15–16.

> creeds and practices within itself, and that power is bent upon realizing the noble unity of an eternal truth.[93]

In a discourse on the significance of the Brahmo Samaj, Tagore contends:

> It is not true that the Brahmo Samaj is an attempt to reform Hindu society in modern times; nor is it a contemporary attempt to bring about the confluence of knowledge (*jnan*) and devotion (*bhakti*) in the minds of God's worshippers. The Brahmo Samaj is the modern self-expression of an eternal India.[94]

The modernity of India is identified with the modernity of the Brahmo Samaj which, Tagore affirms, lies in the idea of universalism:

> The history of the Brahmo Samaj denotes that India will establish a perfect image of Brahma-worship in the world – a mode of worship that brings everyone within its ambit and can unify all, a means through which life attains its true completeness within the universal.[95]

India has acquired and cultivated this spirit of universality through her legacy of extending hospitality to different cultures at different points of time in her history; the arrival of the West has re-awakened that spirit again:

> This time the western guest has been invited to India's store-house of wisdom – there is no cause for alarm, there is no want. At the feast that will now be held, the East and the West will be placed on the same chord.[96]

The idea of universalism is treated with more philosophical profundity in other essays. One such notable essay is 'Visvabodh' (Universal Consciousness), given as a lecture at Santiniketan in 1909. In it, Tagore states that the focus of India's spiritual pursuit has been to acquire a Universal Consciousness, to be the part of a unifying experience. 'The more a person extends his sense of perception or experience', Tagore argues, 'his desire for mastery gradually withers.'[97] Though Tagore does not mention anything explicitly, we feel that this statement is directed against all forms of power struggle, both within and outside India.

93 Rabindranath Tagore, 'Hindu Brāhmo' in *RR*, Vol. IX, 1999, p. 729.
94 Tagore, 'Brāhmosamājer sārthakatā', p. 607.
95 Ibid., p. 611.
96 Ibid., p. 608.
97 Rabindranath Tagore, 'Viswabodh' (Universal Consciousness) in *RR*, Vol. VII, 1988, pp. 723–725.

But Tagore's universalist argument is not the figment of a poet's imagination. Nor is it unaccommodative. 'Is the thing called universalism then a fantasy?' he asks rhetorically and proceeds to answer that:

> [T]he thing called universal could undoubtedly be a fantasy if it denied all kinds of boundaries, all kinds of specificities. ... Since everything has its own distinction, the realisation of a unity in the midst of immense diversity constitutes the real pursuit of universalism.[98]

The key 'problem facing the world', he points out elsewhere, is not 'how to drown our differences and become one – but how unity can be achieved with all differences maintained'.[99] In this context, he identifies the categorical difference between the *soi-disant* universalism of the West and the universalism of India. The universalism of the West manifested in its 'consciousness of imperialism' aims at binding together peoples of different European nations, but this unity is superficial and is acquisitive in nature.[100] On the other hand, the 'Universal Consciousness' pursued by India is spiritual and immutable in nature.[101] Thus, Tagore offers a powerful critique of the universalism espoused by many European Enlightenment thinkers, and foregrounds an alternative form of universalism rooted in spirituality and the spirit of sacrifice – a universalism that encounters the universalism of the West that masks its materialist and acquisitive intention. We shall consider briefly in the following two sections how Tagore's universalist ideas are manifested in his literary and institutional work.

98 Rabindranath Tagore, 'Hindu Brāhmo' in *RR*, Vol. IX, 1999, pp. 725–726.

99 Rabindranath Tagore, 'Hindu Viswavidyālaya' (Hindu University) in *RR*, Vol. IX, 1999, p. 606.

100 Indeed, Tagore's critique of European Enlightenment would be corroborated by many modern scholars; while they agree that the Enlightenment with its emphasis on reason, science, freedom, and human rights fostered liberation from religious dogmas and created ideas of civil and political freedom, they also argue that the Enlightenment project with its homogenising idea of progress and universal rationality was an imperialist discourse to write off all local cultures and traditions. Some others have stressed the Eurocentrism of Enlightenment thought, leading to the marginalisation and exclusion of the non-West.The literature on the Enlightenment is too vast to mention here. However, a few of the finest critiques for our present purpose are, Gayatri Chakravorty Spivak's *A Critique of Postcolonial Reason: Towards a History of the Vanishing Present* (Cambridge, MA: Harvard University Press, 1999) and Uday Chand Mehta's *Liberalism and Empire: India in British Liberal Thought* (New Delhi: Oxford University Press, 1999). Daniel Carey and Lynn Festa, eds *The Post-colonial Enlightenment: Eighteenth-Century Enlightenment and Postcolonialism* (Oxford: Oxford University Press, 2009) has a number of important essays. Jonathan Israel's excellent *Radical Enlightenment: Philosophy and the Making of Modernity 1650–1750* (Oxford: Oxford University Press, 2001) pursues a trajectory challenging the established ideas of the Enlightenment.

101 Tagore, 'Viswabodh', p. 724.

Ireland, India, and the world: nationalism, internationalism, universal humanism

Cousins migrated to India while the First World War raging. Within a few months of his arrival, the Easter Rising in Dublin (in April 1916) would shatter the dreams of the Revivalists such as Yeats and AE, and political violence would replace their efforts to bring about national reawakening and unity in Ireland through literary and cultural activities. Yeats bemoaned that 'all the work of years has been overturned'.[102] Though Cousins shared the belief of other Irish Revivalists in a literary-cultural solution to the Ireland's nationalist problem, he, nonetheless, expressed support for the revolutionaries in a series of articles in *New India*. His articles invited the censure of the English administrators in India and led to his dismissal from the newspaper by none other than Annie Besant. In an article in *New India* of 3 May 1916 he wrote:

> The outbreak is simply and solely the reaction of a quick and proud race to the vacillation and ineptitude in regard to the passing of the Home Rule Bill displayed by the Liberal Government. … [T]he lesson of history has been lost on the ruling caste, that frankness and generosity are the way to love and loyalty, while prevarication and shuffling are the parents of revolt.[103]

He followed it up with a few short biographical pieces on some rebel leaders such as Constance Markievicz, Patrick Pearse, and James Connolly. He wrote another article on Dublin in which, while delineating the urbanity and the glories of the city, he bemoans the great divide between its poverty and its wealth, implicitly accusing the English rulers in Ireland for the uprising.[104] Cousins paid a moving tribute to Francis Sheehy-Skeffington, his close friend, when the latter was shot dead without a trial after his arrest, in the poem 'In Memory of Francis Sheehy-Skeffington'. Cousins describes Sheehy-Skeffington as 'shak[ing] the world' in his 'fall' and concludes on a bitterly ironic tone:

> You whom no threat or danger awed;
> Whose hand would heal where sharp it fell,
> Smite Error on the Throne of God,
> And smile on Truth though found in Hell.[105]

102 Yeats to Lady Gregory, 11 May 1916. *InteLex CL* 2950.

103 Cited in Lennon, *Irish Orientalism*, p. 335.

104 James H. Cousins, 'Dublin: The City of Revolutions' in *The Modern Review*, Vol. XX, July-December 1916, pp. 450–454.

105 Cousins, *Collected Poems 1894–1940* (Madras: Kalakshetra, 1940), p. 166.

He also wrote the following lines in another poem, 'To Ireland before the Treaty of December, 1921':

> But for your night of agonies
> I give dark songs I cannot sing.[106]

But the dream of a romantic Ireland persisted, and back in Ireland in 1925, a decade after he had left it in 1915, he paid a 'simple' tribute to his homeland in the form of a 'prayer' in the poem 'Ireland after Ten Years':

> Land of my birth! again I greet
> Thy grey-wing sky, green earth, sweet air
> And, passing hence, lay at thy feet
> The tribute of a simple prayer;[107]

On 1 October 1902, Annie Besant gave a lecture entitled "Theosophy and Ireland"; Cousins attended the lecture and was so overwhelmed that he soon became a member of the Dublin Theosophical Society. From Besant's lecture, he had gathered the idea that 'Ireland was ultimately to emerge as the spiritual mentor of Europe, even as India had long ago been to Asia'.[108] So India offered him the home where he could forge a common anti-colonial Indo-Irish cultural agenda, but he was simultaneously thinking beyond India and Ireland. Cosmopolitan and internationalist ideas were taking shape in his mind. He justifies this in a book of essays he inscribed to Tagore:

> So subtly, however, had the Aryan influence intermingled with the culture of Ireland that when, once again, at the beginning of the twentieth century, the ancient Asian spirit touched Ireland through the philosophy of India, as conveyed to it through the works of Edwin Arnold and the Theosophical Society, there was an immediate response. Two poets (AE and Yeats) found their inmost nature expressed in the Indian modes.[109]

For him, Tagore was the paradigm of India's unity with Ireland in modern times; he writes passionately of his deep conviction that the 'simple profundities and exaltations' of Yeats, AE, and Tagore 'reached depths and heights beyond the bearings of race and country and language'. Recalling Henri Jubainville, the

106 Ibid., p. 285.
107 Ibid., p. 286.
108 Cousins and Cousins, *We Two Together*, p. 75.
109 James H. Cousins, *The Cultural Unity of Asia* (Madras: Theosophical Publishing House, 1922), pp. 7–8.

French Celticist's analogy between the ancient religions of Ireland and India, he continues:

> We were one in spirit, we pioneers of the new Irish movement in poetry, and the poet from India. And those who are one in spirit, the dissimilarities in expression are even more generous in suggestion of the spiritual through the material, which is the essence of mysticism in arts, than the similarities that the archaeological mind values.[110]

Cousins's attempt to see the unity of Ireland and India on the spiritual plane was a formative step towards a cultural order where nations of the world, both of the East and of the West, would be united through their literature and art. As Gauri Viswanathan, in her brilliant essay, so aptly put it: 'Indeed, he [Cousins] argued that through literature and art, and not through the political order, that the new internationalism was being forged.'[111]

At the same time, Cousins was extremely conscious of the fact that contemporary internationalism advocated by western nations was all but a disguise for prolonging the economic exploitation of the weaker nations by the stronger nations of Europe. In a short, hard-hitting essay, he exposes how internationalism has been supplanted by nationalism because 'the Internationalism dreamt of was not real Internationalism in any sense but a projected commercial bucking up of big political trusts. … The Internationalism that will be worthy of contemplation will be found in a spiritual comradeship.'[112]

Cousins elaborates his idea of the 'spiritual comradeship' in his book on modern English poetry. He begins on the premise that in Fitzgerald's recreation of Omar Khayyam, Laurence Hope's fevered songs of India, and Edwin Arnold's poetical recreation of Buddhism and Hinduism in *The Light of Asia* and *The Song Celestial*, 'it will be seen that for the invasion of India by the English language, the East has taken a spiritual revenge by invading English poetry'.[113]

A literary cosmopolitan such as Tagore, who inhabits multiple linguistic and cultural worlds, runs Cousins's argument, brings

110 James H. Cousins, 'Introduction' in *Three Mystic Poets: A Study of W B Yeats, A E and Rabindranath Tagore*, ed. Abinash Ch Bose (Kolhapur: School and College Bookstore, 1946), p. vi.

111 Gauri Viswanathan, 'India, Ireland and the Poetics of Internationalism' in *Journal of World History*, Vol. XIV (1), March 2004, p. 23. I have discussed in detail how Yeats, Tagore, and Cousins thought of culture as a domain alternative to politics. See Majumdar, *Yeats and Tagore*. See also Sachidananda Mohanty's *Cosmopolitan Modernity* on the cosmopolitan ideas of Cousins and Tagore. Cousins uses the term 'internationalism'. Gauri Viswanathan has followed Cousins in her essay cited above.

112 James H. Cousins, *Footsteps of Freedom: Essays* (Madras: Ganesh & Co, 1919), p. 74.

113 James H. Cousins, *Modern English Poetry: Its Characteristics and Tendencies* (Madras: Ganesh & Co, 1921), pp. 10–11.

> the best of each towards the other, in a true free spiritual kinship. He sets the heart of India … right against the heart of the world; and … will … profoundly move English poetry towards a broader view of the nature of humanity and the universe.[114]

Critics of postcolonial literature now argue that this kind of literature while making 'direct or oblique' references to the violence embedded in imperialism, also facilitated 'the no less fascinating and sometimes rather auspicious forms of contact and communication' that ultimately engendered and implanted 'cosmopolitan forms of relationship that would be required to create and to legitimize a global society'.[115] The seminal ideas of Tagore and Cousins had already set the tone for this kind of thinking in the early twentieth century. Tagore, we may note, did not merely write in both Bengali and English; he was born and grew up in a family whose culture was expressly modern and cosmopolitan. Members of his family were poets, artists, musicians, philosophers, and playwrights; they were also avid readers of English and European literature, much of which they read in the original. Tagore himself took great interest in world literature and read not only English writers, but also Dante, Goethe, Heine, and others in English translation;[116] he even wrote essays on Dante, Petrarch, Goethe, and Anglo-Saxon and Anglo-Norman literature in his younger days.[117] Moreover, he set the modernist tone in Bengali literature, making innovations in language and style while also blending many generic, formal, and thematic elements of English and European literature in his writings. In this sense, Susan Steadman Friedman has very appropriately subsumed Tagore into her wide-ranging framework of 'planetary modernism'.[118]

Irish poets too used English, Cousins notes, and '[t]here is an affinity in their [Tagore's and Irish poets'] poetry which is deeper than emotion or thought and can only be signified by the term spiritual'. Thus, while Irish poets 'aim[ed] at national expression' there was 'behind her [Ireland's] professed aim … an urge to spiritual conquest'.[119]

So, the 'sentiments of comradeship' that literature can potentially foster is shattered by nationalist ambition. Cousins concedes that patriotism is necessary as a voice of protest against 'voluntary domination by foreign ideals … or involuntary domination by foreign institutions in countries, as in Ireland and

114 Ibid., pp. 14–15.

115 Robert Spencer, *Cosmopolitan Criticism and Postcolonial Literature* (Basingstoke: Palgrave, 2011), pp. 1–3.

116 Of many such scattered references in Tagore's autobiographical writings see, particularly, the lecture entitled 'Autobiographical' in *Talks in China*, pp. 40–41.

117 These essays in Bengali are in *RR*, Vol. XVII.

118 Susan Stanford Friedman, *Planetary Modernisms: Provocations on Modernity across Time* (New York: Columbia University Press, 2015).

119 James H. Cousins, *Modern English Poetry*, p. 15.

India', but the need of the moment is 'internationalism'.[120] The poetry of nations like India and Ireland with a rich spiritual tradition can only bind all human beings into a unity; this is the only way for real internationalism to flourish. It is in Tagore's poetry that he finds internationalism and universal humanism. Incidentally, Tagore himself became aware of the universal impact of his own role. To Amiya Chakravarty, a poet and academic and his close associate, he wrote: 'If you came out of the country, you would realise how extensively I am related to the world — that relationship has significance — it is making a contribution to the history of the world which is deeper and more valuable than local politics.'[121]

Cousins does not diminish or repudiate the importance of patriotic sentiment; rather, he argues that internationalism becomes meaningful only in the context of patriotism. But he calls for only that kind of patriotic poetry which will bear the 'corrective influence of the international ideal on the national'. True nationalism is that which is at home with 'world consciousness'. As he points out:

> Hitherto, the international note in poetry has been mainly expressive of acquisition on the part of strong nations, and the setting up of relationships, based not on the principle of mutual service, but of self-interest ... but few have sung the ideal of human comradeship. When Tagore prays his prayer for his country, [Where the mind is without fear ...] it is not for India alone but for all lands.[122]

In other words, great writers transcend the confines of their national cultures and appeal to entire humanity. It is their universal humanism that must be reckoned with:

> The great masters of literature are translatable into the language of all countries and all ages, not because they renounced patriotism, but because their patriotism was lifted and completed by humanism, sometimes as a conscious *ism*, sometimes as an intuition.[123]

While James Cousins expounded how literature could be a vehicle of internationalism, Margaret Cousins believed that internationalism could grow through 'mutual understanding between the various existing nations' and 'understanding arises from some bases of intercommunication and some medium of exchange of ideas'. She points out that music, as the 'language of emotion' both in the East and the West alike, could be an 'international pathway to world-harmony'. As

120 Ibid., p. 202.

121 Tagore to Amiya Chakravarty, 25 March 1929 in Rabindranath Tagore, *Chithipatra* (Letters), Vol. XI (Calcutta: Visva-Bharati, 1974), p. 92. (My translation).

122 Ibid., pp. 202–203.

123 Ibid., p. 204.

against nationalistic affiliation, she projected a radically different utopian world where 'perhaps a person in the near future will choose his or her country according to temperamental affinities (including the special kind of music) rather than by birth'.[124] With this, we turn to Tagore.

In a letter to Tagore, Cousins mentions that 'you are "frightfully famous", as a person once said of James Joyce'.[125] There is apparently no evidence to suggest that Tagore and James Joyce (1882–1941) knew each other. But what connects them is that both were subjects under British imperial rule. Only recently, a few scholars have woken up to the fact that their response to imperialism may have some affinities. Susan Friedman, for instance, has argued that since there are '[m]ultiple and recurrent modernities' which are 'not only distinctive but also linked to other modernisms in vast relational networks'; Joyce and Tagore through their 'interactions with the colonizing cultures' and their 'rooted[ness] in their own vernaculars and cosmopolitan traditions' became iconic figures of 'colonial modernities' in the Irish Renaissance and the Bengal Renaissance, respectively.[126]

In *A Portrait of the Artist as a Young Man*, we come across some of Joyce's reactions to English imperial rule in Ireland. One important incident in the novel is Stephen Dedalus's encounter with the English dean of studies, 'the countryman of Ben Jonson'; the encounter makes Stephen acutely conscious of the status of English for the native speaker in Ireland; Stephens's musing after his encounter illustrates the pain and paradox of using the coloniser's language: 'The language in which he is speaking is his before it is mine. … I cannot speak or write … without unrest of spirit. His language, so familiar and so foreign, will always be for me an acquired speech. … My soul frets in the shadow of his language.'[127] English was imposed on the Irish through the erasure of the native language and culture over several centuries of colonial rule. However, in his extraordinary virtuosity of its usage, particularly in *Ulysses* and *Finnegans Wake*, Joyce virtually re-invented English and appropriated it for himself. This was Ireland's linguistic revenge on English,[128] much like the 'spiritual revenge' of India on English poetry as remarked by Cousins above.

The position of English in India and Ireland is, undoubtedly, different. Tagore occasionally wrote in English, but he mostly translated into English to reach a global audience; his poetry, beginning with the English *Gitanjali*, had introduced into world literature a new idiom and ambience. Still, we find in him a strong

124 Margaret E. Cousins, *The Music of Orient and Occident: Essays towards Mutual Understanding* (Madras: BG Paul & Co, 1935), pp. 2–4.

125 See Letter No. 45 in this volume.

126 Friedman, *Planetary Modernisms*, pp. 8 &261–262.

127 James Joyce, *A Portrait of the Artist as a Young Man*, ed. Seamus Deane (London: Penguin, 1992), p. 204.

128 See, particularly, Colin McCabe, 'Finnegans Wake at Fifty' in *Critical Quarterly*, Vol. XXXI (4) (Winter 1989), p. 4.

note of resistance, and he refused to surrender his poetic autonomy to 'the attraction of the literary world which with its offer of rewards tries to standardise creative visions according to criterions[*sic*] distractingly varied and variable', as he wrote to Edward Thomson, rather defiantly.[129] In another letter, he wrote more self-assuredly of his 'reputation' even without his place in English literature, and that, he had 'written and published both prose and poetry in English, mostly translations unaided by any friendly help … in order to express my ideas, not for gaining any reputation in the use of a language which can never be mine'.[130]

Incidentally, *A Portrait* and Tagore's *Ghare Bāire* (*Home and the World*, English translation, 1919) were contemporary novels and were published in the same year – 1916. Joyce, ostensibly, has nothing to do with India in *A Portrait*, but in his recall of the Latin phrase '*India mettit ebur*'[131] meaning, India sends ivory, Stephen implies a wide range of imperial oppressions in the non-western colonies which Ireland, as a western colony, also suffered.

But the affinities between the two novels run somewhat deeper than has been thought. In the final chapter of *A Portrait*, we find that Stephen refuses to subscribe to a denominational (Jesuit) 'universal brotherhood of man' and asserts: 'I believe in man … the mind of man independent of all religions.'[132] Still later, when his friend Davin questions his Irishness, Stephen blurts out that Irish nationalists such as Wolfe Tone and Parnell had been betrayed by their own people, saying: 'You talk to me of nationality, language, religion. I shall fly by those nets' because, to him, Ireland is 'the old sow that eats her furrow.'[133]

If Stephen rejects the nationalism in which his friends seem absorbed, he is, nonetheless, committed to Ireland in his own way; at the end of *A Portrait*, Stephen proposes that by escaping from Ireland, he will 'forge in the smithy of my soul the uncreated conscience of my race'.[134] In other words, he thinks of recreating a different Ireland in his imagination. Joyce's modernist cosmopolitanism, which resembles that of Tagore (and Cousins), can thus be seen as an attempt to liberate Ireland from the narrow confines of the literary provincialism and propagandist writing advocated by nationalists.

Tagore was similarly critical of nationalists, and in *Ghare Bāire*, his ironic stance puts him on a similar footing with Joyce.[135] *Ghare Bāire*, unlike *A Portrait*, is not a bildungsroman; rather, its principal concerns are nationalism, gender, patriarchy, and social harmony. In its fictional guise, it explores the limitations and the destructive consequences of political nationalism in India. The novel

129 Tagore to Edward Thompson, 20 September 1921 in *A Difficult Friendship*, p. 132.
130 Tagore to Rothenstein, 26 November 1932 in *Imperfect Encounter*, p. 346.
131 Joyce, *A Portrait*, p. 193.
132 Ibid., p. 215.
133 Ibid., p. 220.
134 Ibid., p. 277.
135 See Rahul Rao, *Third World Protest: Between Home and the World* (Oxford: Oxford University Press, 2010), pp. 113–126 for the idea of 'ironic nationalism'.

is set against the backdrop of the *swadeshi* movement that rocked Bengal from 1905 to 1908 in protest against the partition of the province by the colonial administration, allegedly, to emasculate the Bengali intelligentsia as much as to create a communal split between Hindus and Muslims. Tagore, through the protagonist Nikhilesh, the landlord, a liberal-minded humanist and cosmopolitan, questions the moral import of political swadeshism and boycott of English goods that causes immense suffering to the poor.

Sandip, the delusive, crafty, politician and demagogue, is an incarnation of a belligerent political nationalism; Tagore exposes the fatal consequences of such nationalism in Sandip's seduction of Bimala, Nikhil's wife, and in the communal violence that it engenders towards the end of the novel. Sandip is unapologetic about his unprincipled manoeuvring for his selfish ends; he tells Nikhil: 'This is not the time for us to differentiate between good and evil, right and wrong ... we have to be ruthless and unfettered; we have to anoint sin with holy markers.'[136] To Nikhil's decent, rational mind, all this sounds inherently delusive, as good as an opiate:

> In my opinion, those who do not find inspiration to serve the country by thinking of her simply and honestly as the country and respect her people as human beings, but need the intoxication of chanting aloud the mantra of addressing her as the mother, as a goddess, their love of the motherland is not as intense as their addiction to the charm. To cast a thick veil of obsession on any principle of truth is a sign of our inherent disposition towards slavery. As soon as our minds are freed, we become weak. ... As long as we do not get the taste of simple truths, as long as we have the need of such intoxications, we have to understand that we have not yet acquired the power to think of the country as our own.[137]

Way back in 1908, Tagore had recoiled from the *swadeshi* movement when it had turned violent; in a letter, he had explained his position refusing to align himself with parochial nationalism:

> Patriotism cannot be our soul's ultimate refuge; I have embraced humanity – I shall not buy glass for the price of diamonds – I cannot allow patriotism to triumph over humanity in my life ... if I cannot envision religion, if I cannot envision universal man over and above my country, if national prejudice overshadows my God, I am deprived of my soul's sustenance.[138]

136 Rabindranath Tagore, *Ghare Bāire* (*Home and the World*), in *RR*, Vol. IV, 1987, p. 491. (My translation).

137 Ibid., p. 33.

138 Tagore to Aurobindo Mohan Bose, 19 November 1908, reprinted in *Visva-Bharati Patrika* (Shravan-Ashwin) 1362 BS, p. 2. (My translation). The entire letter is translated and included in *Selected Letters of Rabindranath Tagore*, pp. 71–72.

Within a few months of the publication of *Ghare Bāire*, Tagore went on more assiduously to indict the myth of nationalism in his lectures in Japan and America in 1916–1917; the lectures were published in a book form as *Nationalism* in 1917. In the lecture in Japan, he accuses Japan of imitating the West in the name of modernisation, having abandoned the principle of *maitri* (fellowship or friendship), thereby 'brewing evil menace towards neighbours and other nations through devious means'. By accepting 'the motive force of the Western nationalism as her own', Japan was losing her 'social ideals' and thus 'poisoning the very fountainhead of humanity'. Western nationalism was destroying 'the universal brotherhood of Man', and he recalls the 'closest tie of friendship' when 'eastern Asia from Burma to Japan was tied to India'.[139] His lecture disappointed many, and even elicited sharp reactions in certain quarters in Japan.

At the same time, Tagore admired Japan's spirit of 'maitri'– '"maîtri" with men and "maîtri" with Nature"'.[140] But neither the adverse reaction in Japan nor the raging First World War in Europe deterred him, and his zeal for condemning nationalism continued undaunted in his lectures in America. In the lecture 'Nationalism in the West', Tagore views the question of nationalism through the prism of India, which he elegantly describes as a nation of 'No-Nation'. 'Neither the colourless vagueness of cosmopolitanism, nor the fierce self-idolatry of national worship can be the goal of nations', argues Tagore, because '[a] nation turns a people mechanical for political and economic ends'; it is a dehumanising machinery that undermines humanity.[141]

The motive force behind western nationalism in its ugly form, Tagore contends, is economic, which also informs its politics. Hence, Tagore does not denounce the nation per se, but the nation as a political and economic entity devoid of its social and humanistic dimensions. Instead of the nation, Tagore advocates the social ideal that has sustained India so long. 'The ideals that strive to take form in social institutions', he points out, 'have two objects. One is to regulate our passions and appetites for the harmonious development of man, and the other is to help him in cultivating disinterested love for his fellow creatures.'[142] But this ideal of universal humanity is ignored by laissez-faire materialism which lies at the root of nationalism.

It might apparently seem that Tagore's ideas are self-contradictory, since he indicts the West while he upholds the unity of all nations. But a careful reading of the text of *Nationalism* would dispel this misunderstanding, because he makes a subtle distinction between what he calls 'the spirit of the West' and 'the Nation of the West'. By the 'spirit of the West' Tagore means the literary, cultural, moral, and ethical values of the West as embodied in its literature and its ideas of 'justice

139 Rabindranath Tagore, *Nationalism* (New York: Macmillan, 1917), pp. 47–94.
140 Rabindranath Tagore, *The Spirit of Japan* (Tokyo: Indo-Japanese Association, 1916), p. 11.
141 Tagore, *Nationalism*, pp. 1–46.
142 Ibid., p. 120.

and freedom', its truthfulness in 'friendship'. It is through this 'spirit' that the East and the West can come together:

> We are complementary to each other because of our different outlooks upon life which have given us different aspects of truth. Therefore if it be true that the spirit of the West has come upon our fields in the guise of a storm it is all the same scattering living seeds that are immortal.[143]

Therefore, for Tagore, the hiatus between the East and the West, based on asymmetrical political and economic power, can be bridged on the cultural, intellectual, moral, and affective planes. This vision of internationalism and universal humanism leads him to take a utopian view of history. For him, the history of mankind is an undifferentiated history. 'There is only one history – the history of man', he claims, and '[a]ll national histories are merely chapters in the larger one.' In a prophetic note, he hopes that though India has temporarily deviated from its destined path, it will ultimately be the redeemer – 'sweeten the history of man into purity' with 'holy waters'.[144]

Simultaneously with Tagore's *Nationalism* another book on a nearly similar subject was published in America. The book was Paul Richard's *To the Nations*, to which Tagore wrote an introduction. Tagore had met in Japan, among others, Paul and Mirra Richard,[145] probably through William Pearson. Prasantakumar Pal, Tagore's biographer, notes that on Pearson's request, Tagore had recommended Richard's book to George Bret, the American editor of Macmillan, which published Tagore's English works. Bret agreed to publish the book if Tagore were to edit it and write an introduction to it. But his better advice was that the poet should pull himself back from the undertaking 'as the message of this book can be more fully given and more adequately represented in the poet's

143 Ibid., p. 26.

144 Ibid., p. 46.

145 Paul Antoine Richard (1874–1967) was a Frenchman who enlisted in the French army, left it, studied law, and was a theologian and occultist. He was closely attached to Sri Aurobindo's Pondicherry Ashram as the second husband of Mirra Alfassa (The Mother). Both Paul and Mirra were in Japan between May 1916 and April 1920. It is in Japan that Tagore and Cousins met Richard. Though Richard professed some kind of socialism, his ideas appeared convincing to Tagore. Richard was a cosmopolitan who said in an interview to Bhagawat Sharan Upadhyay in New York in 1950 that 'I always felt that the whole world was my home.' He was a believer in the unity of all cultures, and saw no difference between the East and the West. Whane asked about the differences between the civilisation of the East and the West he replied that '[h]uman culture is one. It is the spirit of man throwing great waves of light from East to West and from the West again toward East.' The interview was published in the *Amrita Bazaar Patrika*. See https://overmanfoundation.wordpress.com/2013/08/10/a-rare-interview-of-paul-richard/.Accessed 08 February 2021.

own work'.[146] Tagore, nonetheless, wrote an introduction hurriedly, and was dissatisfied, and conveyed his feelings to Pearson:

> Please give my kindest regards to Monsieur and Madame Richard and remember me to Mr Speight.[147] If the July number of *Modern Review* reaches you, you will find my introduction to "To the Nations" in an enlarged form. You know how hastily I had to write it and I was not quite satisfied with it.[148]

A major addition in the 'enlarged' version is the expression of his aversion for the 'crowd mind' which he describes as 'essentially primitive' and its power, 'elemental'; an individual loses all his power of reasoning when in a crowd, and politicians exploit this 'crowd psychology':

> Crowd psychology is a blind force. … [R]ulers of men who out of greed and fear are bent upon turning their peoples into machines of power try to train this crowd psychology for their special purposes. They hold it to be their duty to foster in the popular minds universal panic and unreasoning pride in their races and hatred of the others.[149]

Gustave Le Bon's psychological study of the unconscious actions of crowds *The Crowd: A Study of the Popular Mind* was published in 1896 and Wilfred Trotter's very influential *Instincts of the Herd in Peace and War* in 1916. It would not be wrong to think that Tagore was aware of these and other books on crowd psychology and was influenced by them. Earlier, in *Ghare Bāire*, Tagore had shown how political demagoguery sways people's minds into committing violent irrational acts. It was the same popular instinct that was played upon for garnering support for the First World War by the respective national leaders. With all this may have been combined Tagore's disappointment with the unenthusiastic public reactions to his lectures on nationalism in some of the American

146 Prasantakumar Pal, *Rabijibani* (Tagore's Life) Vol. VII 1914–1920 (Calcutta: Ananda Publishers, 1997), pp. 245–246.

147 Ernest Edwin Speight (1871–1949) was a Professor of English at the Tokyo Imperial University in Japan, and later, at Hyderabad University in India. Cousins had visited his rooms in Japan in 1919. Among Speight's Irish friends were WB Yeats and GB Shaw, and his Indian friends included Aurobindo Ghose and MK Gandhi. During his first visit to Japan, Tagore had to shift to Speight's house in Tokyo because of certain inconveniences at his initial accommodation. Both Mirra Richard and Speight attended Tagore's lecture on 11 June 1916 in Japan. Tagore had a long friendship with Speight and their letters are in the Rabindra-Bhavna Archives. Speight contributed poetry and essays to *The Modern Review* and *The Visva-Bharati Quarterly*. Pearson and Speight had co-translated Tagore's poem no. 94 from the volume *Naibedya* and it was published with the title 'To India' in *The Modern Review* in 1917. Note added.

148 Tagore to Pearson, 4 July 1917. RBA File No. 287(1).

149 Rabindranath Tagore, 'The Nation' in *The Modern Review*, Vol. XXII, Nos 1–6, July–December 1917, p. 1.

cities.[150] Cousins, on his part, was greatly impressed with Tagore's introduction to Richard's book and implored the poet to enable him to use it 'as the first pamphlet … of a new cultural mission' in India.[151] Stephen Hay remarks that though *Nationalism* and *To the Nations* address the same subject and were thoughts 'along converging lines', Tagore 'rejected the nation as something evil in itself' while Richard 'accepted it as a necessary fact but sought its transformation'. Referring to an entry in Romain Rolland's journal *Inde* about a conversation between Richard and Rolland, Hay also notes that it was in response to one of Richard's stirring questions that Tagore had told him of his plan of setting up an international university.[152]

Tagore was not alone in India in his espousal of internationalism; similar ideas were shared by other contemporary intellectuals in India as well. For instance, Ananda Coomaraswamy, for long Tagore's close associate, also believed that, more than political movements, it was intellectual and moral autonomy which was required in India. He wrote in 1910 that national cultural movements in India, Ireland, and elsewhere across the world were 'a protest of the human spirit against a premature and artificial cosmopolitanism, which would destroy in nations … the special genius of each'.[153] A staunch advocate of national cultural identity, he, nonetheless, unambiguously states that 'Nationalism is inseparable from the idea of Internationalism, recognising the rights and worth of other nations to be even as one's own.' To him, internationalism symbolised the progress of a nation under imperial domination to a state of freedom, political and economic, intellectual and moral.[154]

But Tagore's indictment of nationalism did not make his commitment to his own country less fervent. The Jallianwala Bagh Massacre (in Amritsar of Punjab) of April 1919 provoked him into a vehement protest, and he relinquished his knighthood. In an emotionally charged letter asserting the dignity of his countrymen, he famously wrote to Lord Chelmsford, the then Viceroy:

> The time has come when badges of honour make our shame glaring in the incongruous content of humiliation, and I, for my part, wish to stand, shorn of all special distinctions, by the side of those of my countrymen

150 See Stephen N. Hay, 'Rabindranath Tagore in America' in *American Quarterly*, Vol. XIV (3), (Autumn 1962), p. 449. See also Sujit Mukherjee, *Passage to America: The Reception of Rabindranath Tagore in the United States* (Calcutta: Bookland, 1964), pp. 79–84.

151 See Letter No. 19 in this volume.

152 Stephen N. Hay, *Asian Ideas of East and West: Tagore and His Critics in Japan, China, and India* (Cambridge, MA: Harvard University Press, 1970), pp. 126–127.

153 Ananda K. Coomaraswamy, *Essays in National Idealism* (Colombo: Colombo Apothecaries Co, 1910), p. vii.

154 Ibid., pp. 2–3.

> who, for their so-called insignificance, are liable to suffer degradation not fit for human beings.[155]

The following year he would write to Andrews of his bitterness at the public 'condonation' of Dyer in England:

> The result of the Dyer debates in both Houses of Parliament makes painfully evident the attitude of mind of the ruling class of this country towards India. It shows that no outrage, however monstrous … arouse[s] feelings of indignation in the hearts of those from whom our governors are chosen. The late events have conclusively proved that our true salvation lies in our own hands; that a nation's greatness can never find its foundation in half-hearted concessions of contemptuous niggardliness.[156]

Disappointed and embittered at the English parliamentary response to 'Dyerism and other symptoms of an arrogant spirit of contempt and callousness about India',[157] he wrote to Rothenstein: 'I have nothing to do directly with politics. I am not a Nationalist, moderate or immoderate in my political doctrine or aspiration. But politics is not a mere abstraction, it has its personality and it *does* intrude into my life where I am human.'[158]

Tagore's opposition to the cult of nationalism received glowing recognition from western intellectuals. In June 1919, Romain Rolland[159] sent him a

155 In *The English Writings of Rabindranath Tagore*, Vol. III, ed. Sisir K. Das (New Delhi: Sahitya Akademi, 1996, reprint 2002), p. 751.

156 *Letters from Abroad*, pp. 7–8.

157 Ibid., p. 11.

158 *Imperfect Encounter*, p. 277. Emphasis original.

159 Romain Rolland (1866–1944) was a French writer and dramatist and a mystic; he was awarded the Nobel Prize for Literature in 1915. On 10 April 1919, Rolland wrote to Tagore to enlist his support for the Declaration of Independence of the Spirit, a manifesto to forge unity among the nations in post–First World War Europe. The signatories included, among others, Albert Einstein and Hermann Hesse. Rolland's thoughts on Indian cultural, intellectual and spiritual tradition are recorded in his diary *Inde*, and he also wrote books on great Indian personalities. Among his books are: *Life of Ramkrishna* (1929), *Life of Vivekananda and the Universal Gospel* (1930) and *Mahatma Gandhi: A Study in Indian Nationalism*, translated by L. V. Ramaswami Aiyar (1924). Incidentally, the book on Gandhi was reviewed by AE who concludes his review with the comment which is worth noting: 'If we had a Tagore in Southern Ireland and a Gandhi in Northern Ireland what a revolution would take place in our politics.' AE, 'Literature and Life: The Leaders of Indian Nationalism' in *The Irish Statesman*, October 4, 1924, p. 112. For Tagore-Rolland relationship, see Chinmoy Guha's scholarly introduction in *Bridging East and West: Rabindranath Tagore and Romain Rolland Correspondence 1919–1940* (2018), pp. i–lxxii. Rolland also had a massive correspondence with the famous Indologist Kalidas Nag. See Chinmoy Guha edited, annotated and French letters translated, *The Tower and the Sea: Romain Rolland and Kalidas Nag Correspondence (1922–1938)* (New Delhi: Sahitya Akademi, 2010). Rolland's correspondence with Gandhi has been published in English translation as *Romain Rolland and Mahatma Gandhi Correspondence (Letters, Diary Extracts, Articles, etc.)*, translated by R. A. Francis (New Delhi: Publications Division, Govt. of India, 1976).

request to sign the 'Declaration of Independence of the Spirit', as he found in him a companion who would fulfil his 'dream that one day we might see the union of these two hemispheres [East and West] of the Spirit' and applauded Tagore 'for having contributed towards this more than anyone else'.[160] In reply, Tagore gladly agreed to be a part of the 'project' and wrote that 'truths that save us have always been uttered by the few and rejected by the many', lauding Rolland that 'the higher conscience of Europe has been able to assert itself in one of her choicest spirits'.[161] Alex Aronson writes that Rolland's mind had turned to Asia following the First World War and he had read a number of books on the East while he was in Switzerland. 'His recent adoption of an internationalism which would embrace all the nations of the earth – and particularly its best intellectual representatives – led him to scrutinize those manifestations of the human mind which were of a universal appeal.'[162] Rolland, before he came to know Tagore personally (Tagore and Rolland met first in 1921 and then in 1926 and 1930 in Europe), had translated some parts of Tagore's lecture, 'The Message of India to Japan', given in Japan in 1916, and had incorporated it into his anti-war pamphlet 'Declaration of Independence of the Spirit'. Aronson concludes that 'there is no doubt that Tagore's lectures in Japan further stimulated Rolland's interest in Eastern thought'. Thus, while Rolland found a kindred mind in Tagore, the latter's anti-war and anti-nation tirade brought the French writer and thinker into a still closer bond with India.[163]

We have noted that in his lecture 'Nationalism in the West' Tagore speaks of India's onus of sweetening the history of mankind. In this, he was no ineffectual dreamer. While he rejected the idea of the nation as a political entity and denounced the evils of nationalism which it produced, he was also thinking of the means through which India could be united with the world. To his son Rathindranath Tagore, he wrote on 11 October 1916:

> I also remember that the Santiniketan school must be developed into a thread linking India with the world. It is here that a centre for the cultivation of universal humanism must come up ... the victory flag of the universal man must be sown here. The efforts of my last years shall be to uncoil the world from the bondage of national sentiment.[164]

160 Reprinted in *The Modern Review*, Vol. XXVI, Nos. 1–6, July–December 1919, p. 80.

161 Ibid., p. 81.

162 Alex Aronson, *Romain Rolland: The Story of a Conscience* (Bombay: Padma Publishing House, 1944), p. 149.

163 Ibid., p. 154.

164 Rabindranath Tagore, *Chithipatra* (Letters), Vol. II (Kolkata: Visva-Bharati, reprint 2012), p. 70.

Indeed, as early as 1913, Tagore had written to Andrews of his idea of extending the mental horizon of his school:

> In the letter you will find an idea of mine as to how to cultivate the feeling of international fellowship among the boys of our school and that of some schools in the West. ... In India the range of our lives is narrow and discontinuous, that is the reason why our minds are beset with provincialism – in our ashram we must have the widest possible outlook for our boys and worldwide interests on every side – not merely through reading books, but dealing with the wider world.[165]

Within a few years, Tagore would embark upon the programme of giving concrete shape to his idea. On 22 December 1918, he laid the foundation of his international institution, Visva-Bharati, a centre where 'all her resources of knowledge and thought, Eastern and Western, [would meet] in perfect harmony'.[166] It was formally inaugurated on 22 December 1921 as a university.

It needs to be noted that Visva-Bharati was not a new establishment; it had evolved out of the Santiniketan School (Brahmacharyashrama) which Tagore had founded in 1901. Prasanta Chandra Mahalanobis, a close associate of the poet, recalls:

> On 22 December 1918, a special meeting of students, teachers, ex-students and well-wishers of the Santiniketan Ashram was held in the mango grove in Santiniketan in which Rabindranath explained his ideas about the (new developments) creation of an institution which would be a true centre for the different cultures of the East. The poet coined the word Visva-Bharati at this time. *Visva* in Sanskrit means the world in its universal aspect; *Bharati* is wisdom and culture. The Visva-Bharati was to be the centre of learning for the whole world.

Mahalanobis adds that the initial focus was on the study of Sanskrit, Pali, Buddhist, Prakrit, Tibetan, and Chinese literature; more significantly, he mentions that '[a]rt and music had always occupied an important place in Rabindranath's scheme of education, and in 1918 he had succeeded in establishing Kala-Bhavana, the School of Art and Music, as an integral part of the educational institutions in Santiniketan'.[167] Tagore himself bemoaned that '[w]e almost ignore the aesthetic life of man', and that, 'music and the fine arts are among the highest means of national self-expression without which the people remain

165 Tagore to Andrews, 16 October 1913, RBA, File No. 1.

166 Rabindranath Tagore, *The Centre of Indian Culture* (Madras: The Society for the Promotion of National Education, 1919), p. 38.

167 Prasanta Chandra Mahalanobis, 'The Visva-Bharati' in *The Calcutta Municipal Gazette: Tagore Supplement*, ed. Amal Home (Calcutta: Calcutta Municipality, 1941), pp. 3–4.

inarticulate'.[168] We shall see below how the arts occupied a pre-eminent position in Tagore's educational programme in Visva-Bharati.

While Tagore called his institution a 'centre of culture', implying that it would focus on intellectual and artistic activities, his vision was far more extensive; to put it differently, he did not stop at culture; his idea of complete education involved integrating culture with agriculture (and allied activities) on the 'co-operative principle', even bringing adjoining villages within its ambit. In September 1921, Leonard K Elmhirst arrived in Santiniketan, and the Institute of Rural Reconstruction or Sriniketan at Surul near Santiniketan was founded on 5 February 1922. It started functioning as Elmhirst took charge of the institution. Tagore's integrated vision of Visva-Bharati thus began to acquire full shape.

In a lecture in 1922, Tagore elaborated on what his idea of complete education meant. While emphasising the importance of intellectual training, Tagore does not lose sight of the economic aspects of life. He observes:

> Economic life covers the whole width of the fundamental basis of society because its necessities are the simplest and the most universal. Educational institutions, in order to obtain their fullness of truth, must have close association with this economic life. ... Society is based on economic co-operation, and economic co-operation should be made the basis of our University.[169]

He reiterates and elaborates his view expressed in *The Centre of Indian Culture* in 1919, pointing out that:

> Our centre of culture should not be the centre of intellectual life of India. It must co-operate with the villages round it, cultivate land, breed cattle, spin cloths, press oil from oil-seeds ... [i]ts very existence should depend upon the success of its industrial activities carried out on the co-operative principle.[170]

With this in view, Tagore set up Siksha-Satra (literally meaning a place that imparts free education) in 1924, a school that would impart education to students from rural background. In a letter to Elmhirst written in 1937, Tagore expressed his bitterness at how his ideal was being undermined, and reposed his faith in the potential of Siksha-Satra to give shape to his ideal:

> Outside the bhadralogue [gentleman] class, pathetic in their struggle for fixing a university label on their name, there is a vast obscure multitude

168 Tagore, *The Centre of Indian Culture*, p. 42.
169 Rabindranath Tagore, *Creative Unity* (New York: Macmillan, 1922), p. 191.
170 Ibid., p. 192.

> who cannot even dream of such a costly ambition. With them, we have our best opportunity if we know how to use it, and there only we can have our freedom from offering to our country the best all-round culture not mutilated by the official dictators.

Tagore did not merely stop here; Siksha-Satra meant much to him as the letter reveals. He continues: 'I am therefore all the more keen that the Siksha-Satra should justify the ideal I have entrusted to it and should represent the most important function of Sriniketan', for he had set up Sriniketan to train its students 'in an atmosphere of rational thinking and behaviour which alone can save them from stupid bigotry and moral cowardliness'. He concludes the letter on a note that is surprising:

> I myself attach much more significance to the educational possibilities of Siksha-Satra than to the school and college of Santiniketan, which are everyday becoming more and more like so many schools and colleges … borrowed cages that treat the students' minds as captive birds.[171]

In pursuit of the fulfilment of his objectives, Tagore, in a letter to Cousins on agricultural co-operation cited above, implores Cousins to remind AE 'that my mission is not (as he [AE] seems to have suggested in some of his late writings) to offer intoxicating fumes of vague idealism to our people in place of bread which they need so much'.[172]AE was certainly aware of the advances in rural welfare for his own subjects that Tagore had made in his own estates in Eastern Bengal, and of including agriculture and rural welfare through the co-operative system even in his educational institution. Moreover, as we have seen above, AE greatly admired Tagore. It is, therefore, difficult for us to understand why he should make such uncharacteristic remarks about Tagore's experiments with agricultural co-operatives.

In this respect, Tagore's discussion with Sir Horace Plunkett[173] can be said to have been more fruitful. Plunkett had set up the Irish Agricultural Organization Society (IAOS) in 1894 to help Irish farmers adapt themselves to the realities of

171 Tagore to Elmhirst, 19 December 1937. RBA File No. 107.

172 Tagore to Cousins, Letter No. 22 in this volume.

173 Sir Horace Plunkett (1854–1932) was the architect of the co-operative movement in Ireland. He founded the Irish Co-operative Organisation Society in 1894. He published a book entitled *Ireland in the New Century* in 1904, the year Tagore delivered his famous lecture 'Swadeshi samāj' in which he expounded his idea of the ideal indigenous community. Tagore strongly held the view that India's indigenous social organisation could not be replaced with the idea of the 'Nation' which was more appropriate to European society. Tagore also met Plunkett in 1920 in London and had discussion with him. In 'The Cult of the Charka' cited above, Tagore pays a handsome tribute to Plunkett saying that his 'success was not confined to Ireland alone; he achieved also the possibility of success in India.' See *The English Writings of Rabindranath Tagore*, Vol. III, p. 546.

a modernising economy. Rathindranath Tagore notes that in 1920, Tagore had a discussion with Plunkett who 'was aware of the similarity of conditions in the West of Ireland and India'. Plunkett also advised Tagore that it would be 'more instructive' for him to study the experiences of the co-operative movement of Ireland rather than of Denmark.[174]

In 1920–1921, Tagore went on a long visit to several European countries and to America with the intention of garnering intellectual support for Visva-Bharati. By that time, Gandhi had launched the Non-Co-operation movement in India. Both Tagore and Gandhi held each other in high esteem, but they had their strong disagreements as well. The times were difficult, and Tagore seemed split between his respect for Gandhi on the one hand and his commitment to his ideal of East–West co-operation on the other. He disapproved of some of Gandhi's principles, and he explained his ideological differences with Gandhi succinctly thus: '"No" in its passive moral form is asceticism, and in its active moral form, violence.'[175]

Many of the letters Tagore wrote during those testing years bear witness to his agonies. He wrote to Andrews from Chicago: 'I am striving with all my power to tune my mood of mind to be in accord with the great feeling of excitement sweeping across my country. But, deep in my being, why is there this spirit of resistance?'[176] In a moment of self-critical reflection, he wrote: 'What irony of fate is this that I should be preaching co-operation of cultures between East and West on this side of the sea when the doctrine of non-co-operation is preached on the other side?'[177]

Tagore also did not hesitate to chastise Gandhi about some aspects of the Non-Co-operation movement: 'What I heard on every side was that reason, and culture as well, must be closured. It was necessary only to cling to an unquestioning obedience. Obedience to whom? To some *mantra*, some unreasoned creed!'[178] In a similar vein, he also opposed Gandhi's idea of *charka*,[179] for he believed that such a movement fostered 'a blind faith on a very large scale' which would 'lure' the people to 'short cuts'.[180]

174 Tagore, *On the Edges of Time*, pp. 118–119.
175 Ibid., p. 77.
176 Tagore, *Letters from Abroad*, p. 74.
177 Ibid., p. 79.
178 Tagore, *The English Writings*, Vol. III, p. 419.
179 The word literally denotes a spinning wheel. But it has a larger connotation in Gandhian thought. In *Hind Swaraj* (1909), Gandhi proposed that Indian middle-class people should use handmade cotton produced in their own spinning wheels. The charka gradually became central to his thought and came to symbolise self-reliance, restoration of an indigenous skill, and national pride, among other things. During the Non-Co-operation movement in the 1920s, Gandhi promoted it as an 'embodiment of willing obedience'. It is this attempt of Gandhi to impose virtue that Tagore opposed.
180 Ibid., p. 540. On Tagore-Gandhi relationship, see *The Mahatma and the Poet: Letters and Debates between Gandhi and Tagore 1915–1941*, ed. Sabyasachi Bhattacharya (New Delhi: National Book Trust, 1997).

On the other hand, Tagore felt intellectually at home in the West. 'My communication with western humanity has been a communication of life',[181] he wrote, and believed that 'Santiniketan will not bring forth its fullness of flower and fruit, if, through me, it does not send its roots to the Western soil.'[182] Spiritual emancipation, he affirmed, was more important than political freedom. 'Swaraj' to him was 'maya', an illusion, as he stood for a higher ideal. 'Our fight is a spiritual fight – it is for Man. We are to emancipate Man', he wrote to Andrews.[183]

Tagore was so disaffected with politics that he even admonished Andrews to '[k]eep Santiniketan away from the turmoils of politics', claiming that '[w]here I have politics, I do not belong to Santiniketan.'[184] For him, politics in any form meant the manifestation of power, and '[p]ower, whether in the patriotic or any other form, is no lover of freedom. It talks of unity, but forgets that true unity is that of freedom'. Indeed, he was a patriot for whom human freedom counted most. 'I love India', he wrote, 'but my India is an Idea and not a geographical expression. Therefore I am *not* a patriot – I shall ever seek my compatriots all over the world', he told Andrews, adding, '[y]ou are one of them, and I am sure there are many others.'[185]

In 1927, Tagore went on a visit to Southeast Asia accompanied by scholars and artists such as Suniti Kumar Chatterjee, Surendranath Kar, and Arnold Bake, among others. This visit enlarged his vision of the 'Idea' of 'India' into that of a 'Greater India', an idea articulated by many intellectuals around that time. In the long letter he wrote to Rani Mahalanobis, wife of Prasanta Chandra Mahalanobis, on 15 July 1927, he comments on the contrast between India and Europe in their respective influence on other nations. Europe, driven by its 'greed', had become a menace to Asian and African countries (it colonised), and was itself aflame and devastated by war. In contrast, India too, in ancient times, had extended herself beyond her boundaries, but her purpose was to disseminate her culture which had been assimilated by 'Tibet, Mongolia, the Malay Islands', among others. So, to Tagore, this visit was a 'pilgrimage' undertaken to 'witness the historical traces of India's entry into the universal'.[186]

A Greater India Society had been formed in 1922 by a few intellectuals; Kalidas Nag, an eminent scholar, argued in a paper entitled 'Greater India: A Study in Indian Internationalism', that while India had ignored composing her history in the manner of Europe, she had actually developed an 'International

181 Ibid., p. 6.
182 Ibid., p. 16.
183 Ibid., p. 73.
184 Ibid., p. 31.
185 Ibid., p. 95.
186 Tagore, 'Jāva-Jātrir patra' (Letters of a Traveller to Java) in *RR*, Vol. X, 1999, p. 503.

History', and that, her 'obsession of the Eternal … has a counterpart in the obsession of the Universal in her national history'.[187]

In a lecture in Bombay (now Mumbai), before his departure for Southeast Asia, Tagore had outlined his idea of Greater India thus: 'The only true expression of India was in all that she gave openly and freely. The surplus of her cultural life … was the core of her personality. … Thus from India Abroad we may catch a glimpse of that eternal grace of India', concluding that 'the grand message of Fraternity must dawn within us.'[188] This demonstrates that alternative forms of universalism and internationalism had emerged from Asian nations which were 'subtly different from an abstract globalism'[189] and also, how free mutual diffusion and exchange of intellectual and cultural knowledge could create relationships devoid of the odium of dominance or oppression.

While Tagore's visit was meant to study the remains of ancient Indian culture, and also to disseminate the ideals of Visva-Bharati among the people of these neighbouring nations, it reinforced cultural interaction as well; he was fascinated by the different versions of the ancient Indian epics, the *Ramayana* and the *Mahabharata*, and wrote a nuanced interpretation of these variant forms.[190] The cultural baggage he brought back from Java included, among other things, the art of Batik printing and certain forms of dance and dance-costumes which were introduced in Visva-Bharati.[191]

The poetics and aesthetics of education

These new artistic elements gathered from other kindred cultures invariably added a new magnitude to the aesthetic ambience and the cosmopolitan spirit of Visva-Bharati. Tagore did not merely emphasise cultivating the aesthetic sensibility of his students. His educational ideas, as already suggested above, need to be seen in aesthetic terms. Visva-Bharati is the creation of a poet and artist's imagination.[192] Tagore himself called his school 'a poet's school', and he virtually thought of Visva-Bharati as a work of art. 'I am an artist and not a man of sci-

187 Kalidas Nag, 'Greater India: A Study in Indian Internationalism' in *Greater India Society Bulletin I*, November 1926, p. 3.

188 Rabindranath Tagore, 'Greater India' in *VBQ*, Vol. IX, NS 1943–44, pp. 5–7.

189 Sugata Bose, *A Hundred Horizons: The Indian Ocean in the age of Global Empire* (Cambridge, MA and London: Harvard University Press, 2006), p. 234.

190 See Tagore's letter to Rani Mahalanobis dated 7 September 1927 in *RR*, Vol. X, pp. 513–515.

191 A detailed account of this visit is to be found in Suniti Kumar Chatterjee's *Rabindrasangame Dwipomoy Bharat o Shyamdesh* [Visiting the Indian Archipelago and Indonesia in Tagore's Company] (Calcutta: Prakash Bhavana, 1940, reprint 2010).

192 See Kathleen M. O'Connell, *Rabindranath Tagore: The Poet as Educator* (Kolkata: Visva-Bharati, 2012). Martha Nussbaum pertinently observes that Tagore encouraged the cultivation of an 'inclusive sympathy' which could be 'cultivated only by an education that emphasizes global learning, the arts, and Socratic self-criticism'. Martha C. Nussbaum, *Not for Profit: Why Democracy needs the Humanities* (2012; Princeton & Oxford: Princeton University Press, 2012), p. 68.

ence, and therefore, my institution has necessarily assumed the aspect of a work of art and not that of a pedagogical laboratory', he declared publicly in 1931.[193] This statement should not, however, be misconstrued as the shifting stance of a poet who had begun to paint a few years before, and was, therefore, applying an artist's perspective on education; Tagore's 'lyrical' ideals of education, as Alex Aronson[194] so elegantly calls it, and the ideals of Visva-Bharati are best understood through a broad, aesthetic frame.

Tagore was vehemently against the mechanistic and utilitarian form of education introduced by the English in India. In several of his Bengali essays (one of the most celebrated being 'Sikhsār Herpher' [Anomaly in Education, 1892]), he argued for the need for an alternative form of education which is inclusive, creative, and enables the flowering of the human 'personality'. Tagore's idea of personality is elaborated in the lectures he delivered in America and published as *Personality* in 1918. Significantly enough, the inaugural essay in the volume is entitled 'What is Art', and it leads us into his insightful view of personality. Tagore distinguishes between what he calls the 'physical man' and the 'personal man'; the latter he considers to be the 'highest in man' which comes in contact with the 'great world' to 'satisfy his personality'. Elsewhere, he defines man as the 'Angel of Surplus'.[195] The surplus in man is his 'fund of emotional energy', which Tagore explains thus:

> Man has a surplus where he can proudly assert that knowledge is for the sake of knowledge. There he has the pure enjoyment of knowledge, because there is freedom. This surplus seeks its outlet in the creation of art. … This surplus is what makes up man's personality which finds its expression in art.

The expression of man's personality is possible only through the 'language of picture and music'. For Tagore, art is superior to science which is constituted of analysis and abstract reasoning and calls for the application of the intellect, whereas art evolves out of the human personality and leads towards its full manifestation. Tagore refuses to define art for he believes that art pertains to a 'region where both our faculties of creation and enjoyment have been spontaneous and half-conscious' and asserts that, in art, man creates his 'own heaven, the heaven of ideas shaped into perfect forms, with which he surrounds himself, the inexhaustible abundance through which he comes to know the Supreme person who has fashioned the universe'.[196]

193 Rabindranath Tagore, 'My Educational Mission' in *The Modern Review*, Vol. XLIX, No.6, June-December 1931, p. 621.

194 Alex Aronson, 'Tagore's Educational Ideas' in *International Review of Education*, Vol. VII, No. 4 (1961), p. 389.

195 Rabindranath Tagore, *The Religion of Man* (London: George Allen & Unwin, 1931), p. 27.

196 Rabindranath Tagore, *Personality* (New York: Macmillan, 1918), pp. 5–40.

These ideas and statements offer us the perspective from which we can approach Tagore's foundational ideas of Visva-Bharati. Tagore believed that 'man by nature is an artist'. In the lecture, 'An Eastern University' in *Creative Unity*, he dwells at length on how his educational ideas have an aesthetic dimension. We shall see briefly how Tagore explains his idea.

'Universities', Tagore cautions, 'should never be made into mechanical organisations for collecting and distributing knowledge. Through them the people should offer their intellectual hospitality, their wealth of mind to others.'[197] In an essay which is rarely referred to, Tagore brings out the cardinal idea of Visva-Bharati:

> It made me realise that a great responsibility was laid upon me to seek to bring about a true meeting of the East and the West, beyond the boundaries of politics and race and creed. I was convinced that my own institution at Santiniketan must now open wide its gates. It must offer to those who might come from the West that generous hospitality which India had traditionally offered to those who have visited her shores. Thus, gradually this idea of founding a centre of Indian culture, with which I started, was enlarged. The fuller idea of Visva-Bharati now included the thought of a complete meeting of East and West, in a common fellowship of learning and a common spiritual striving for the unity of the human race. The stress was now to be laid on the ideal of humanity itself.[198]

The following year he would write on a loftier note:

> I believe I have the power of vision which seeks its realisation in some concrete form. Unless our different works in Visva-Bharati are luminous with the fire of vision I myself can have no place in it. That is why … I was intently wishing that it should not only have a shape, but also light; so that it might transcend its immediate limits of time, space and some special purpose. If Visva- Bharati comes to attain truth through the life of those who serve her then she will illumine the path of pilgrimage. … A lighted lamp is for the end of us and not a lump of gold. I could have taken the path of politics or social service and be idolised by my people, but I naturally avoided it and incurred the displeasure of my countrymen. … Let us bring all our power of imagination and create a world.[199]

197 Tagore, *Creative Unity*, p. 172.

198 Rabindranath Tagore, 'The Visva-Bharati Ideal' in *The Visva-Bharati Ideal*, eds. Rabindranath Tagore and C.F. Andrews (Madras: G A Natesan & Co, 1923), pp. 9–10.

199 Tagore to Leonard Elmhirst, 16 June 1924, RBA File No. 107.

He mentions in another essay that he himself had 'felt the meeting of East and West in my own individual life' and it had made him aware 'for the first time universal Man marching across all physical boundaries'; therefore, India should give up her 'obstinately provincial' frame of mind and open herself up to external influences.[200] The West, he argues, had created new opportunities for India 'for the creation of a new thought-power', and in order to strengthen Indian culture, western culture should be truly accepted and 'assimilated'.[201] With this in view, he invited many experts from all across the globe to teach at Visva-Bharati in its formative years. Orientalist scholars such as Sylvain Levi from France and Moritz Winternitz from Prague and Carlo Formichi and Guiseppe Tucci from Rome, the Scottish sociologist Arthur Geddes, the Dutch musicologist Arnold Bake, the Irish linguist Mark Collins, the French painter Andree Karpeles, the Viennese art historian Stella Kramrisch, the Norwegian archaeologist Sten Konow are among the distinguished international scholars who taught at Visva-Bharati. An invitation to James Cousins to teach a course at Visva-Bharati was made in the same vein. We have noted that Elmhirst was given the responsibility of organising Sriniketan. Through his American friends, he enlisted the services of Gretchen Green, a paramedic, for the clinic at Sriniketan. Dr Harry Timbers, a malaria expert, and his wife also came from America and served at Sriniketan for three years.

Tagore wanted to forge through Visva-Bharati the 'spiritual unity of all races' and create a 'brotherhood where men of different countries and different languages can come together';[202] but he was equally alert to the fact that 'mathematics' did not rob the attention of students from the 'thrills' that the 'kiss of rains' brought to the surrounding trees.[203] A life in harmony with nature is in itself emblematic of an aesthetic way of living; this aesthetic sensibility could be reinforced by inculcating in his students an interest in art. With this in view, he had invited eminent artists to work in Visva-Bharati, and had established Kala-Bhavana in 1919, one of the earliest schools to come up at Visva-Bharati.

We may recall that in his first public statement (in English) on Visva-Bharati in 1919, Tagore had described it as the centre of 'Indian culture'. This suggests that, for Tagore, education is synonymous with cultural excellence. In many of his English writings, he uses the word 'culture' rather than 'education' to express his views. For instance, when the Bengali essay, 'Shikshār Milan' [Unity of Education] (1921), written in the backdrop of the Non-Co-operation movement, was translated into English, it was titled 'Union of Cultures'.

In an illuminating passage in 'An Eastern University', Tagore makes it clear that education, for him, does not denote a customary pedagogical exercise, a

200 Rabindranath Tagore, 'The Ideal of Visva-Bharati' in *Proceedings of the Bengal Education Week*, Vol. I, 1936 (Calcutta: Working Committee of the Bengal Education Week, 1936), pp. 79–81.

201 Tagore, *Creative Unity*, p. 186.

202 Tagore, 'My Educational Mission', p. 622.

203 Ibid., p. 623.

mechanical acquisition of information. It carries a deeper value and is synonymous with culture: 'Man's intellect has a natural pride in its own aristocracy, which is the pride of its culture. Culture only acknowledges the excellence whose criticism is in its inner perfection, not in any external success.'[204] The achievement of cultural excellence has not been possible in modern India because '[o]ur educated community is not a cultured community but a community of qualified candidates'. The purpose of Visva-Bharati, therefore, is to take education beyond the confines of what he, rather pejoratively calls, 'grammar and laboratory'.[205] To him, the ideal aim of education 'should lie in imparting life-breath to the complete man, who is intellectual as well as economic, bound by social bonds, but aspiring towards spiritual freedom and final perfection'.[206]

Tagore names that perfection cultural excellence, as we have just seen. To him, education does not mean a dry intellectual pursuit; it is creative and inclusive in nature and thus acquires the aspect of the aesthetic: 'For intellectual knowledge also has its aspect of creative art, in which the man who explores truth expresses something which is human in him.'[207] At the same time, since art is universal in its appeal, it is perfectly in consonance with the universalist ideals of Visva-Bharati, as he records in a late essay: 'it [art] is unique in its manner and universal in its appeal; it is hospitable to the All because it has the wealth which is its own; ... it carries its special criterion of excellence within itself'. So he enjoins that:

> It is the duty of every human being to master, at least to some extent, not only the language of intellect, but also that personality which is the language of Art ... to be brought up in ignorance of it ... is to remain deaf to the eternal voice of Man that speaks to all men the messages that are beyond speech.[208]

Cousins shared with Tagore certain views on art and education. We might recall Cousins's perceptive review of *Creative Unity*, and, its ideas had deeply influenced him. Some of his writings bear testimony to this, but they cannot be compared with Tagore's in terms of philosophical depth and profundity, as we shall see.

We have noted above that Tagore had sought Cousins's assistance for Visva-Bharati, and that Cousins had agreed to do his part in his personal capacity. Tagore's invitation was an urgent one: 'I am obliged by circumstances to ask you to give us a continuous period of one or two years your help in the building up of the educational side of Visva-Bharati. We have now long been in need of one who may undertake to organize the higher courses of study at Santiniketan.'[209]

204 Tagore, *Creative Unity*, p. 173.
205 Ibid., p. 189.
206 Ibid., p. 196.
207 Ibid., p. 180.
208 Ibid., p. 189.
209 See Letter No.23 in this volume.

Cousins's cautious response needs an explanation. In 1922, the Theosophical Society decided to wind up their National University; Cousins proposed that they should start a 'school of a universal culture at Adyar' as an alternative institution. The school that came up was called Brahmavidya Ashrama (school of universal culture); it adopted a 'synthetical approach to knowledge' drawing upon the ideas of the French Enlightenment. Cousins explains that these ideas 'were not quite new: the French Encyclopaedists of the eighteenth century had made a start in the way of bringing knowledge together'. But there would be a difference between the approach of the French Enlightenment, which was 'quantitative', and Cousins's approach, which would be 'synthetical: that is, the relating of matters apparently diverse, the discovering of their affinities, and the understanding of their apparent incongruities'.[210] It is on the basis of his idea of the Brahmavidya Ashrama that Cousins sought an affinity with Tagore's idea of Visva-Bharati; this is evident from a letter he wrote to Tagore:

> Personally I find the Theo-Sophia (which is the same thing as Brahma Vidya) sufficiently inclusive to enable me to merge myself in others and realize that they are as inevitable as myself. … I might be able to help you to find a plan of work which, once inaugurated and watched for a while, would give the same sense of progressive security as we have in the Ashram here. … Such experience and capacity as I have would, if circumstances so permitted, be bent to fulfilling your ideals, not pushing any notions of my own save as they were in affinity with yours.[211]

No detailed record of Cousins's activities in Visva-Bharati, however, seems to exist; we can, at best, have fleeting impressions of his experiences at Santiniketan from his own accounts. Cousins's first visit to Santiniketan followed Tagore's visit to Madanapalle; about that visit, Cousins writes:

> During my brief call Rabindranath had summoned a conference of such teachers of the school as were not on essential duty and myself to discuss various aspects of education. … Our affinity in ideals was apparent; but three years were to pass before I realised from the copy of his "Creative Unity" that the poet sent me how close our minds were in the philosophy and technique of what we believed to be true education.[212]

This was followed by a second visit when he was accompanied by his wife Margaret Cousins, from 4 to18 October, before the formal opening of Visva-Bharati in 1921; this time, the experience was different: 'A fortnight's visit to Santiniketan … gave us the regeneration of spiritual and aesthetic uplift', Cousins writes; they had

210 Cousins and Cousins, *We Two Together*, pp. 390–393.
211 See Letter No.24 in this volume.
212 Cousins and Cousins, *We Two Together*, pp. 343–344.

the privilege of talking to Tagore 'at any time that suited him [Tagore]', exchanging 'opinions on all kinds of high topics, and on his [Tagore's] scheme for creating an International University' while enjoying rehearsals of his [Tagore's] plays.

But more memorable were the 'roof-talks' which guests and inmates of the school attended; occasionally, they participated in 'expositions of religious, philosophical, artistic and educational subjects by Gurudev[213] [Tagore]' as well. Cousins splendidly recounts one of his most rapturous experiences:

> On this particular occasion, he [Tagore] drew out some of the basic principles of the Upanishads, and took us behind cold terms and phrases to their realities. He gave us his idea of personal relationship with the life of the Universe. This could only be fulfilled through some kind of intermediary. Hence, the monotheistic religions, and the psychological reason for their existence. Our long, happy intercommunication was not the comparing of mind and mind, but of that deeper instantaneous stratum of consciousness, soul and soul. When, in the starlit silence, the exalted communion ended, and the rapt group retired, it was some kind of pain to pull back into activity. We had no words with which to jar the ecstatic with the formal. All I could do, in signifying departure, was to touch Gurudev's feet; and Gretta [Margaret Cousins] kissed his hair.[214]

Cousins composed the poems 'Gorgeous Lies', 'The Miser and the Coin', 'The Giant and the Pomegranate', and 'The Prodigal's Return' under the broader title of 'Surya-Gita'(Sun Songs) while he was at Santiniketan. In 1922, he published a volume of his poems with the title *Surya Gita*. A third, short visit followed for four days in July 1923, when he:

> [A]gain prophesied, talked on the Irish literary revival, met and listened to Dr Radhakamal Mukherji and Dr Winternitz, and had private conversations with Rabindranath on the possibility of translating his Bengali poetry into English verse-forms, and discussions with his staff on education.

But that short stay was also no less an enriching experience to him because, as he continues, '[a] great original creative genius pervaded the atmosphere and pivoted attention from prayers under trees at sunrise to celestial wisdom on a roof at moonrise'.[215] This was followed by a fourth (probably the last) visit in February 1930 when Cousins was told to talk to Tagore about occultism and spiritualism.[216]

213 The word means a spiritual teacher or guide, a preceptor. It was M K Gandhi who gave Tagore the appellation of 'Gurudev', meaning, a guide, a preceptor, while Tagore called Gandhi the 'Mahatma' which means a great soul.

214 Ibid., pp. 387–388.

215 Ibid., p. 400. Cousins had contributed an essay entitled 'The Irish Renaissance' to *The Modern Review*, Vol. XIX, April 1916, pp. 423–426.

216 See Cousins and Cousins, We Two Together, p. 511.

One of Cousins's major intellectual preoccupations was with geography, or with imaginative geography; his geographical ideas were informed by theosophy. Theosophy professes the spiritual unity of all races while giving importance to cultural and national differences; the underlying spiritual unity of all mankind then leaves no room for any kind of hierarchy and dominance in the social and political sphere.

In Cousins's scheme of geography one should be loyal to one's local region, to one's nation, to one's culture, and see oneself as separate from others. But it simultaneously ensures equality and a non-hierarchical order of relationship among nations and peoples. This sharply contrasts with the imperial idea of geography which saw the world as a unity but inhabited by peoples and cultures arranged in a hierarchical order over which the West dominated.[217] India offered to Cousins a classic case of his idea of geographical unity. Despite her physical, cultural, and linguistic variety, and despite the absence of unifying social and political movements, India, he argues, is one country 'knit into an invisible unity by the spiritual imagination'.[218] In other words, to Cousins, India, more than being a geographical reality, was an idea, an imaginative space, much like the 'Idea of India' Tagore had written to Andrews about.

Like Tagore, Cousins also believed in the importance of art in education. In a pamphlet of 1924, Cousins argues for the social value of art which, he thinks, are mainly three – material, aesthetic, and intellectual. The full potential of art can be realised if it is introduced in schools. The artistic sensibility can be fostered further, he contends, through institutional means such as the local museum and a Ministry of Arts and Crafts.[219] This is different from Tagore's approach; Tagore believed that the impulse to create is inherent in man, and the creative impulse finds its expression when appropriate opportunities are offered to the student. His own institution was meant to create those opportunities.

Cousins was not merely distressed by the gross neglect of art in education. In the essay, 'Art and Education', he emphatically points out that this neglect has resulted in 'the appallingly inartistic life of humanity and that most inartistic and inhuman of human activities, warfare'.[220] He argues that art should be made a part of education not because it enhances man's aesthetic sensibility, but because it awakens his spiritual power, which will ultimately dissuade him from destructive activities like war. As he put it more explicitly elsewhere: 'Art in education is not a merely aesthetical matter. It is, in the profoundest sense of the term, a spiritual necessity, and, in the profoundest sense of the term, a spiritualising

217 Catherine Nash, 'Geo-centric Education and Anti-imperialism: Theosophy, Geography, and Citizenship in the Writings of J.H. Cousins' in *Journal of Historical Geography*, Vol. XXII, No. 4, 1996, pp. 399–411. See the discussion of Nash's point in Majumdar, *Yeats and Tagore*, pp. 133–134.

218 Cousins, *The Renaissance in India*, p. 8.

219 James H. Cousins, *The Social Value of Arts and Crafts* (Mysore, 1924), pp. 1–7.

220 James H. Cousins, 'Art and Education' in *VBQ*, Vol. I Part 1, NS, May-July 1935, p. 11.

power.'[221] Thus while Cousins thinks of the therapeutic and remedial potential of art in education, Tagore sees art in creative and expressive terms. In fact, not only education, but all activities had an aesthetic dimension for Tagore. He once wrote: 'Practical work too has its own art just as painting or dance or music has. Its poverty is mitigated only by its completeness.'[222]

Cousins also believed that art should be an integral part of daily life. As he put it in an essay: 'the impulse to art is universal, and should have free course for its expression first in education and afterwards in daily life'. Not only that; in a world where national antagonisms lead to self-destructive wars, art can become a vehicle for the resolution of such conflicts and the promotion of international understanding. He continues: '[W]hen art is as common in life as other essentials, [it] will form the basis of universal sympathetic understanding between the nations'. He recalls in the same essay how he had demonstrated the internationality of art by exhibiting before a small audience in Florence in 1925, miniatures of the Bengal School of Oriental Art: 'My brushing in of the historical background and the foreground of contemporaneous circumstances of the movement was received with complete understanding' and the audience found, in what they saw, 'the law of inner unity and outer diversity, of internationality in spirit and nationality of expression.'[223]

In a lecture delivered in Geneva in 1928, Cousins, drawing upon ancient Indian texts and philosophical ideas, demonstrates the 'modernity' of the ancient ideals of the Orient in education. He distinguishes between the liberty guaranteed by education in Europe and the meaning of liberty in education as understood in India and points out that 'in the Indian conception, the ultimate liberty of a nation depends on the liberation of its individuals'. This liberation is to be understood in its wider philosophic and humanistic senses, that is, it means the liberation of the individual from its lower impulses. 'The ideal of India,' asserts Cousins, 'is … to eradicate all disruptive tendencies in the individual.'[224] The chief intention of ancient Indian education was to 'provide generously for the expression of the intellectual capacities of the student'. Art is an integral part of this education since art has the 'power of liberation'. The function of art, Cousins argues, as enunciated in ancient Indian tradition, is to enable an individual become 'a better citizen' and, by awakening his aesthetic sensibility, cleanse him of his lower impulses. As such, 'the whole environment of the student should radiate aesthetical influences of the highest kind'.[225] This is his

221 James H. Cousins, *Three Lectures on Educational Principles and Practice* (Palghat: The Scholar Press, 1935), p. 37.

222 Tagore to Amiya Chakravarty, 21 February 1929, in *Chithipatra* (Letters), Vol. XI, p. 80. (My translation).

223 James H. Cousins, 'Individuality, Nationality and Internationality in Art' in *Faith of the Artist: Essays* (Madras: Kalakshetra, 1941), pp. 84–89.

224 James H. Cousins, *Oriental Ideals in Education* (Karachi: Seva Kunj, n.d.), pp. 3–4.

225 Ibid., p. 10.

attempt to weave education and art into the process of nation-building. He concludes the lecture by noting that this ancient Indian ideal finds its modern manifestation in Tagore's educational programme, and reiterates that Tagore's poem in the English *Gitanjali* (poem no. 4) 'throws into modern poetry the whole genius of the nation and links up the past and the present'.[226]

Cousins also believed that education should be geared towards the development of the 'reflective capacity of the student'. In this, art has a great role not only in setting the imagination free, but in creating 'the taste for higher things in life'. As he wrote to Tagore, 'I find there is an aesthetic for other activities than art.'[227] His ideas of aesthetic education, and of thinking of all activities in aesthetic terms, naturally brought his mind closer to Tagore's.

Conclusion

A perusal of the letters in this volume gives us the impression of how the intimacy of Tagore and Cousins grew with the passage of years; this would also be evident from the gradual change in the mode of address in the letters. Initially, Tagore addresses Cousins formally as 'Dear Mr. Cousins', but it changes to 'Dear Cousins' very soon and then to 'Dear Friend' from 1923 onwards; towards the end, it is 'My dear Cousins'. The initial formal tone grows intimate, and both 'Dear Friend' and 'My dear Cousins' suggest this growing intimacy.

On Cousins's part, it is always 'Dear Gurudev'. Tagore never protested, even mildly, to Cousins addressing him as 'Gurudev'; he did not express any kind of embarrassment as he had done in the case of William Pearson. In a letter, Tagore somewhat irritatingly had written to Pearson: 'You have got into some conventional habits, such as calling me "Gurudev." … Drop them. For I know that there are occasions when they hurt you, and for that very reason are truly discourteous to me.'[228] Should this again suggest that Tagore's relationship with the Englishmen he befriended suffered occasional strains because they were Englishmen? The modes of naming, of addressing, as much as of communicating, definitely throw some light on the nature of a friendship. But a friendship may have greater things beyond all this. In our case, Tagore considered himself and Cousins as 'fellow voyagers'.[229] On the other hand, Cousins, in his last letter to Tagore, wrote: '[w]e shall have much aspiration and work together in our next incarnation.'[230] Some friendships, we are led to conclude, are treasured to a life beyond this life.

226 Ibid., p. 13.
227 Letter No. 24 in this volume.
228 Tagore to Pearson, 13 December 1920. RBA File No. 287(1).
229 See Letter No. 46 in this volume.
230 See Letter No. 57 in this volume.

THE LETTERS

The fifty seven letters that Tagore and Cousins exchanged between them pertain to several areas of thought, creativity, and practical action. They are marked by shared ideas in art, literature, and education and issues of nationalism and internationalism. For Tagore, Cousins was a 'fellow-voyager' (Letter 46), while Cousins saw Tagore as 'eternal friend' (Letter 37) and his relationship with Tagore as 'high comradeship' (Letter 32). The early letters discuss issues of art and literature, particularly differences of approach in eastern and western art and literature; there are good-humoured exchanges on translation, proposals for collaborative translation, and Tagore's contribution of occasional poems. A few letters dwell on issues of nationalism, particularly in the context of Tagore's lectures on nationalism; strangely, their impression of Japan is similar as one letter shows. Some of the letters show Tagore desperately seeking Cousins's support for Visva-Bharati – both for academic purposes and for agricultural co-operation; there are also letters in which both share the importance of art in education. A few letters are about the ideals of Visva-Bharati and the Theosophical Society – their differences and affinities. 'Jana gana mana' features prominently in the exchange; some of the letters show mutual praise for each other's works. Their intimacy is reflected in Cousins's request to Tagore for recommending him for the Nobel Prize, which Tagore does. The strength of this friendship is proved by the fact that refusal on the part of any of the friends did not lead to any kind of bitterness. The letters thus narrate the story of a friendship built on mutual understanding and interdependence.

DOI: 10.4324/9781003149354-1

1) TAGORE TO COUSINS

Shilida
Nadia
November 14, 1915

Dear Mr. Cousins,

Many thanks for your letter and the copy of the *New India*[1] which were delayed in reaching me owing to my erratic movements of late. I fully agree with you in what you have said in your paper about the temptations our artists are subject to from foreign criticisms, especially from friendly advice. We must see things with our own minds – for art is not logical like science or mathematics, it is extremely personal; its function is to express what universal truths there are in that highest mystery of creation – personality.[2] Happily with regards to pictorial art our minds are free as yet from barbed wire entanglements of fixed traditions or those machine-made enjoyments which are turned out of mere habits. I believe we shall truly be able to help the West if we only can resist her allurements or her browbeating.[3] I do not mean to say that we have to turn the table and try to teach her ourselves – for teaching is not man's proper business – our supreme object being to truly reveal ourselves. And art is one aspect of that revelation – freed from all necessity and from conformation to external and artificial standards.

I am glad to have this opportunity of knowing you who are a friend of Mr. Yeats,[4] for whom I have a deep love and respect.

1 *New India* was a newspaper started by Annie Besant and published by the Theosophical Society. Cousins was appointed its literary sub-editor when he migrated to India in 1915. Cousins sent Tagore a copy of *New India* containing his 'leading article' entitled 'The Art of the East'. The relevant section of the essay about which Tagore speaks in the letter reads: 'It is certain that the painters and sculptors and writers of the Society [Indian Society of Oriental Art in Calcutta] are engaged in no mere academic amusement, but are busy on the inspiring work of expressing through the arts the Soul of India. ... It is well that the Art of India should be enriched by the advancement in technique and knowledge of the West; but enrichment will assuredly be turned to poverty if the artists of India allow themselves to be lured away from their own vision and their own method.' Cited in *We Two Together*, p. 260. See also Cousins's two later essays, namely, 'The Bengal Painters – First Impression 1916' and 'The Bengal Painters – Second Impression 1918' included in his *The Renaissance in India*, pp. 61–114.

2 These ideas are fully developed in the lectures collected in *Personality* (1918).

3 See excerpt of Tagore's letter to Edward Thompson dated 20 September 1921 in the Introduction to this volume.

4 William Butler Yeats (1865–1939) was the leader and the greatest figure of the Irish Literary Revival and, according to WH Auden, the greatest poet in the English language of the twentieth century. Cousins, who was a part of the Irish Literary Revival and a member of the Irish National Theatre Society in his early years, earned Yeats's displeasure, who even refused to stage Cousins's play *Sold*. Cousins was also a part of the faction with nationalist commitment that opposed Miss

Yours sincerely,
Rabindranath Tagore

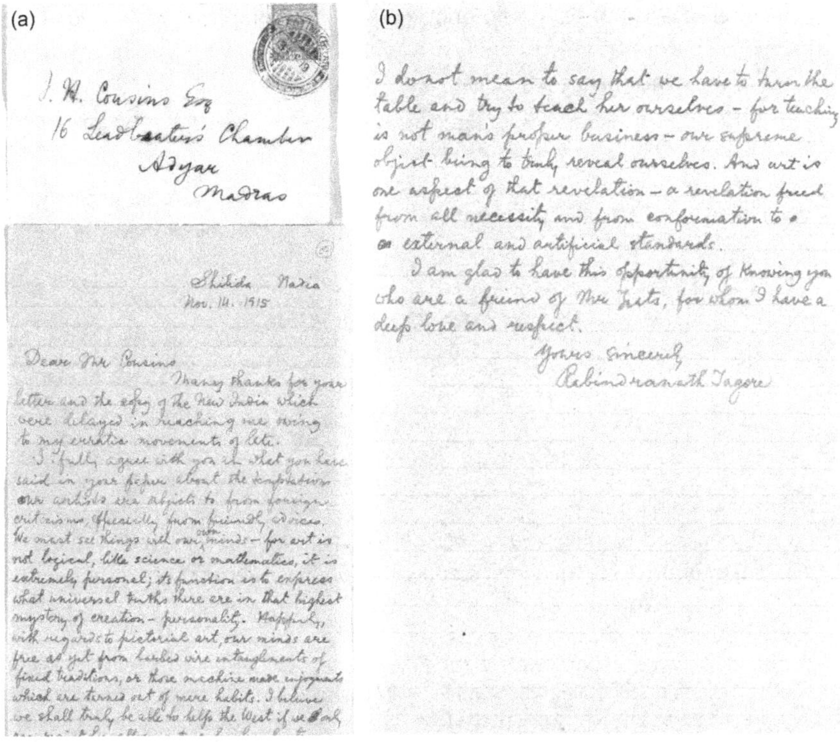

(a) (b)

FIGURE 1a/b Facsimile of Rabindranath Tagore's first letter to James Cousins, dated 14 November 1915. Source: Rabindra-Bhavana Archive, Visva-Bharati, West Bengal, India. Reproduced with permission

---

Hornimann's move to make the Abbey Theatre in Dublin professional. However, because of Yeats's opposition, Cousins resigned from the Society in 1903. See Peter Kuch, *Yeats and AE: 'The Antagonism that Unites Dear Friends'* (Gerrards Cross: Colin Smythe, 1986) for more details. Yet, this did not prevent Cousins from writing an appreciative account of Yeats's poetry in his collection of essays *New Ways in English Literature* (1917), nor did it prevent Yeats from recommending Cousins for the Nobel Prize for Literature in 1934.

2) TAGORE TO COUSINS

Shilida
Nadia
February 9, 1916

Dear Mr. Cousins,
Please do not worry yourself about the *Phalguni* synopsis.[5] At first I felt myself accountable for it to Ramanandababu[6] having received something from him in exchange, but since then I have come to consider the money as paid to the famine relief[7] and not to myself. And now my only complaint against you is that you could not be present on the occasion. We missed your possible enjoyment of the performance and felt sorry.

Yours sincerely,
Rabindranath Tagore

3) TAGORE TO COUSINS

Shantiniketan
Bolpur
April 18, 1916

Dear Mr. Cousins,
I greatly enjoyed reading your paper on 'Literary Ideals',[8] for which I thank you. Literature reflects the writer's outlook upon life – generally speaking, an

5 *Phālguni* was translated into English as *The Cycle of Spring*. The synopsis was made by Tagore himself, rather hurriedly, and somewhat in an explanatory manner, for circulation among the audience when the play was staged in Bengali at Jorasanko in Calcutta on 29 and 30 January 1916. From his letters to Gaganendranath Tagore on this issue (published in *Rabindra Biksha* XIV, 1915), it would be evident that Tagore was anxious for the need to provide an explanatory synopsis of the play. Tagore must have sent an invitation to Cousins, and may have talked to him about the synopsis, as the letter seems to suggest. But Cousins had gone back to Madanapalle by that time with the intention of organising an exhibition of paintings in Madras from 19 February to 4 March 1916 with the help of the Indian Society of Oriental Art.

6 Ramananda Chatterjee (1865–1943) was the founder-editor of two very important periodicals – *Prabasi* (Bengali, started in 1901) and *The Modern Review* (English, started in 1907). Tagore had contributed most of his writings to *Prabasi*; Chatterjee was Tagore's close friend and associate till the end. The Bengali word 'bābu' has an extensive connotation; in a general way, the word is used to refer to an educated, middle-class gentleman in Bengal.

7 *Phālguni* was staged for raising money for the Bankura Famine Relief Fund. Tagore himself acted in the play in the roles of 'Kabisekhar' and the 'Bāul'.

8 The essay is included in *The Renaissance in India*. Cousins mentions Tagore as an exemplary poet writing in his native tongue. The relevant passage on which Tagore's observations are based is: 'It is here, I think, that we find the vital distinction between the literary ideals of east and west. The predominant activity in Europe is analysis, separation, specialization, not merely in the

Indian's outlook is philosophical, therefore, philosophy naturally assumes a living form in Indian literature. When a European says he fully wants to live he does not mean to say that he wants to live the life of truth but that it is a wish to live the life of passion – and his literature reflects his desire. It is not light that he wants but conflagration. He consumes himself and his world – and the present war is the best illustration of that.

Very sincerely yours,
Rabindranath Tagore

I am very much touched by Mr. Bain's letter to me – I shall write to him.

4) TAGORE TO COUSINS

Shantiniketan
Bolpur
May 4, 1917

Dear Mr. Cousins,
Thank you very much for the booklet.[9] I shall try to send one of my teachers to your Summer School meeting at Poona[10] to attend your lectures. Professor Geddes[11] is going to have his course of lectures for teachers at Darjeeling in the

affairs of daily life, but in the things of the mental life. A poet is a poet, and a philosopher is a philosopher. ... Such a divorce between the arts and religion and philosophy is the development of the individualistic and materialistic character of European thought. ... India however, gave me the complete confidence that is necessary to literary creation. She showed me the examples of Mirabai, Tukaram and Rabindranath Tagore, in whom life, religion and philosophy are one.' The essay is also significant as Cousins advises Indians to write in their own language and not in English; and if they should write in English at all, they should follow the example of the Irish who write Irish-English. Indian writers similarly should write what he calls 'Indo-Anglian', Indian in spirit ... and English only in words.' See *The Renaissance in India*, pp. 71–84.

9 The booklet is probably *New Ways in English Literature* (Madras: Ganesh & Co, 1917). It contains the essay 'First Impression of Tagore in Europe'. Aurobindo Ghose, in his review of the book in his journal *Arya* (1917), praised it very highly; the review appears as the opening essay in Ghose's *The Future Poetry*.

10 No reference to a Summer School lecture at Poona occurs in *We Two Together*. Cousins visited Poona in 1918 on his National Education lecture tour where he had two contrary experiences. The 'intellectual' Poona did not pay much importance to his idea of national education, but the 'less brainy and more vital' Poona offered to seek affiliation for schools with the Theosophical Society for the Promotion of National Education. See *We Two Together*, pp. 318–320.

11 Sir Patrick Geddes (1854–1932) was an eminent Scottish biologist, sociologist, town planner and educationalist. He came to India in 1914 as evident from an introductory letter from the writer William Archer to C F Andrews. It is uncertain when Tagore and Geddes met, but that they had grown intimate by the time of this letter is evident from the fact that Tagore dedicated to him *The Parrot's Training* which is his own English translation of 'Totā-Kāhini'.

FIGURE 2 Rabindranath Tagore in America, 13 March 1921. Note: Tagore gave lectures on nationalism in America in 1916–1917. This image of him in America is from a later period. Source: Rabindra-Bhavana Archive, Visva-Bharati, West Bengal, India. Reproduced with permission

---

In a letter of 10 November 1922 to Tagore, Geddes, while discussing the poet's idea of his 'International University', mentions having run Summer Schools in Edinburgh, but does not mention anything he had done in Darjeeling. Tagore did visit Darjeeling in June 1917, but there is no record of his activities during his stay, nor is there any mention of Geddes. Incidentally, Geddes had many other Indian friends, and wrote a book on the renowned

first fortnight of June where I have promised to join him. But I am sure, I should have done better to have kept away from all kinds of engagements for some time to come. I need complete rest after the strenuous time I had in America.

Yours sincerely,
Rabindranath Tagore

5) COUSINS TO TAGORE

Theosophical College
Madanapalle
July 26, 1917

Dear Sir Rabindranath,

Thank you for having the copy of the *Atlantic*[12] sent to me. I shall return it if desired. It is an indictment that must surely bring revelation to many in the West. I, who have lived through and escaped from 'the Nation',[13] know

---

Bengali scientist Jagadish Chandra Bose titled *An Indian Pioneer: The Life and Works of Sir J.C. Bose* (1920). Bose was one of Tagore's intimate friends. See *The Tagore – Geddes Correspondence*, ed. Bashabi Fraser (Kolkata: Visva-Bharati, 2004).

12 Tagore's lecture 'The Cult of Nationalism', given in different cities in America in 1916, was published in *Atlantic Monthly* CXIX (March 1917), on pages 290, 294, 296, 300 and 301. Tagore's lectures on nationalism, one of the most powerful and audacious critiques of nationalism in human history, were published together in book form as *Nationalism* (1917) by Macmillan. Tagore had wanted to dedicate the book to Woodrow Wilson, who, while campaigning for re-election to presidentship, had remarked that Tagore had 'kept us [America] out of war', but could not get Wilson's consent as the latter's office was advised by the British special liaison officer in America on 6 April 1917 that it would be an unwise move in view of the persisting belief that Tagore 'had got tangled up in some way' with Indian revolutionaries in America who were trying to conspire with Germany to overthrow the British in India. While Tagore initially received an enthusiastic response to his lectures, his later experience was bitter; he cut short his trip and returned home. Indeed, when some Indian revolutionaries were tried in a federal court, Tagore's name was implicated. Tagore learnt of all this much later from newspapers and shot back a letter to President Wilson on 9 May 1918; its concluding part reads: 'I have been outspoken enough in my utterances when my country needed them, and I have taken upon myself the risk of telling unwelcome truths to my own countrymen … therefore I owe it to myself … to assure your countrymen that their hospitality was not bestowed upon one who was ready to accept it while wallowing in the sub-soil sewerage of treason' (State Department Index No. 862.20211/1401), cited in Stephen N. Hay, 'Rabindranath Tagore in America' in *American Quarterly*, Vol. XIV, No. 3 (Autumn 1962), p. 451.

13 There was intense controversy in Ireland between the Literary Revivalists led by Yeats and the political nationalists over whether literature should be political. One of the most powerful critics of the literary revivalists was D P Moran, the editor of the paper *The Leader*, who advocated the idea of Irish-Ireland arguing that Irish literature should be written in Gaelic and not in English. Cf his *The Philosophy of Irish Ireland* (1905). The controversy between Tagore and the nationalist politicians in India and that between the Anglo-Irish Revivalists and Irish nationalists had thus

how close to truth you have got. I fancy you are aware that AE (whose prose resembles yours in vision and utterance) is fighting against 'the nation' too, under the name of the 'State' and believes that in the co-operative movement[14] there is the possibility of human organization in small and vital communities that will give the needful order to the conduct of affairs, and give the maximum of personal contact and freedom. I am trying this principle in College; and it is good to see boys who come to us with all the symptoms of repression from the machine-made system of education, rapidly blossoming into frankness and expression. I trust the national scheme will be pushed on. There is a great opportunity before it.

Certain passages in the enclosed pamphlet as to art[15] may interest you.

I shall put some extracts from the *Atlantic* into *New India.*

Yours sincerely,
James H. Cousins

6) TAGORE TO COUSINS

Santiniketan
January 24, 1918

Dear Mr. Cousins,

I must write these few lines to thank you for your books though I am forbidden to read or write letters for at least two months. But the Defence of Realm Act[16] has no connection with this imposition. The possibility of a breakdown with which I had been threatened has suddenly overtaken at last and it has

---

a close affinity. For Cousins, see note No. 2 above. However, in 1914, Cousins wrote a pamphlet called *War: A Theosophical View* in which, though he mentioned the brutalities of the First World War, his primary intention was to provide a philosophical dimension to death on the basis of the idea that life is, after all, eternal, and man undergoes incarnations through different rebirths. In other words, the pamphlet was not a denunciation of the War, but an attempt to make people accept death with resignation.

14 AE, the pseudonym of George William Russell (1867–1935), was an Anglo-Irish poet, critic, and editor. See note No. 13 to Introduction to this volume for more details.

15 Cousins had published a leaflet entitled 'The Art of the East' in 1916, already referred to above, and he may be referring to it in this letter.

16 On 12 August 1914, a week after Britain declared war on Germany and entered the First World War, the British parliament passed the Defence of the Realm Act, imposing several restrictions on its citizens and revoking several civic rights. As a sequel to it, the British government in India also passed the Defence of India Act in 1915, empowering itself thus to thwart all revolutionary activities.

come to me as a relief to know for certain I am entitled to all the undisputed rights of the sick.

Very sincerely yours,
Rabindranath Tagore

7) TAGORE TO COUSINS

Santiniketan
Bolpur
January 31, 1918

Dear Mr. Cousins,
The following poem has been written by me for your National Education week as requested by Mr. Arundale.[17] I send it to ask you if it is at all suitable for the occasion. If you do not think it is, please reject it without the least hesitation.

Yours sincerely,
Rabindranath Tagore

The lamp is trimmed. Comrades, bring your own fire to light it.
For the call comes again to you to join the star pilgrims crossing the dark towards the shrine of sunrise.
The day was when you went forth to your glad adventure of light
And the star of hope thrilled in the sky and kissed your banner.
But as the dusk deepened you fell behind in the march and slept with your light gone out
While your dreams grew discordant like the ominous cries of night birds.

17 George Arundale (1878–1945) was an Englishman who migrated to India in 1909 and took up a teaching assignment in Varanasi. He was an active theosophist and freemason, and became the president of the Theosophical Society in Adyar in 1934. He married Rukmini, the daughter of the noted historian of South India Nilakanta Shastri, who was also a theosophist. Rukmini Devi Arundale was a celebrated classical dancer. Tagore had written to George Arundale on 31 January 1918: 'The message which you ask from me for your National Education Week I send you herewith in the form of a short prose poem. I hope it will be acceptable.' Arundale's letter to Tagore could not be located in the Rabindra-Bhavana Archive (RBA), but Arundale had acknowledged the receipt of the poem and must have expressed his gratitude which elicited a response from Tagore on 8 February 1918. Tagore wrote: 'I am glad you think the poem suitable for your purpose. I send you herewith a copy of the revised version of it which you are at liberty to publish in the newspapers.' RBA File No. 32.

Yet, though it is dark and the wind in the forest is like the wails of lost souls
Has not the breath of that prayer already touched your foreheads
Which comes from the past echoing from age to age,
"Lead me to Light from the dark, from death to Everlasting life!"
Sleepers, rise up from your stupor of dim desolation
And know once more that you are children of Light.[18]

8) TAGORE TO COUSINS

Santiniketan
Bolpur
February 4, 1918

Dear Mr. Cousins,

Many thanks for the cuttings. I shall show them to Surendra Kar[19] who, you know, is in my school. He will be delighted with the appreciative reference to his works in your paper. As I am not allowed to tax my mind with attempts at original composition, I try to translate some of my Bengali writings into English to lighten the burden of unmitigated leisure.[20] I have been told by some of my critics that my English is not modern, and therefore, it sounds strangely remote and inadequate to the present-day readers. As I can have no conscious choice of my English style, never having the advantage of an analytical training in the acquirement of your language, I cannot judge my own performance in English. I am not very sure of my grammar, and I have no doubt that I make absurd mistakes in my English which would be tragic in a university examination paper. Of course, I know that a mere absence of mistakes is not vital in literature, being aware that my own Bengali is only often too incorrect from the schoolmaster's point of view. Yet your language being foreign to me I cannot fully trust my instinct about the atmosphere of the words I use and I am still more uncertain whether my ideas assume their aspect of truth to an English reader of an average receptivity of mind. This is the reason why I send you the accompanying translation. Please tell me if the English of it is appropriate,

18 The poem is to be found in Ms 111, p. 127 in RBA and was composed originally in English on 31 January 1918. See Tagore's letter to Cousins dated 10 February 1918 in this volume.

19 Surendranath Kar (1892–1970) was a prolific artist of the School of Oriental Art founded by Abanindranath Tagore and Gaganendranath Tagore. He came to Tagore's school at Santiniketan along with Nandalal Bose, Abanindranath's famous disciple, in April 1914. Kar helped Tagore found Kala Bhavana, the school of fine arts at Santiniketan, of which he subsequently became the Principal. Kar had also accompanied Tagore on his Southeast Asian tour in 1927; at Java, Kar learned the art of Batik printing which he introduced in Visva-Bharati.

20 Tagore seems to have translated at least five poems at this time of which four were published in *The Manchester Guardian* of 28 March 1918. For details see Prasantakumar Pal, *Rabijibani*, Vol. VII (Calcutta: Ananda Publishers, 1997), pp. 310–311.

if the meaning of it is clear enough to be attractive to an English reader, not judging them from your own standard, your mind being at home in India and having the poetic insight. Please know I am genuinely sincere when I ask you to be unsparingly frank with me and to have your full revenge against myself for the trouble I am giving you.[21]

Yours very sincerely,
Rabindranath Tagore

I find that the copy of the National Education week poem which I sent to Mr Arundale is incorrect in a few places. Kindly send him the copy which is with you if you think it at all acceptable.

9) TAGORE TO COUSINS

Santiniketan
February 10, 1918

Dear Mr. Cousins,
The message which I sent for the National Education week is not twice-born. It was written for the occasion in English at the instigation of Mr Arundale. So you can use your freedom in moulding it into any metrical form you choose. But the one which I sent you later on has its original in Bengali and it is written in what you call *vers libre*. No mere transliteration will give you the cadence. You will have it recited when we meet.

I shall try to be present at the opening ceremony of the University[22] if I am not asked to preside or take any part in the function.

Yours,
Rabindranath Tagore

21 Tagore was unsparing in the criticism of his own English renderings. He had written in a similar vein to Edward Thompson, to WB Yeats, and to William Rothenstein. But as a poet, he knew that it was impossible to translate his poems with all their nuances into English. As such, he found prose translations a more effective medium. This is evident from what he wrote to J D Anderson. 'It was the want of mastery in your language which originally prevented me from trying English metres in my translations. But now I have grown reconciled to my limitations through which I have come to know the wonderful power of English prose. ... I think one should frankly give up the attempt at reproducing in a translation the lyrical suggestions of the original verse and substitute in their place some new quality inherent in the new vehicle of expression.' RBA File No. 10.

22 The National University was set up by the Theosophical Society in Adyar in 1918 but was formally opened on 7 January 1919.

10) TAGORE TO COUSINS

Santiniketan
February 20, 1918

Dear Mr. Cousins,
In the following you will find my own revision of the poem which I sent you sometime ago.

Very sincerely yours,
Rabindranath Tagore

11) TAGORE TO COUSINS

Calcutta
March 5, 1918

Dear Mr. Cousins,
I thank you most heartily for your criticism and suggestion about my poem. I feel penitent for having put you to such an amount of trouble over this, especially as I myself am in that state of fatigue when one longs to take off one's thinking mind altogether like an office dress in a hot summer afternoon.

About the Englishness of my English, I have to be careful, as the language is not my own, but about ideas I think it is best to have a defiantly independent attitude of mind. For instance, for the sake of my average readers, I define the Eternal Runaway, giving it a name, such as, life, then it would be like giving the butterfly to pin it into its Latin name.

The subject of my poem is the Evermoving Spirit of Existence whose body is the infinite series of changing forms. It is pure because of its detachment, because the filling up of the cup and pouring it out belongs to the one and the same process. There is a spirit of perfection towards which it is moving, rhythm of whose music it follows. When we individuals harmonise our cadence of life with the dance – steps of this eternal love-quest, then we find our deliverance.

We in the Orient are not afraid of shifting our images that symbolize some idea that is not stationary. The picture of the Ganges as a stream of water may be followed in the next moment by that of a woman without having the effect of pulling us up. In fact, our readers find a special pleasure in having the many imaginative facets of some one truth turned round before their minds. It is not the consistency of only one particular image which is important but the in-effableness of truth which in its expression must be made fluid by its very inconstancy of form.[23]

But I must stop here, for writing letters has become too irksome for me. I hope I shall have a full discussion of this subject when we meet. Thanking you once again.

I am very sincerely yours,
Rabindranath Tagore

FIGURE 3 Rabindranath Tagore looking out of a train window in Japan in 1916. Source: Rabindra-Bhavana Archive, Visva-Bharati, West Bengal, India. Reproduced with permission

23 The poem opens Tagore's book of poems called *The Fugitive* (1921). It is the translation of poem No. 8 in the Bengali volume of verse, *Balākā* (Flight of Swans). For the two drafts of the poem see the Appendix to this volume. See also note No. 21 above on Tagore's views about his own mastery of English and his translations. The differences between the two drafts and the final version according to the following letter show that Tagore was meticulously careful about his translations.

12) TAGORE TO COUSINS

Calcutta
March 7, 1918

Dear Mr. Cousins,
Three more changes and then I think I shall have done with my poem. These are as follows:

1) 'at the shock of whose bodiless rush the stagnant space frets into froth of things'
2) 'and fire-pearls roll in your path torn from your necklace of mist'
3) 'Your fleeting steps kiss the dust of the world into sweetness'

Yours,
Rabindranath Tagore

PS: The original contains a succession of images which is non-transferable.

13) TAGORE TO COUSINS

Calcutta
May 12, 1918

Dear Mr. Cousins,
I have a letter from Macmillan asking me if it was my wish to make arrangements with you to compile a reader from my works. You may remember that I told you that Andrews[24] had undertaken to do this work and Macmillans had corresponded with him. But what with his Fiji[25] engagements and other things his work was interrupted and the last time when he was in Australia I thought he would never have time to finish it. But after his return I find that he has done a part of the work and the rest will be ready soon. I hope you will not mind if he in collaboration with me finishes this work. My help will be needed, as I wish some new stories to be translated and included in this book.[26]

24 Charles Freer Andrews (1871–1940). See note No. 13 to the Introduction to this volume.

25 Andrews, along with Pearson, was sent by the Indian government to Fiji in 1915 to inquire into the misery of indentured Indian labourers. Pearson visited Fiji again in 1917 for the same purpose. Andrews's report was published in *The Modern Review*, Vol. XIX, No. 109, June 1916, pp. 615–621.

26 The 'Reader' that Tagore mentions here is *Hungry Stones and other Stories* (1918) which is a collection of thirteen short stories translated by several hands, including Tagore and Andrews. The Preface records that the 'Reader' was meant for school children in India to provide them with

Perhaps you know I was preparing to leave India but am prevented to do so. I am still in a maze of entanglements, but I hope I shall come out of it and be able to keep my promise to see you in Madanapalle.

Yours very sincerely,
Rabindranath Tagore

14) TAGORE TO COUSINS

Santiniketan
June 17, 1918

Dear Mr. Cousins,
After some vacillations I have finally made arrangements to start for America sometime in August.[27] This will prevent my going to Adyar in July as I proposed to do – for I shall have to be busy in putting things in order in my school till I leave.

I have got a letter from Yeats in which he confesses to having been married. I wonder what will happen to the fairies with whom he was in speaking terms and also to his wonderful room in Woburn.[28]

Very sincerely yours,
Rabindranath Tagore

---

reading material with whose environment they were familiar. The collection also has notes, and both the notes and the preface were probably written by Andrews. The letter from Macmillan that Tagore mentions is not in the Tagore–Macmillan Correspondence File at the RBA.

27 Tagore went to America in October 1920, on his third visit, and not in 1918 as stated in this letter.

28 It is only here that we learn that Tagore visited Yeats's room in Woburn Buildings in London, where, apart from many other things, Yeats held his famous Monday morning meetings. Yeats married the twenty-five-year-old Georgie Hyde Lees in 1917, whom he had met at the Order of the Golden Dawn. Yeats had written to Tagore on 24 April 1918 about his marriage, adding that his wife 'cares for your work.' Though Tagore mentions Yeats's fairies rather jocularly, they were more than real to Yeats and were a part of his imaginative world since his childhood in Sligo. Particularly significant here are his stories in *The Secret Rose*. Rathindranath Tagore, the poet's son, who had accompanied the poet on his visit to England in 1912 and held long talks with Yeats observes: 'We always carried back the impression that Yeats lived and had his being in a world of imagination, a fairy world which was very real to him. It was difficult to believe he was a Westerner.' *On the Edges of Time* (Calcutta: Visva-Bharati, 1958), p. 104.

15) COUSINS TO TAGORE

Madanapalle
Madras Presidency
July 11, 1918

My dear Gurudev,

Thank you very much for the American edition of your new book.[29] I read many of the pieces to our students on my verandah last night, and will read more again. I wonder how far those who are temperamentally in affinity are associated on the inner planes of thought and feeling, and actually impart something to one another that appears on the outer planes in what is called exoterically plagiarism. Your first poem on the Taj[30] comes to me just as I am in the middle of a series of sonnets voicing emotions and thoughts stirred in me by that wonderful monument last April, and some of your phrases are quite parallel to mine. Also I wrote last afternoon in my tamarind grove a sonnet – which still wants a line to complete it – and lo! one of your poems says exactly the same thing.[31] I am heartily glad to come towards you in thought and feeling, even if I stumble along far behind in expression. Next incarnation I shall attain freedom of expression.

I think we can arrange satisfactorily for Dewal.[32] He spent a few days here, and made a good impression all round. He would find new impacts

29 Cousins refers to *Lover's Gift and Crossing* which was published by Macmillan in 1918 in London. A corresponding edition was published in America, a copy of which Tagore sent to Cousins.

30 The Taj Mahal was built in the seventeenth century by the Mughal Emperor Shahjahan (1592–1666), in memory of his deceased wife, Mumtaz, and is one of the most exquisite works of architecture in the world. The poem on Shahjahan and the Taj with which the volume of poems, *Lover's Gift* opens, is poem No. 7 in the Bengali volume of verses called *Balākā*. The original poem is long whereas Tagore makes a paraphrase of it in the prose translation.

31 See Cousins's series of four sonnets 'The Taj Mahal' in his *Collected Poems: 1894–1940* (Madras: Kalakshetra, 1940). The last one, 'The Builder's Rest', has an affinity with the closing words of Tagore's poem. See Appendix for both Tagore's and Cousins's poems. The other 'sonnet' that Cousins refers to could not be determined. The volume of poems he published in 1922 entitled *Surya Gita* contains 'The Taj Mahal' and other poems written at Madanapalle, but none of them is a sonnet. It is possible that Cousins may not have included the sonnet in any of the volumes, not even in his *Collected Poems*.

32 Narayan Kashinath Dewal was a student of the Santiniketan School whom Tagore sent to England for training in sculpture. He returned to India in 1916 and was employed at Bichitra or The Bichitra Studio for Artists of the Neo-Bengal School, a model institution set up at Jorasanko for imparting training in music and art along with other general subjects. Nandalal Bose, Surendranath Kar, Mukul Dey, and Asitkumar Halder were appointed on a monthly remuneration of sixty rupees at Bichitra. When Dewal returned from England, he too was appointed at Bichitra. But Bichitra did not work out well and it had to be wound up. Thereafter, Dewal stayed at Santiniketan for some time. See Prasantakumar Pal, *Rabijibani* (Tagore's Life), Vol. VII, p. 157. Pal remarks that nothing more is known about Dewal from that point onward. C F Andrews wrote an appreciative account of Dewal as a promising sculptor. See C F Andrews, 'A Young Indian Sculptor' in *The Modern Review*, Vol. XXIII, No. 1, June 1917, pp. 654–657. In

on his genius in our environment which might provoke a big piece of work. And he can do a great deal to help me in awakening taste and expression in South India which is dreadfully backward artistically. He is calling on Mrs Besant[33] on his way to Bolpur, and I have proposed a scheme to her which will, I trust, bring him back in a couple of weeks. We shall give him a studio and in short holidays we shall visit some places of special sculptural interest, spending probably the Dasara[34] week among the ruins of the wonderful city of Vizianagar near Hospet.[35]

We shall be delighted if you can come to us for a short or long time in October. I am sure that the change to our clear and cool air and our little hills would be acceptable to you. We have a clean guest-house with simple but sufficient appointments, and our life would be, I think fragrant to you, particularly if you come with the October moon. I may have to go to the north-east on University Extension work, and perhaps we could come south together, if you wish to escape Madras, which may then be in its monsoon, and which is always clammy and hot (and probably you could come down here from Bezwada). Then you might look in casually at Adyar on your way home. Of course I make these suggestions in ignorance of any other engagements that you may have in view, and remembering your former wish to be preserved from public engagements.

I have only learned of your loss of your daughter.[36] I too know what it is to lose friends of the heart and brain, and give you the right hand of the Comradeship of Sorrow and the left hand of the assurance of joy in the realization of the One Undying life.

Yours sincerely,
James H. Cousins

fact, Dewal migrated to South India to work at the Theosophical College as a teacher of art and craft, as evident from this letter, with Tagore's help. See *We Two Together* for further details. On Bichitra, see Rathindranath Tagore, *On the Edges of Time*, pp. 76–81.

33 Annie Besant (1847–1933) was a Fabian socialist, theosophist, social reformer, women's rights activist, educationalist, and Home Rule leaguer. Born in England, she claimed that three-quarters of her blood and heart were Irish. She was the second president of the Theosophical Society at Adyar, and helped found the Home Rule League in India. She was also elected president of the Indian National Congress and was interned by the British government in India for three months in 1917 against which Tagore protested strongly.

34 A major festival of Hindus celebrated on the concluding day of the worship of the goddess Durga to mark her victory over the buffalo demon or Mahishāsurā, symbolising the defeat of oppression and evil. The festival is also known as Vijayādashami and Dussehrā in some parts of India.

35 Margaret Cousins notes that both James Cousins and she accompanied by Dewal went to Hampi 'in quest of clay moulds of old bas reliefs in the Vijayanagar temples'. *We Two Together*, p. 336.

36 Tagore's eldest daughter, Madhurilata died of consumption on 16 May 1918.

16) TAGORE TO COUSINS

Shantiniketan
December 27 (?) 1918

Dear Mr. Cousins,

Certainly this time I shall never fail to see you at Madanapalle. But my heart quakes to imagine what is awaiting me at your Presidency, and I hope I shall be able to keep up my courage upto the last moment and take the final desperate step towards the South. Death's door is called the southern door in Bengal and I hope it won't claim me as a duly consecrated victim sacrificed to the myriad-tongued divinity of the Public Meeting. However, it would not be possible for me to be present at your Art Exhibition and I shall not be free to move before the last week of January. But should I not warn you not to put too implicit a faith upon my promises?[37] Chanakya[38] advises never to trust women and kings but I think poets should top the list of all unreliables.[39]

Very sincerely yours,
Rabindranath Tagore

37 Tagore went to Madanapalle which he named 'the Santiniketan of South India' in February 1919 from Bangalore. This visit is historic because it is here that Tagore translated *Jana gana mana* into English as 'The Morning Song of India'. Cousins rightly remarks that Tagore had created 'literary history' by giving humanity 'the nearest approach to an ideal national anthem'. There is a detailed and fascinating description of Tagore's reception and activities in *We Two Together*, pp. 340–344. See also the Introduction to this volume.

38 Also known as Kautilya and Vishnugupta, Chanakya (371BC to 283 BC) was a proverbial philosopher, jurist, economist, and royal adviser to Mauryan kings, and is known for the pioneering ancient Indian political treatise, *Arthashāstra*.

39 In a letter to Dorothy Wellesley, Yeats wrote, 'poets are good liars', and this bears a great significance in the context of the letter. For poets and writers, lying broadly denotes the fictional nature of their work. The word is never meant to be taken in its literal, everyday sense. Unfortunately, Sourindra Mitra, in his book *Khyati Akhyatir Nepathyey* (In the Background of Fame and Infamy,1981) accusing Yeats of being 'envious' of Tagore, takes this expression in its literal sense and turns it against him!

17) TAGORE TO COUSINS

Shantiniketan
April 13, 1919

Dear Cousins,

We shall be ready from the next June to receive students here[40] who want to have their art training from Nandalal[41] and others of his kind. Twenty rupees a month will be needed for board, lodging and tuition and, I am sure, another five rupees will be enough for other costs.

I am looking forward to meeting you in our ashram before you sail away from Calcutta. I am asked by doctor to keep to bed for at least a fortnight and it gives me much pleasure to take this opportunity to break his injunction and sit up to answer your letter.

Yours,
Rabindranath Tagore

From the liberty I allow myself against doctor's advice you can guess Andrews is away.

18) TAGORE TO COUSINS

Santiniketan
Bolpur
July 22, 1919

Dear Cousins,

Your letter reminded me of my own visit to Japan and for a moment I felt a strong wish to renew my experience once again. But I have come to that period of life when one knows that merely getting more is not getting the best, and that the fullness may be better contained in the smallness than in

40 Kala Bhavana, the school of fine arts, was founded in 1919 and continues to be the most distinguished school of art in India since then.

41 Nandalal Bose (1883–1966) was one of the foremost artists of the Bengal School pioneered by Abanindranath and Gaganendranath Tagore. He was a teacher at the Kala Bhavana in Visva-Bharati and became its Principal in 1922. Apart from his own achievements as an artist, he had designed the covers of many of Tagore's books. He was also a very vocal advocate of the inclusion of art as part of general education. See his essay 'The Place of Art in Education' with which his slim volume of small observations on the methods of artistic creation, *Silpakathā*, (Speaking of Art, 1999) opens. He also decorated the original manuscript of the Constitution of India.

the bigness. Disenchantment is very often another name for the mental dyspepsia. It comes from knowing more than is good for one and not being able to assimilate the details of knowledge into an organic unity of enjoyment. At the shock of novelty our mind is stimulated to put forth all its power to grasp, but when that impetus is gone the mind becomes lazy and puts out most of its lights, wrongly thinking that they are no longer required. This dullness of illumination in our own mind makes the outer world appear dull. This will serve as an introduction to my resolve not to repeat my experience of the delightful country where I was received with such unexpected warmth of heartiness.[42]

Invitations have come to me from Australia which I have accepted. It is a country whose youthfulness is still unimpaired joyfully carrying in its vigorous immaturity its unrealized future. This, I am sure, will attract me greatly, all the more because my own country is obsessed with its past – the past which has made our future anaemic drawing away all its life-blood to itself – like a dying parent uselessly draining away blood from the veins of a devoted child. However, my visit to Australia is not going to be before the next summer – and in the meanwhile I shall have to be busy with my institution whose scope I am trying to extend.

I am sure you get all the news of India from various sources – therefore, I shall not add to your torment by repeating them – they are not things of beauty.[43]

I know you will love Japan where she is purely herself, but things have got terribly mixed up nowadays and a great flood of physical and moral ugliness has drowned the modern world in a monotonous expanse of efficiency.

Yours affectionately,
Rabindranath Tagore

42 Tagore visited Japan first in 1916 on his way to America. It was in Japan that he first delivered his lecture on nationalism called 'The Message of India to Japan' which was unfavourably received by many. He visited Japan again in 1924 and 1929. Whatever the Japanese reaction to Tagore's decrying of their imitation of western nationalism, Japan had gripped his imagination which is evident from the mesmerising travelogue he wrote in Bengali, *Jāpānjātri* (Traveller to Japan). We may add here Cousins's comment on the Japanese response to Tagore and his own impression of the Japanese mind. Comments Cousins: 'Rabindranath Tagore had delivered a lecture three or four years previously, and had somewhat spoiled matters by delivering a lecture not merely to the crowd but at them – which gave me an oblique spy-hole into the psychology of the new Japan.' James H. Cousins, *The New Japan: Impressions and Reflections* (Madras: Ganesh & Co, 1923), p. 22.

43 Tagore here probably refers to the Jallianwalabagh Massacre that took place on 13 April 1919 when, on the orders of Colonel Reginald Dyer, British forces opened fire on harmless citizens of Amritsar in the Punjab who had gathered on the occasion of Baisākhi celebrations. Nearly four hundred people were killed and fifteen hundred injured in the firing. Tagore relinquished his knighthood conferred on him in 1914, in protest. The post-War period also witnessed intensification of nationalist activities in India. Baisākhi is a very important Sikh festival observed annually on 12 or 13 April to mark the birth of the Sikh order.

FIGURE 4 Rabindranath Tagore outside Okakura's villa residence in Japan, 1916; photograph by K Maekawa. Note: This image is of the time when Tagore gave lectures on nationalism in Japan in 1916. Source: Rabindra-Bhavana Archive, Visva-Bharati, West Bengal, India. Reproduced with permission

19) COUSINS TO TAGORE

Keio University
Tokyo, Japan
September1, 1919

Dear Gurudev,

I am interested to hear that you intend to go to Australia[44] next summer. You will probably have Mrs. Cousins as far as Singapore on her way here to join me for a year in Japan.[45]

The intrusion of a second long vacation and hot weather has kept me getting fully into Japanese life save that of holiday makers. I spent a month with the Richards at a village up the slope of a volcano, and am now spending three weeks with Speight[46] at Nikko revelling in his fine library of modern poets – and, dear me! What a muddle is it of uncertainty, cocksureness, modernity, ancient simplicity, art, ugliness, thought, brainlessness, and anything but poetry. They are bawling for the new age, but they wouldn't know it if it hit them between the eyes, they are so blind with their own little preconceptions regarding it. They go red-cheeked over such tremendous questions as rhyme or no rhyme, dustbins (as subject matter) versus flowers and stars. There is no hint of such a thing as soul – such 'stuff' is good enough for back numbers like AE and the singer of Gitanjali.[47] Well it is all very amusing, and very tragic, and I suppose we are all compelled to do what we are compelled to do (if I make myself clear), and a sense of humour is a great help to sanity.

I hope your plans for the asram will work out satisfactorily. I wish again and again that my karma enabled me to be of real help to you. May be the wish is, as so often happens in my life, a prophecy. When you get back from Australia, and Mrs. Cousins and I from Japan, we shall see what we shall see.

44 There is no record of Tagore having visited Australia. But the University of Melbourne had sent an official invitation to Tagore (letter dated 10 July 1919) and other universities such as the University of Western Australia, University of Adelaide, University of South Australia, University of Sydney, and University of New South Wales also offered to lend financial support to his visit. RBA File No. 16.

45 Cousins was in Japan between May 1919 and April 1920. He was a guest professor of English Literature at Keio University. His lectures on English poetry in Japan were later published as *Modern English Poetry*. In fact, Cousins too was critical of some of the western imitations of the Japanese which he records in *We Two Together*.

46 Speight refers to Ernest Edwin Speight. See note No. 131 to the Introduction to this volume.

47 In his book on Japan, Cousins gives a short description of his experience at the gathering of Japan's modern poets thus: 'There is no keenness, no sparkle, no fire – yet who knows what energies were working behind this superficial dullness?' adding that these 'poetical iconoclasts who, though they may never sing a line against things as they are, are introducing new mental and emotional rhythms that may shatter the moulds of national thinking and feeling.' Cousins, *The New Japan*, pp. 72–73.

Yes, I get the Indian news from many sources, and the less said of it, the better. I shall just whisper that many people have sung chants of joy at your answering their prayer.

Curiously I saw Romain Rolland's[48] letter to you and your reply, just after Paul Richard[49] and I had concocted a scheme for bringing together in India a few of you bog-eyed ones who see things straight, in order that you might make a pronouncement as to the spiritual unity of all humanity, and give the necessary inspiration and authority to a band of workers to elaborate the central declaration into the details of life. A move has been made to ask you to meet Bernard Shaw,[50] Aurobindo Ghose,[51] Abdul Baha,[52] and Annie Besant, perhaps before you go to Australia. A collective pronouncement from you Big Five would make a great impact on a large number of good people, and find perhaps that the band round the world of which you speak in your preface to Monsieur's 'To The Nations'.[53]

About which preface I have something to say. I have very carefully revised the book (author's text only, of course!) from the point of view of expression, and Monsieur has written for permission to Ganesh to make such alterations as may be necessary in his text to avoid official friction. He wants the substance spread. He tells me emphatically that you placed no restrictions on the use of the preface which you wrote for the American edition. I trust this is so, and that you will write Ganesh & Co., Thambuchetty Street, Georgetown, Madras, permitting them to reprint. Monsieur and I have a plan in mind for making

48 Romain Rolland (1866–1944) was a French writer and dramatist and a mystic; he was awarded the Nobel Prize for Literature in 1915. Rolland wrote to Tagore that he had put in passages in French translation from Tagore's 'The 'Message of India to Japan'. Tagore replied on 24 June 1919 agreeing to be one of the signatories, and also apologising as he had received Rolland's letter and the English version of the Declaration in a 'magazine.' RBA, File No. 321 (i). Tagore's letter and the Declaration were published in *The Modern Review*, July 1919, pp. 80–82. See also the Introduction to this volume.

49 Richard refers to Paul Antoine Richard (1874–1967) whose anti-nation and anti-materialistic ideas Tagore shared. This led him to write an introduction to Richard's book *To the Nations* (1917). See note No. 132 to the Introduction to this volume.

50 George Bernard Shaw (1856–1950), of Anglo-Irish descent, was a famous playwright and thinker associated with Fabian Socialism. Tagore met Shaw in London in 1912, but the two do not seem to have developed any friendship.

51 Aurobindo Ghose (1872–1950) was a revolutionary patriot who was accused and tried in the Alipur Bomb Case. The case involved the assassination in 1908 of Douglas Kingsford, the British district judge of Mazzafarpur, now in the Indian state of Bihar. Ghose was charged but after a protracted trial was acquitted. Later, Ghose abandoned politics and became a mystic and set up his ashram at Pondicherry which has since become a leading centre of Indian culture. Ghose not only wrote essays on spiritual subjects, but was a literary critic and a poet. His *Sāvitri* (1940) is one of the finest specimens of mystic poetry in the world. Tagore addressed a poem to him which begins: 'Aurobindo, accept Rabindra's salutation'.

52 Abdul Baha (1844–1921) was the son of Bahaullah, the founder of the Bahai Faith, which believes in monotheism and in the spiritual unity of all mankind.

53 Cousins refers to Tagore's introduction to Paul Richard's *To the Nations* (1917).

India a great centre for the dissemination of true spiritual culture, and the elimination of those caricatures of Indian thought and practice which come from America. I can find agents here and in America, and with a good start we can greatly help India by developing the printing and publishing business. I am getting some of my students at Madanapalle to learn type-setting and bookbinding, so that we may have a press and capable staff under our control in a couple of years. Help us please, by allowing Ganesh to use your introduction to 'To the Nations'. We want it to be regarded not a money-making book, but as the first pamphlet, so to speak, of a new cultural mission.

Speight joins me in hearty greetings.

Yours affectionately,
James H Cousins

20) COUSINS TO TAGORE

Adyar, Madras
December 16, 1921

Dear Gurudev,

The extension of my paper on 'The Cultural Unity of Asia' into a book of 100 pages, with 8 illustrations, for the Asian Library, is now almost complete. The chapters are as follows:

i) The Cultural Origins of Asia
ii) The Great Buddhist Migration
    a) From India to China and Korea
iii) The Great Buddhist Migration
    b) From India via Korea to Japan
iv) Japan – the Modern Insular Synthesis of Continental Asian Culture
v) Continental Cultural Movements–
    a) Burma and Siam; Turkistan and Tibet
vi) Continental Cultural Movements–
    b) Arabic, Persian, Mughal
vii) The Island Cultures – Ceylon, Java
viii) India – the Mother of Culture

Unless you get an injunction against me, I shall dedicate the book to the Founder, Staff and Students of Visva-Bharati! This is the least I can do to sympathise with your big idea. I shall do more when my karmic periphery becomes more elastic. Somewhere after next August, I shall start the circumnavigation of the globe for several purposes – 1) To satisfy myself that it is an all-round affair, notwithstanding the flatness of a good many of the people and things on the surface; 2) To find and link up in companionship as many men and women of goodwill and culture as possible, and to prepare for the publication of an all-world magazine of the international spirit which will voice the Visva-Bharati idea, not, of course, as an opponent of any magazine you yourself may start in the meantime.[54] If you do start – it will help; if you do not start, then it may be used by you. 3) To see Ireland again; 4) To expound your poetry to many good people who love it – but do not know what the deuce it is all about. When I get back to India in 1923, I shall be free to help your work. My trip will probably be – Java, Australia, China, Japan, Korea, America, Canada, Ireland, Britain, France, Italy.[55]

The book on Asian culture will go round in advance and pave the way. The publishers may say that a short introduction from you would greatly help it. It certainly would – but I have never in my life asked for an introduction for any of my books. However, this is an impersonal matter, with an intention entirely in support of your ideas; and if the request is not repugnant to you (and time permits) I pass on their desire to you. Such an introduction need not go beyond 1200 words.[56] The chapter headings given above show the scope of the book. All through it I emphasise the tendency towards fusion which arises

54 Tagore sought Cousins's help in starting a journal for Visva-Bharati. The first issue of *The Visva-Bharati Quarterly* was published in 1923 to which Cousins contributed an essay on Shelley entitled 'Poetry and World Problems'. See *We Two Together*, p. 396. Incidentally, Tagore himself delivered a lecture on Shelley at Presidency College on the poet's death centenary.

55 Both James and Margaret Cousins visited Europe and America from April 1928 to September 1929. Cousins gave lectures on Indian painting, architecture, and sculpture and addressed gatherings at Theosophical Lodges. Significantly enough, on 26 August 1929, at a congress of the Theosophical Society in Chicago, Cousins and Rukmini Devi Arundale had sung 'Jana gana mana' as the national anthem of India, and Cousins comments that through this 'Indo-Irish duet … India was given a proper musical place among the nations.' However, again in 1930, Cousins recited 'The Morning Song of India' at Washington while speaking on Tagore. He remarks that it had struck him to be 'the international anthem of humanity'. See *We Two Together*, pp. 499, 520. It was during the tour of 1928–1929, that Margaret Cousins gave lectures on 'The Awakening of Asian Womanhood', which were subsequently published in a book form.

56 *The Cultural Unity of Asia* was published in 1922. Cousins dedicated the book to Tagore, the Staff and Students of Visva-Bharati, as he wanted. Tagore did not write any introduction to it. In the book, Cousins made small changes in the titles and sub-titles of a few chapters. Below are the chapters as they appear in the book:

i) The Cultural Origins of Asia
ii) The Great Buddhist Cultural Migration
    a) From India to China and Korea
iii) The Great Buddhist Migration
    b) From India via Korea to Japan
iv) Japan – the Modern Insular Synthesis of Continental Asian Culture
v) Continental Cultural Movements –
    a) Burma and Siam; Turkistan and Tibet
vi) Continental Cultural Movements –
    b) The Mughal Expansion
vii) The Island Cultures – Ceylon and Java
viii) India – the Mother of Asian Culture

out of the fundamental Asian realization of the spiritual unity in which all the variety of manifestation is rooted. Words from you on the value of the Asian attitude would be valuable to the world. You want the world to realize that Asia had (and has) a mind as well as devotion. The book will do this within its limited space, and give indications of larger study.

If you prefer to wait and see the proofs, they can be sent by and by, but perhaps this is not essential.

And I shall (probably) be just as pleased if you say no – for then I shall feel that you can be quite frank and sincere with me.

I have come across a fine collection of Mughal and Rajput paintings not seen for some centuries – stored away in a palace! They are being catalogued (79), translated and studied.[57] I hope to take them (and some) Bengal work on my tour.

I trust you are quite well again.

Yours sincerely,
James Henry Cousins

21) TAGORE TO COUSINS

Santiniketan
January 31, 1923

Dear Cousins,
There will be no harm if Dr. Kramrisch[58] is detained in the South. Let her utilize this opportunity to the fullest extent. We shall consider it as Visva-Bharati's own duty if she is helped in her study of Indian Art, also in her interpreting it to the

57 Cousins presumably refers to the paintings that would be put up at the Jaganmohan Chitrasala, an art gallery founded in 1924 in Mysore under the auspices of the Maharaja of Mysore; the gallery was organised by Cousins. The gallery put up 90 (and not 79, as Cousins mentions in the letter) paintings; Cousins wrote an introduction to the Catalogue and also the notes to the paintings.

58 Dr Stella Kramrish (1895–1993) was an academic exponent of Indian art. Tagore first met her in London in 1920 and invited her to Santiniketan. Among her many books are *Principles of Indian Art* (1924), *Indian Sculpture* (1932), *A Survey of Paintings in Deccan* (1937), *Indian Terracottas* (1939), *The Hindu Temple* (1946), and *The Arts and Crafts of Travancore* (1948). In 1923, she was appointed Bageswari Professor at Calcutta University, while she also lectured on the history of western art at Kala Bhavana in Santiniketan. She was one of the earliest of art critics who found close affinity of Tagore's paintings with modernist western paintings.

(This is a draft letter in pencil in the poet's own hand with an instruction in Bengali written to Cousins.)

people who require her help. Visva-Bharati is not merely for the students who live within the limited area of Santiniketan.

Owing to the late flood which has nearly ruined our own estate the financial condition of Visva-Bharati is not as it should be. I do not think we can afford to invite any more European teachers for some time to come. We need very badly someone who can teach us European languages but our material needs have become still more urgent.

Andrews is away and my burden of work has grown enormously heavy.

Yours,
Rabindranath Tagore

22) TAGORE TO COUSINS

Undated 1923(?)

I am sure you will be able to help our Visva-Bharati[59] by the experience you gain in your European tour.[60] We specially want you to study Agricultural Co-operation in Ireland and let us know how far its methods can be adapted to our Indian condition. We shall be very thankful to you if you can persuade some experienced man who has worked with AE, to come and help us in our village work for about six months or longer if it is possible. Of course on our side we shall be only too glad to offer you the pecuniary help you need so much, the amount of which will be fixed in our committee meeting according to our financial capacity and communicated to you without delay.[61]

As my intention was to proceed to China in the beginning of the present autumn I did not send your invitation letter to AE which you had left with me

59 Cousins paid a four-day visit to Santiniketan in the first week of July 1923 after lecturing at Calcutta University on 2 and 3 July. At Santiniketan, he gave talks on the Irish Literary Revival and held discussions with Tagore. See *We Two Together*, p. 400. He had visited Santiniketan earlier along with Margaret Cousins from 4 to 18 October 1921.

60 Cousins's European tour did not come off until 1928. See note No. 49 above.

61 It is pertinent to point out that Tagore had started the co-operative in Sriniketan in the teeth of the opposition unleashed by the non-cooperation movement. He had had a densely argued debate with Gandhi over the latter's idea of *charka* and sought Leonard Elmhirst's help in establishing co-operation and rural reconstruction as part of his Visva-Bharati scheme. The work for rural reconstruction in the village of Surul, two miles away from Santiniketan, began on 5 February 1922. By 1924, much progress had been made, but troubles had also cropped up between Elmhirst and other associates such as Kalimohan Ghosh and Santosh Majumdar, ultimately leading to Elmhirst's estrangement. He accompanied the poet to Europe in 1924 but did not return to Santiniketan. It is presumably under these compelling circumstances that Tagore appealed to Cousins seeking AE's help.

at our last meeting. I did not want him to come during my absence. I have been compelled to put off my engagement in China to March next year.[62] We shall be glad if you exercise your influence on AE[63] and try to send him to us in the cold season of 1924. Please assure him that my mission is not (as he seems to have suggested in some of his late writings) to offer intoxicating fumes of vague idealism to our people in place of bread which they need so much. He must have misunderstood me owing to his not being able to follow me outside my literary adventure of a purely poetical kind.

Andrews is in Beneras lecturing to the students.

23) TAGORE TO COUSINS

6 Dwarakanath Tagore Lane
Calcutta
November 11, 1925

Dear Friend,
It is with hesitation that I write this letter, for I am not sure if my proposal will suit your own plans of work. I am obliged by circumstances to ask you to give us a continuous period of one or two years your help in the building up of the educational side of Visva-Bharati. We have now long been in need of one who may undertake to organise the higher courses of study at Santiniketan.[64] I cannot recollect at present any one who may so worthily fill the office of Principal of our Department of Collegiate Studies as yourself.[65] May I know if your engagements would permit you to join us and help us at least for a year or two?

I wish I could personally come to your place and fetch you to Santiniketan, but the journey may prove to be too heavy a strain in the present state of my health.

62 Tagore, on an invitation, visited China in April 1924 with the avowed intention of establishing what he called 'spiritual communication' between the two civilisations. For a comprehensive revaluation of Tagore's relationship with China see, among others, the volume of essays *Tagore and China*, eds. Tan Chung, Amiya Dev, et al. (New Delhi: Sage, 2011).

63 For AE's and Tagore's interest in the Irish Co-operative movement see note No. 11 above. Tagore does not seem to have met AE. However, Ranjee G Shahani, in a letter to Tagore, wrote that AE often spoke to him about Tagore. RBA File No. 247.

64 In 1924, the academic structure of Visva-Bharati underwent change with the formation of three sections, namely *Patha Bhavana* (school education), *Sikhsa Bhavana* (collegiate education), and *Vidya Bhavana* (higher education and research). A number of European scholars came to Visva-Bharati to teach. Tagore is writing desperately to Cousins under these circumstances.

65 Cousins had the experience of carrying out the responsibilities of the Principal of Madanapalle College, a position to which he had been promoted in 1918. Tagore wanted to bank on his experience. But Cousins could not take up this offer.

FIGURE 5 Foundation of Visva-Bharati Parisad-Sabha at Amrakunja, 23 December 1921. Note: L-R, Sitting: Acharya, Brojendranath Seal, Sylvain Levi, Rabindranath Tagore, Nilratan Sarkar, CF Andrews, Vidhusekhar Sastri, Mahasthavir Dharmadhar, Tapan Mohan Chatterjee L-R, Standing: Surendranath Kar, Nepal Chandra Roy, Rathindranath Tagore. Source: Rabindra-Bhavana Archive, Visva-Bharati, West Bengal, India. Reproduced with permission

With kindest regards to your wife and yourself,

Yours very sincerely,
Rabindranath Tagore

24) COUSINS TO TAGORE

Adyar, Madras
April 4, 1926

Dear Gurudev,

I kept the matter of your two letters of November in mind pending some sign as to how my future work would develop. I knew that extensions were coming on, and I am sure you will agree that I did right in keeping your request to myself so that no external circumstances might complicate the minds of those planning out a great world scheme of educational reform in which I knew I would be wanted to help. What has happened is this: I have been relieved of any teaching work save that of the Ashram between October and March. This work now runs smoothly, and it might be possible for me to get away from it for short spells regularly even during the lecturing session: But in the time between March and October I am free from routine. What I have now to do is to act as general Editor of the reformed text-books of the Theosophical World University, and write some of them myself. This is a big work, but I can do much of it away from here as well as here.[66] But if you think that I could be of practical service to you in shaping the plans towards the fulfilling of your ideal, I think I could go to you for a month or two before October, either in July, August or September as suited you. We could then see exactly how, if at all, I could be useful. As I am not a wage earner it would be necessary for Visva-Bharati to pay my travelling expenses and give me board and lodging. I have to put my future plans before Mrs Besant next week before she goes to Europe and America. If there is any likelihood of such partial service being any good to you, you might send me a wire saying what month I might go to you in, so that your wishes could be taken as a factor in our arrangements here.

I wonder if you have thought of the probable effect of my association with Dr. Besant and the Theosophical Society on any work which I might undertake for Visva-Bharati. You yourself are beyond any narrowness in this respect, but others in various parts of India are not so broad. Personally I find the Theo-Sophia (which is the same thing as Brahma Vidya)[67] sufficiently inclusive to enable me to merge myself in others and realize that they are as inevitable as myself. The last thing I would think of would be an attempt to turn anyone from their own modes. But I would also claim the same freedom of polite expression of my own ideas as I would gladly grant to others. I think your staff like me, and I think I might be able to help you to find a plan of work which, once inaugurated and watched for a while, would give the same sense of progressive security as we have in the Ashram here. I say this without knowing what has developed in Visva-Bharati since you wrote me in November. I have no ready-made specific for running the universe! Such experience and

66 Cousins's proposal for setting up what he named Brahmavidya Ashrama (school of universal culture) at Adyar was accepted by Annie Besant. The school would teach 'mysticism, religion, philosophy, art, and science' under the five main aspects of humanity: 'substance, form, vitality, consciousness, superconsciousness'. Cousins spurned the offer of a professorship in Northern India and was appointed protem Registrar of the school. The school began functioning from October 1922. These were Cousins's engagements during this period. For details on this, see *We Two Together*, pp. 392–394.

67 In 1922, Annie Besant proposed the winding up of the National University and Cousins suggested the opening of a school to be called BrahmavidyaAshrama, as stated in note 62 above. It is evident from Cousins's scheme of studies noted above that this was more in tune with theosophical ideas and beliefs. As such, it bears little or no affinity with Tagore's ideas of education followed at Santiniketan.

capacity as I have would, if circumstances so permitted, be bent to fulfilling your ideals, not pushing any notions of my own save as they were in affinity with yours.[68] I find there is an aesthetic for other activities than art. As soon as I find it, I take joy in it. That, I think, is the explanation of the way in which I outrage the sense of propriety in some of my friends by taking a ferocious delight in the most hopelessly unpoetical matters. The qualities that give life to art are also inherent in the art of life. When we touch them we live. I am hot on the organizing of our library here on a new plan. It is a splendid adventure in creation. It is better (meanwhile) than verse-making, for while the poet in me makes little universes of words, the present librarian is hustling around the masters of literature (including RT) making them dance themselves into a new cosmos.

Well, we shall see. I learn that you are somewhat better. I think you would be still better if you felt your ideals moving and consolidating. If I can be of use to that end I shall indeed be happy.

Yours affectionately,
James H. Cousins

25) TAGORE TO COUSINS

April 8, 1926

Dear Friend,
Your letter brought me very welcome tidings. I am very grateful that circumstances have allowed you freedom to come and help us in our work. For the fulfillment of which I have often had to struggle hard almost single-handed. I have already wired to you the period during which we should wish to avail ourselves of your services. Visva-Bharati will most gladly bear your expenses for travelling, board and lodging.

I am in complete agreement with what you say regarding your relationship towards the Visva-Bharati and the Theosophical Society. There should not be the least cause for misunderstanding and differences of opinion and allow such freedom of expression to others as we should like enjoy ourselves. It is a matter of sincere regret that I shall be in Europe during the whole period of your stay in our asrama, but arrangements will be made so as to make your stay

68 See note 59 and 67 above.

comfortable and happy.[69] It is almost impossible for me to refuse the invitation from Italy which I have long tried to postpone.

With kindest regards to your wife and yourself,

Ever yours,
Rabindranath Tagore

26) COUSINS TO TAGORE

Adyar, Madras
April10, 1926

I received your wire, and saw Dr. Besant. She gladly gives me a general permission to be of the best service possible to you without, of course, injuring the work here. I hoped to have your letter today giving me some details, but will not withhold this information longer. I leave tomorrow night for Nandi Hill Mysore State where I shall be till the end of May. I shall not write in detail now but it looks as if I can join you about June 20, if not before, and have time to talk matters over fully with you before your session begins.

I am intensely happy at the prospect of being of use to you even in a partial way.

Yours warmly,
James H. Cousins

27) COUSINS TO TAGORE

Till May 28
Cunningham Bungalow
Nandi Hill, Mysore State
April 13, 1926

Dear Gurudev,

Your letter of April 8 reached me at Adyar just as I was leaving to come here for a physical and mental clean-up in coolness and solitude. I arrived too late yesterday to catch the mail.

69 There appears to be no surviving record of what Cousins had done for Visva-Bharati, and there is no reference to his visiting the university to help Tagore in his work as would be evident from letters below, though he was made a member of the Court of the university in 1922.

I fear my first letter was not sufficiently explicit as regards the actual time I could give to the work you have in view. A continuous period of three months would not be possible. I can manage from a month to six weeks round about July, and a fortnight in January or later. If I take you up rightly (and you have not given me an idea of the work) I think you want a scheme that, once satisfactorily set going, will give you a sense of security as to its continuity. I think this can be done. But I must first have close contact with your mind, and get to know as much as I can (beyond what I already know) of your thoughts as to how your ideals may be incarnated more fully in the organization. Knowing this, I shall set to work with imagination and experience to see how the materials at hand in the ashram can be more effectively used. If you and I decide on a plan, you must give it the authority of your approval, not as a finality, but as a way to be thoroughly and loyally tried by all concerned. Your being away from July[70] will make matters less easy than they could be in your presence. Humanity does not like innovation, if we find such to be necessary; and criticism is rather a prickly plant in Bengal! But a thorough discussion with you, a tentative plan, and your benediction on it during your absence, would help us round corners. When do you leave for Italy?[71] And where and when can I see you personally? I can join in June whenever you are staying. What date does the ashram resume work in July?

With happy anticipations,

Yours warmly,
James H. Cousins

28) TAGORE TO COUSINS

April 20, 1926

Dear Friend,

I well understand the little anxiety you express in your last letter in regard to the work which you hope to start here but which would be somewhat difficult of proper fulfillment during my absence in Europe. I may sail for Europe on May 15, or if that were not possible, on June 1. It will not be quite easy to

70 Between May and November 1926, Tagore visited many European countries, including Italy.

71 It is rather surprising that Cousins should ask Tagore, above anything else, about Italy. He himself had visited Italy in 1925, and his account of it in his duo-autobiography is mostly of Italian art and architecture. In contrast, Tagore's visit was much more eventful and controversial. For a recent profusely documented critical appraisal of Tagore's Italian visit see Kalyan Kundu's *Meeting with Mussolini: Tagore's Tour in Italy 1925 and 1926* (Delhi: Oxford University Press, 2015).

arrange for a meeting and a discussion with you during the short interval of time at our disposal. Will it not be better to let this question stand over until I return from Europe towards the end of this year? You may then visit us in January as you suggest in your letter and the whole plan of work may be then thought out and discussed and shot into execution. You will remain in our thoughts all the while and our welcome to you will be all the warmer because of this waiting.

With my warmest regards to your wife and yourself.

Yours affectionately,
Rabindranath Tagore

29) COUSINS TO TAGORE

Adyar, Madras
April 25, 1926

Dear Gurudev,
I was hoping to have word from you as to where and when it would be most convenient to see in you in order to get fully in touch with your mind as to the matters in which I may be able to help you.

In order to be within easy call I have found a place at Kalimpong (near Darjeeling) where Mrs. Cousins and I will stay from May 5 to 31 or even a little longer. From there I can hunt you up, and I can extend my stay in the hills until the Visva-Bharati opens. I can work in it until the end of August, and by that time we should have found our stride.

Will you please wire me probable date of your departure; where and when you can be found before it; date of opening of Visva-Bharati.

If you have already given these particulars in a letter that may be awaiting me at Adyar (I am writing from Mysore, but am leaving for Adyar today), you need not wire.

If special lectures on Geology, Animal psychology and Craniology would be useful, I can send you good men next winter for travelling expenses and hospitality. They are coming to Adyar to give lecture courses. I have also an Egyptologist coming.

Hoping to see you soon, and to find means of service in your great work.

Yours sincerely,
James H. Cousins

30) COUSINS TO TAGORE

Adyar, Madras
April 26, 1926

Dear Gurudev,
Your letter of 20th has come. Since I have the time between now and September, I think it would be a pity not to take up the work. I wrote you yesterday from Mysore. I find it now certain that I shall be in Calcutta on the 3rd or 4th of May. I can see you either at Bolpur or Calcutta though Calcutta would be more convenient, if it was likely that you would be there. If we can have a chat then, I can go on to Kalimpong for a holiday, and go to Santiniketan some days before the opening of the session. Then I can do whatever is required up to the end of August, or even a week longer. So please send me a wire saying if I can see you at Calcutta or Santiniketan – Calcutta on May 4, Santiniketan on May 3 to allow me to get back to Calcutta for Kalimpong train on 4th afternoon. Better get things on the move now than wait till January, I think.

Yours sincerely,
James H. Cousins

31) TAGORE TO COUSINS

Santiniketan
March 7, 1928

Dear Cousins,
I hope we shall meet somewhere somewhen in Europe during our tour there. I have my engagement in Oxford about the end of October – that is the only fixed point in my programme.[72] I do not know when I shall be able to leave India or when I return. In the meanwhile I shall have to be very busy writing lectures and finishing my works that are urgent.

With affectionate regards

Ever yours,
Rabindranath Tagore

72 Tagore was at Oxford in 1930, where he delivered the Hibbert Lectures for that year on 19, 21 and 26 May entitled 'The Religion of Man'. In these lectures, Tagore focuses on the plebeian and folk religious and devotional traditions of Bengal and other parts of India as against the high canonical ideas enshrined in the Upanishads from which he drew much of intellectual and spiritual ideas.

FIGURE 6 Rabindranath Tagore taking class in Santiniketan. Source: Rabindra-Bhavana Archive, Visva-Bharati, West Bengal, India. Reproduced with permission

32) COUSINS TO TAGORE

Madanapalle
Madras Presidency
July 23, 1934

Dear Gurudev,

Every working morning 'Janagana' is sung by hundreds of young people in our big hall. We want to extend its purifying influence by sending copies of it to other schools and colleges in India, and by making it known abroad.[73]

I send you a copy of a leaflet giving its first two stanzas. Before I broadcast them I am in duty bound to request your permission to do so.

How I wish we could have you with us sometime for a week's rest and high comradeship. We have now a fine home to offer you and a charming garden to ruminate in.

With deep affection and reverence.

Yours sincerely,
James H. Cousins

73 On this point see the Introduction to this volume.

33) TAGORE TO COUSINS

July 29, 1934

Dear Cousins,

I am thankful for arranging to broadcast my 'Janaganamana'.

I still have 'Bard's Pilgrimage'[74] on my desk and am peering into its pages whenever I have time. The poems are helpful when days are crowded with claims of duty; they create leisure by their magic.

I remember Madanapalle and vainly desire to visit once again but flesh is weak.

Yours sincerely,
Rabindranath Tagore

34) COUSINS TO TAGORE

Madanapalle
October 24, 1934
Bezwada for Waltair

Dear Gurudev,

I am very happy to learn from the papers that you are housed beside the great banyan tree and Adyar river. I trust your health will profit by your visit – also the Visva-Bharati.

I am on a talking tour (partly also with a view to rupees for the College). I shall lecture for the Andhra University tomorrow and next day, and shall stay at Madras on Saturday night and all Sunday, on my way to Vellore and Madanapalle.

I shall be at Adyar most of Sunday (I shall be sleeping in Madras), and should much like to see you once more, if only for a few minutes, at any time convenient to you. Preferably for me at 9.30 a.m. or thereabouts. Your secretary might drop me a line:

C/o D. Appa Rao Esqr. Bar-at-law
Master of the High Court

74 Cousins's *A Bardic Pilgrimage* was published by Roerich Museum Press, New York, in 1934, and he had sent a copy of the volume of poems to Tagore. The volume includes most of the poems Cousins had written since his first volume of verse in 1894, excluding the juvenilia. Incidentally, the volume includes the poem 'To Rabindranath Tagore'. A reading of the poems bears the impression of Cousins's mystic inclination and the impact of the Celtic revival, particularly, in his use of Irish myths and legends in many of the poems.

'Seshadri', Mylapore

I hope to attend the performance in the Museum Theatre on Saturday or Sunday night.[75]

With namaskarams and cordial good wishes

Yours sincerely,
James H. Cousins

FIGURE 7 Rabindranath Tagore with students of Santiniketan who performed *Sapmochan* in Ceylon in May 1934. Note: It is presumably the same troupe that performed the dance-drama *Sapmochan* in Madras in October 1934. Source: Rabindra-Bhavana Archive, Visva-Bharati, West Bengal, India. Reproduced with permission

75 Cousins does not refer to his lecture at Andhra University in *We Two Together*, but mentions that he had attended the performance of Tagore's dance-drama *Sāpmochan* at the Museum Theatre in Madras on 26 October 1934. Incidentally, he also mentions that Tagore was disappointed with the poor reception of the performance and had asked Cousins to address the audience for a favourable response. Cousins gave an address to the audience which had a good effect. See *We Two Together*, p. 604. On the other hand, the performance was received very favourably the same year in Ceylon. In fact, SWRD Bandaranaike, later to become the first woman Prime Minister of Sri Lanka, who saw the performance, had commented that the play was superior to Yeats's *Four Plays for Dancers*. See Krishna Dutta and Andrew Robinson, *Rabindranath Tagore: The Myriad-Minded Man* (1995; New Delhi: Rupa, 2005), pp. 318–319.

35) COUSINS TO TAGORE

Madanapalle
Madras Presidency
December 22, 1934

Dear Friend,

A group of friends has decided that my work in prose and poetry (literature of an idealistic tendency) should be sent forward to take its chance for the Nobel Prize for Literature. They have picked you out as a 'representative of the domain of literature' qualified (Rule 7) to propose my name as a candidate. But, as kind friends sometimes do, they have scattered on vacation and left me to the rather appalling job of requesting you to propose me (suggested form enclosed).

I shrink from the job, but breathe deep, set my teeth, and do it because, though I have no premonition of success, there is just the chance that my work will fill the conditions, and that no better may be put forward. In that case, the proceeds would solve the financial problem of the educational institution whose future I am trying to assure before the time comes for my retirement from active life.

If you feel disposed to help towards this end, kindly send forward your proposal in the enclosed manner or any modification you feel desirable. As the date of receipt in Stockholm is not later than January 31, the friends suggest that you dispatch the proposal by air-mail (but they do not say anything about who pays for the stamp!)

In any case bear with me, and keep the matter private.[76]

Yours sincerely,
James H. Cousins

76 Tagore did send the recommendation to the Nobel Committee, and though he did not say anything to Cousins, he did it reluctantly. This is evident from what he wrote to Bhagwan Das on 19 January 1935 when the latter asked Tagore's recommendation for Dr Sarvepalli Radhakrisnan, foremost philosopher of modern India, to the Nobel Committee. Tagore turned down the request pointing out that 'I do not know if his fame rests upon his being the foremost of modern exponents of Hindu philosophy or any distinct personal contribution opening out a new vista of thought and philosophical speculation.' On 20 June 1935, when the request was repeated, Tagore wrote back to Das that he had recommended Cousins 'at the insistent demands of a friend [Cousins]' and that he regretted the 'weakness on my part, for it was against my better judgement. But my friendly sentiments were played upon and I yielded.' RBA, File No.79. Incidentally, among those who recommended Cousins for the Nobel Prize for Literature was Yeats. See Appendix for Tagore's letter to the Nobel Committee.

36) TAGORE TO COUSINS

January 4, 1935

My dear Cousins,

I am sorry I could not write earlier. The last few days have been of great trial to me. I had to go through a number of very exacting engagements in Calcutta and have just returned thoroughly exhausted and pining for some quiet and rest.

I have already sent my recommendation to the Nobel committee by air mail and hope it will bear fruit.

With all good wishes for the year,

Yours sincerely,
Rabindranath Tagore

37) COUSINS TO TAGORE

Madanapalle
Madras Presidency
April 25, 1935

Dear Gurudev,

I heartily reciprocate your Vaishakhi greetings. The accompanying sonnet[77] which I wrote years ago at Srinagar, Kashmir, while living in house-boat[78] among reeds and trees, seems to have some affinity with the 'Stray Bird' on your card.

Mrs Cousins joins me in loving greetings from our holiday home 6500 feet up. You are seldom a day out of our thoughts.

Your eternal friend,

James H. Cousins
(Kulapati)

77 The sonnet is entitled 'Birds before Dawn' and is included in his *Collected Poems*.

78 House-boats with all kinds of provisions, including that of accommodation, are available for tourists on the famous Dal Lake in Kashmir.

38) COUSINS TO TAGORE

'Niton' Kotagiri
Nilgiris
May 24, 1935

Dear Gurudev,
Best wishes to you wherever you are vacationing. I am 6500 feet up among trees and flowers and birds, spending my mornings as a very practical college Principal and my afternoons as an Irish poet receiving hints as to the inner meanings of a certain Celtic myth and putting them into lines. One of my myth personages has whispered to me that:

He knew that not a story had been told
But had another story in its mind ...
and yesterday a rumour reached me:
That tales whose purpose is per due
Are never old and never new

However, that is not what I sat down to tap out to you in the uncultured manner of machinery.

I have been asked by the Maharaja and Government of Travancore to plan out two art galleries and a museum of art-crafts. There is much material of a kind for the purpose. But I declined to tackle the work unless provision was made for a group of pictures by living Indian artists to set off the deadness of the imitative European painting that has its home in Travancore, headed by the late Ravi Varma.[79] An insignificant sum for such purpose has been allocated for a start, with a promise of more each year to come. So I want to make as good a show of modern Indian painting and drawing as I can with the small means at my disposal.[80] In addition to buying items from our artists, I am asking for a few gifts. Would you be so kind as to present one or two of your own pictures to the public gallery? I would have them properly framed and

79 Raja Ravi Varma (1848–1906) was the most celebrated painter prior to his displacement by the Bengal School of Art and the arrival of the modernists in the twentieth century. A member of the royal family of Travancore, he is chiefly famous for history paintings drawing upon themes from Indian classics and epics. He combined a Victorian salon art, and his subjects from India's past were greatly admired by nationalists. But his paintings create the atmosphere of the princely courts with which he was deeply familiar. For a re-appraisal of Ravi Varma see, among others, Chapter 5 of Partha Mitter's *Art and Nationalism in Colonial India: Occidental Orientations* (Cambridge: Cambridge University Press, 1995).

80 Cousins gives a fairly detailed account of the setting up of art museums in Travancore under the aegis of its new ruler who had assumed power in 1931. See *We Two Together*, pp. 613–619. Ravi Varma was an ancestor of the Travancore royal family and so his paintings, despite Cousins's dislike, had to be put up at the museum which was called Chitralayam and which was inaugurated on 25 September 1935. Cousins's preference for Bengal Art is clear in his duo-autobiography as in this letter. Cousins knew about Tagore's paintings as well, but he does not refer to them in any of the letters.

hung, and they would give high pleasure to many people for ages to come. P. Hariharan arose in Travancore as compensation to Ravi Varma. I hope to be able to find others to send to the Kala Bhavana, or to get someone from it to go to Trivandrum, perhaps also to Madanapalle.

With affectionate greetings,

Yours sincerely,
James Henry Cousins

39) TAGORE TO COUSINS

On board houseboat PADMA[81]
Chandernagore
June 8, 1935

81 It was a favourite boat of Tagore. It was a family inheritance. The boat was built by Tagore's grandfather, Dwarakanath Tagore, and the poet's father, Devendranath Tagore used to sail along the river Ganges upto Banaras, several hundred miles away from Calcutta, in this boat. The boat had all kinds of provisions; it had two large rooms, a dining space, and other small rooms. The name 'Padma' was given to the boat by the poet himself. He loved sailing or resting in it in order to enjoy the beauty of the river Padma and its surroundings when he made sojourn to his family estates in Eastern Bengal, now in Bangladesh. These travels in the boat across the river gave the poet a sense of absolute freedom. In one of the letters, he writes: 'Not a human being, not a boat in sight. … I was pacing up and down like the last pulse-beats of the dying world. Everyone else seemed to be on the opposite shore – the shore of life – where the British Government and the Nineteenth Century holds sway, and tea and sugar.' Rabindranath Tagore, *Glimpses of Bengal: Selected Letters 1885–1895* (New York: Macmillan, 1921), pp. 53–54. Many of his poems, short stories and, particularly, his letters to his niece Indira Devi were written while he rested or travelled in this boat. In the words of the poet's son: 'The boat *Padma* served my father well. It gave him peace and shelter when the world harassed him. It offered him adventure when he needed it. It took him into the heart of the country and gave him materials for his writing. And above all it gave him abundant pleasure.' Rathindranath Tagore, *On the Edges of Time*, p. 37. Tagore, however, did not write this letter from the Eastern Bengal family estate but from Chandernagore (Chandan Nagar), a few miles away from Calcutta on the river Hoogly, and a French colony for a very long time. The Tagore family did not have a villa at Chandernagore. The place was a familiar haunt of the poet from his youthful days. Jyotirindranath Tagore, one of the poet's elder brothers, had initially rented a house in Chandernagore and then had shifted to a garden-house called Moran's Garden in 1881. Rabindranath Tagore spent many days with Jyotirindranath and his wife, Kadambari Devi, in this garden-house, and had even composed a few of the poems to be included in the volume *Sandhyā Sangit* (Evening Songs); the house is mentioned in his *Reminiscences* and *My Boyhood Days*. The context of this letter would become clear from a letter that Tagore wrote to his daughter-in-law, Pratima Devi, on 24(?) May 1935: 'It has not rained for a long time, the air is dry, and the temperature is gradually rising … I have ignored the summer heat all along, but this time my vanity would not stand. … The boat was anchored at Uttarpara. From there I went to Sreerampore … finally, I have arrived at Pharashdanga. On the first day I was stationed on the Strand Road, but people began to throng the place. So I had the boat shifted and am now stationed at a point where just on the opposite

My dear Cousins,
The excessive heat and the severe drought this year at Santiniketan has forced me to seek shelter in my houseboat on the Ganges. I have been living the last few days a life of glorious inactivity and that will explain the unwonted delay in replying to your letter which has been pitifully claiming attention well over a week now.

You know how difficult it is for me to say 'no' to any request of yours and yet I cannot reconcile myself to presenting any of my pictures to the Gallery at Trivandrum, where as you yourself admit the ghost of Ravi Varma is yet striding with pristine vigour.[82] Money is little consideration for I had once before presented a good collection of my pictures and had been raising a fund for the purpose. I readily parted with them for I knew they would find a welcome which would be as real as intelligent.[83] I would not like my pictures to be at the gallery at Trivandrum where they would have strange bed-fellows and perhaps be nothing but objects of curiosity. I am sure you will fully appreciate my feelings and not mind the refusal.[84]

With kind regards to Mrs. Cousins and yourself,

Yours sincerely,
Rabindranath Tagore

40) COUSINS TO TAGORE

Madanapalle
Madras Presidency
January 9, 1936

---

side lies the two-storied house in which I had spent many days with Jyotidada [Jyotirindranath]. That house is now in shambles. Next to it is a single-storied house. … I shall rent that house.' *Chithipatra* [Letters], Vol. III (Calcutta: Visva-Bharati, 1962), pp. 136–137. (My translation). See also Jagadish Bhattacharya, *Kabimānasi*, Vol. I (Calcutta: Bharabhi, 1997), pp. 155–173.

82 Though Tagore makes this remark here after he himself began to paint, his early impression of Ravi Varma's paintings was different. In 1893, he had written in a letter to his niece, Indira Devi: 'I spent the whole day looking at Ravi Varma's paintings. I quite admire them. After all, how much these indigenous motifs and indigenous forms and sentiments mean to us can be realised from these paintings. In many of the paintings, the hands and legs and the size of the bodies are very disproportionate; but as a whole, they quite touch the mind.' Rabindranath Tagore *Chinnapatrābali* (Scattered Sheaf of Letters) (Calcutta: Visva-Bharati, 1960), p. 146. (My translation).

83 Tagore had gifted some of his paintings to the National Gallery in Berlin and had sold many to raise funds for Visva-Bharati.

84 Despite this, Tagore did send a painting of a bird and it is still housed in the Trivandrum Art Gallery. Strangely enough, the present website of the gallery does not mention Tagore's painting in its list of holdings.

Dear Gurudev,
The enclosed may open up a possibility of a useful exchange of service. I do not know the lady, but if her qualifications fitted with some needs of the Visva-Bharati, perhaps it could give her hospitality and Indian art in exchange. If such cultural barter is feasible, perhaps your secretary might reply to the lady.[85]

With affectionate good wishes,

Yours very cordially,
James H. Cousins

41) COUSINS TO TAGORE

Madanapalle
Madras Presidency
February 3, 1936

Dear Gurudev,
Once up on a time I collided with you on the platform of Sealdah railway station when you were going to Shillong and Mrs. Cousins and I to Kalimpong. I recall this by Pelman association[86] (tho' I never had a lesson in that 'ism') because we are hungry for the hills, and must see them at least once more in this incarnation. Will you kindly pass this note on to someone who can give me an address where we might find a bedroom and sitting room, with use of kitchen, anywhere in sight of the snows, quiet, and not too expensive?

I am also thinking of another short tour to the USA (hence blatant 'folder') to gather some dollars to keep the College going.

With all good wishes

Yours affectionately,
James H. Cousins

85 Anil Chanda, then Secretary to Tagore, wrote back to Cousins on 20 January 1936 that Visva-Bharati was not in a position to welcome the lady (Mrs Noble) for lack of funds and proper accommodation. RBA File No.72.

86 Named after Christopher Louis Pelman, it is a system of training the mind to strengthen memory and remove indolence, forgetfulness and other forms of mental inertia. It was popular in England in the 1890s. Cousins is humorously recalling a past incident which Tagore might have forgotten.

42) COUSINS TO TAGORE

Madanapalle
Madras Presidency
March 29, 1936

Dear Gurudev,

Your original fair copy of your first English translation of 'Morning Song of India' (Janaganamana) turned up recently and so excited us that we at once decided to have it reproduced in exact facsimile—about the size of this sheet of paper. But before we spread it over the globe to lovers of yourself and your writings, I should like to have a note saying that you have no objection to our publishing it. Of course it will go out freely; and we shall probably give with it a Roman script transliteration of the Bengali to let its original musical quality be known. Mrs. Cousins and I are going to Kalimpong and Darjeeling from April 15 to June 15. I wonder if you will be anywhere near.

With every good wish

Yours affectionately,
James H. Cousins

43) TAGORE TO COUSINS

Uttarayan
Santiniketan, Bengal
April 5, 1936

My dear Cousins,

Many thanks for your letter. Yes, you may have my permission to print in facsimile the English translation of my 'Janaganamana', the manuscript of which you seem to possess.

I have just returned after a most strenuous tour in the North and my only consolation is that now forth, I shall be clear of my debts for the Institution.[87]

If you come to Darjeeling way do not fail to look us up.

Yours affectionately,
Rabindranath Tagore

87 In March 1936, Tagore went on a tour of north India with his troupe from Visva-Bharati to perform in different cities with the avowed purpose of propagating the ideals of art of Santiniketan and also to raise funds for the bankrupt Visva-Bharati.

44) COUSINS TO TAGORE

Madanapalle
Madras Presidency
April 7, 1936

Dear Gurudev,
We heartily share your relief in getting a substantial donation for Santiniketan. I have to find Rs 50,000 before April 1937 or be disaffiliated. So I am taking a year for travel with this in view. Poets get put to queer jobs.

We pass through Calcutta on April 12, but will not have time to see you. However, when coming back from Kalimpong I shall look you up.

Affectionately,
James H. Cousins

45) COUSINS TO TAGORE

Madanapalle
Madras Presidency
October 31, 1936

Dear Gurudev,
Mrs. Cousins and I spent four days last week at Mysore at the splendiferous celebrations of the Dasara. At the closing function, the tattoo at which the Maharaja, resuming rulership after being a devotee for nine days, reviews his army, I broke into visible prose in protest against the simpering foreign tunes that were used by the bands for the march past and somewhat vividly expressed the wish that someone would adapt Indian melodies when Indian horses and men march to music: 'Janaganamana' for instance.

At the end of the review came a troop of Boy Scouts, and as soon as they stepped out the brass band began to blare – guess? … correct – Janaganamana.

So you are 'frightfully famous', as a person once said of James Joyce; even if nobody but Mrs. Cousins and myself had thrills from realizing that the sentiment that accompanies the melody would, if translated into life, nullify the spirit behind military display and transform mass-design and movement into dynamic beneficence.

God bless you – even if there isn't one.

Yours affectionately,
James H. Cousins

46) TAGORE TO COUSINS

November 6, 1936

My dear Cousins,

We are fellow-voyagers in the same uncharted seas and I claim to be a pioneering pilot. Visva-Bharati turned me into a beggar long before you conceived the idea of coming out to the East![88]

It is hopeful to know that 'Janaganamana' is getting better known everyday and I have myself heard it sung to the correct tune in various distant parts of the country. I know I have to feel thankful to Mrs. Cousins for her work in this direction.

I am spending a quiet holiday in my other institution Sriniketan where village welfare work is being conducted from. I shall go back after another fortnight or so.

Yours affectionately,
Rabindranath Tagore

47) COUSINS TO TAGORE

Camp Beneras
January 2, 1937

Dear Gurudev,

I am invading Calcutta from Jan 5 to 8 or 9 on the disagreeable mission indicated in the enclosed Circular. I should like to see you (no, not on that mission, but just for love) perhaps on the 6th and/or 7th either in Calcutta or at Santiniketan. I shall put up at the Theosophical Society, 4/3a College Square.

With affectionate regards and best wishes,

Yours cordially,
James H. Cousins

88 Tagore's sacrifice for setting up his dream institution can hardly be enumerated. He is reported to have sold the ornaments of his wife Mrinalini Devi, for setting up his school at Santiniketan. He earned money through lecture tours in Europe and the USA, and also took troupes of performers from Visva-Bharati to perform across India to raise funds. He had even invested his Nobel Prize money in the Patisar Agricultural Bank to revive the sinking bank while utilising its interest for Visva-Bharati. But, after the 1930 Rural Indebtedness Act was passed that exempted all farmers from repaying their loan, the bank collapsed and the capital was lost.

48) COUSINS TO TAGORE

Camp Krishna College
Madanapalle
Madras Presidency
January 27, 1937

Dear Friend,

You have probably seen in the press the announcement by Sir C.P. Ramaswami, Dewan[89] of Travancore, that the Government of Travancore are considering the foundation of a State University before long.

I am very anxious that such an opportunity, in an atmosphere of elevation and expansion such as is now being experienced in Travancore, should be taken to press on the Government the necessity of giving arts and crafts proper recognition, and an inspiration to their revival and restoration to their former eminence in South India, in the University scheme. This can be done by the granting of diplomas and degrees to those who are to become teachers of the arts in the schools of the State, and others who are to become leaders in fostering arts and crafts in the lives and work of the people. The state has already a School of Arts which could be developed into a College providing both the best technical instruction available and knowledge on the history and characteristics of the arts of India, Asia and the world at large.

I request you to write a letter to the Dewan ('Bhakti Vills', Trivundrum, Travancore) urging him to have the fullest possible consideration given to the raising of the status of the arts by giving them academical recognition and encouragement in a College of arts and crafts.[90]

Yours sincerely,
James H. Cousins

89 Diwan or dewan refers to the finance minister or the prime minister of an Indian ruler.

90 There was an initial plan for a department of Fine Arts at the University of Travancore which was inaugurated on 2 November 1937. But it was clubbed with the department of Oriental studies because of official antipathy towards the fine arts. For details, see *We Two Together*, pp. 691–694.

49) COUSINS TO TAGORE

27 January 1937

Dear Gurudev,
It was to give help in regard to this University scheme that I was called away from Calcutta and prevented from visiting you. I think it may prove worth that sacrifice.

Yours affectionately,
James H. Cousins

50) TAGORE TO COUSINS

February 2, 1937

Dear Dr. Cousins,
I have received your letter dated 27.1.37 and am glad to find your enthusiasm for art and education as great as ever. But you must not expect me, with my advancing years and the strain of manifold duties, which I cannot shake off, on my failing health, to take very active interest in all institutions that need to be supported. I hope therefore you will excuse me. I am sure the authority of your appeal will be sufficient to induce the Government of Travancore to accept your scheme.[91]

With regards

Yours sincerely,
Rabindranath Tagore

91 Indeed, Tagore had wisely distanced himself from the matter as Cousins was made the Head of the Fine Arts Department and Art Adviser to the Government of Travancore.

51) COUSINS TO TAGORE

Madanapalle
Madras Presidency
March 31, 1937

Dear Gurudev,

Once upon a time you desired to have my help in your work at Santiniketan. Unfortunately (for me) I was under obligations that prevented my going to you; and since then my roots have gone deeper and broader into the soil of the South – I am awaiting order to go to Travancore to help in the creation of a State University, after having created two art galleries there and reorganised a Museum.

But if you still need help in your work, I think you could have the excellent services of Mr. Duncan Greenlees, MA (Oxon)[92] who has been headmaster in the High School here, but feels the need of a fresh environment. He has completely assimilated himself into Indian life; he is a close friend of Mahatmaji's, is an enthusiast on education, keen on art, and strong on organizing all kinds of useful and interesting affairs. He would accept a small remuneration plus simple living quarters. If there was such a possibility (from the middle of April or before June 30) I should be happy to put him in touch with you.

Affectionately yours,
James H. Cousins

52) COUSINS TO TAGORE

University Building
Trivandrum
August 5, 1937

Dear Gurudev,

Since my return from Java and Bali, in the party of the Maharaja of Travancore, I have only now found time to say how happy I was to find traces of your visit

92 Duncan Greenlees (1899–1966) was an Englishman who moved to India and worked at the Theosophical School at Madanapalle. He was a theosophist and was associated with Annie Besant. Later on, he became associated with MK Gandhi, and was given the responsibility to draft the first education policy of free India. But he does not seem to have worked at Visva-Bharati.

there, and to realize the love and reverence in which you are held. I hope the news won't make you conceited; but perhaps you have, like me, reached the age when neither discretion nor indiscretion matters.

I have moved to Trivandrum to help to organize a State University. I am in charge of the department of Fine Arts, and have to work up a real College of the arts, and put creation on the same eminence as mere knowledge. I am also in charge of English, and hope to extract its poison by sane teaching and good material. Pray for me.

Affectionately yours,
James H. Cousins

53) TAGORE TO COUSINS

Uttarayan
Santiniketan
August 12, 1937

My dear Cousins,
I knew from the papers that you had gone to Java and Bali in the Travancore Party and I am glad you went, for there is no other place of such interest for one who really loves India. My own visit was indeed a revelation to me.[93]

You have undertaken a grave responsibility about the University and I only hope Trivandrum will not be a mere appendix to the doleful chapter of Indian Universities. Create something which will be true to the culture of the soil and yet ever looking forward.

I am again frightfully busy with re-organising the Music School here – the Sangit Bhavana. I want to make it a living centre of Indian music where dancing too will have its proper place of honour. I want to gather here worthy representatives of all the different schools of dancing in the country and I wish you could persuade the Durbar[94] to give us a competent teacher of Dancing from the South Cochin. We maintained a teacher for two sessions and Travancore certainly can do as much. If you think my representation will not be ignored,

93 Tagore visited Java, Bali, and Malaya in July 1927. He had been gripped by the idea of a 'Greater India' since his visit to Holland in 1920 where his acquaintance with Dutch scholars of ancient Buddhist and Hindu culture had convinced him that the roots of ancient Indian civilisation were stretched far and wide across Asia.

94 Durbar refers to the court of an Indian ruler.

would you kindly move in the matter? I ought to have generous treatment from Travancore now that you are one of the royal advisers.[95]

With affectionate greetings,

Yours,
Rabindranath Tagore

54) COUSINS TO TAGORE

"Ann Arbor"
Nathen Codo, Trivandrum
S. India
May 11, 1938

Dear Gurudev,

When I saw it announced that you had gone to Kalimpong for a holiday, I wondered what pranks destiny was playing in sending you there when Mrs. Cousins and I were not there – while we were there in 1936 when you were not there. No doubt we coincide in the eternal; but an occasional coincidence in the temporal would be very welcome.

Our deep love goes to you many times. I often hunger to be near you.

Yours affectionately,
James H Cousins

95 It needs to be noted here that Tagore not only included art; he gradually included music and dance as much as he made provision for training in handicrafts. Tagore not only wrote many dance-dramas; dance and music occupy a place of pride in Visva-Bharati's scheme of education. Tagore had requested the Maharaja of Cochin for a dance teacher to train his students in Kathakali. Earlier, Santidev Ghosh, had obtained training in Kathakali at the Kerala Kalamandalam. In 1934, the Maharaja of Cochin had sent a lady to train students in Mohinyattam. In 1937, Kelu Nair from the Kalamandalam arrived in Santiniketan to give training in Kathakali. Before Kelu Nair, Gopinath and Rukmini Devi had impressed the poet with their Kathakali performances at Santiniketan. But between 1931 and 1941, Kathakali was blended with other forms of Kerala dances and also with Manipuri which had established itself earlier at Visva-Bharati. On this point, see Santidev Ghosh's *Nrityakalā o Rabindranāth* [Dance and Tagore] (Calcutta: Ananda Publishers, 1999).

55) COUSINS TO TAGORE

"Ghat View"
Kotagiri, Nilgiris
April 20, 1940

My dear Gurudev,

Shortly you will finish eighty years of this life. Thank you for staying so long in this queer era of human history, if it is human and sub-human. When incarnated spirits like you are on the planet, there is still a spark of hope for the race.

Of course, I read every line of your doings and sayings that go into the press; but sometimes I have a keen hunger to see you again in person. This however is difficult, as I have many duties to fulfil, founding and developing art galleries and museums, building cultural institutions, restoring an ancient palace that is a gem of indigenous architecture, sculpture, carving and painting, writing.

I sometimes speculate as to how my life might have gone on if I had accepted your invitation long ago to spend some years with you. Yet the good work I have had the privilege of doing in Travancore for future generations is probably the justification for my renunciation of what would have been a crowning honour and joy.

Along with my work for a living I keep up my personal literary activities. I am just preparing a single volume collected edition of my poetry. Next year I shall publish an Irish mythological story in dramatic and lyrical verse, and a volume of essays on art. A year later, my seventieth year, I hope to publish along with Mrs. Cousins, a duo-autobiography. Occasional lyrics come. We keep in touch with the id of life of the psyche, and find a centre of peace towards which all conflicts converge.

Often we refresh ourselves on your poetry; and recently I renewed the joy of reading 'Creative Unity'[96] which will remain as one of the scriptures of creative life.

Our deep affection and veneration go to you for your birthday; also our keen sympathy in the blank left by the exaltation of our mutual loving brother Charlie.[97] I remember the season we spent together and divided lectures at Kala Bhavan in the afternoons, while I gave literary studies in your hut under the tree.

Yours most cordially,
J.H. Cousins

96 Cousins reviewed the book in *The Modern Review* in 1922, the year of its publication. See Appendix for Cousins's review.

97 'Charlie' here refers to Charles Freer Andrews.

FIGURE 8 James Henry Cousins in the 1940s. Source: James H. Cousins, *Collected Poems*, 1894–1940 (Madras: Kalakshetra, 1940)

56) TAGORE TO COUSINS

Mangpoo
May 3, 1940

My dear Cousins,

It is a great joy to hear from you and to know that Mrs. Cousins and yourself are continuing your good work as ever. I feel deeply moved by all that you say about myself and very sincerely reciprocate your kind thoughts.

I miss Charlie very much; his memory and all his good deed will continue in our lives in many ways. You will soon read the translation of the Sermon I gave at our Mandir[98] on the 5th April.[99] I shall eagerly expect to read your 'duo-

98 The word 'mandir' means a temple, a shrine devoted to a Hindu deity. Here, Mandir refers to the prayer-hall in Santiniketan built under the auspices of the poet's father, Devendranath Tagore. The foundation of the Mandir was laid on 7 December 1890, and it was inaugurated on 22 December 1891. The hall had marble floor, tiles for the roof, and its square walls were built of iron frame and coloured glass. Though it was built primarily for Brāhmo prayer service, it was non-denominational in nature; all prayer services, including those on Christmas, were held in this hall. The hall stands today in its pristine form, as the sign of Santiniketan's hallowed tradition, and all prayer services of Visva-Bharati on designated occasions are held in it as usual.

99 Tagore gave an address at the Santiniketan Mandir entitled 'Dinabandhu [Friend of the poor] Andrews', in Bengali, which was translated by Marjorie Sykes and published in the *Visva-Bharati Quarterly*, Vol. VI, Part I, 1940, pp. 1–4. Cousins, as would be evident here, was a regular recipient of the *Quarterly*.

autobiography'[100] when it comes out. Do give my friendly regards to Mrs. Cousins and accept them yourself.

Yours sincerely,
Rabindranath Tagore

57) COUSINS TO TAGORE

Ghat View
Kotagiri
Nilgiris
December 1, 1940

Dear Gurudev,

This is just to say that my love, as also of Mrs. Cousins's, had gone to you in fullest measure these past months. We also have had sags in health, but have recovered.

I asked my publishers to send you a presentation copy of my 'Collected Poems'. You may not be able to have time to look into it, but it will radiate 'prem'[101] from your shelf.

Hoping we shall have much aspiration and work together in our next incarnation.

Yours most affectionate,
James H. Cousins

100 The duo-autobiography is *We Two Together* written by James and Margaret Cousins with chapters alternating between them. It was not published until 1950.

101 'Prem' means love. Tagore was not keeping well over several months of the year 1940, and Cousins probably knew of it. The letter, the last one from Cousins to Tagore, has a strange tinge of melancholy not noticed in any of the earlier letters. Tagore died in Calcutta on 7 August 1941.

(a)

58

"Glen View,"
Kotagiri,
Nilgiris.

Dec. 1940.

GOVERNMENT OF TRAVANCORE

Dear Gurudeb,

This is just to say that my love, as also of Mrs. Cousins, has gone to you in fullest measure these past months. We also have had sags in health, but have recovered.

I asked my publishers to send you a presentation copy of my "Collected Poems." You may not be able to have time to look into it, but it will radiate "prem" from your shelf.

Hoping we shall have much aspiration and

(b)

work together in our next incarnation.

Yours most affectionately,

James H. Cousins

FIGURE 9a/b Facsimile of James Cousins's last letter to Rabindranath Tagore, dated 1 December 1940. Source: Rabindra-Bhavana Archive, Visva-Bharati, West Bengal, India. Reproduced with permission

WORKS CONSULTED

Primary Sources

Archives

1) RABINDRA-BHAVANA:
   Andrews Papers, File No. 3
   Elmhirst Papers, File No. 107
   Pearson Papers, File No. 287
   Tagore–Cousins Papers, File No. 72
   Tagore–Yeats Correspondence, File No. 442
2) NATIONAL LIBRARY OF IRELAND, DUBLIN

Rabindranath Tagore's Works

Tagore, Rabindranath, 'Bandhu' (Friend) in *Rabindra Rachanabali*, Vol. XIII [Collected Works: 125th Birth Anniversary Edition] (Calcutta: Visva-Bharati, 1991) abbreviated as *RR*.

———, 'Bhumikā' (Introduction) to *Patradhārā*, 3 vols (Santiniketan: Santiniketan Press, 1938).

———, 'Brāhmosamājer sārthakatā' (The Significance of the Brahmo Samaj), in *RR*, Vol.VIII, 1988, pp. 606–611.

———, *The Centre of Indian Culture* (Madras: Society for the Promotion of National Education, 1919).

———, 'Charlie Andrews' in *The Visva-Bharati Quarterly*, Vol.VI, Part j, NS, May–July 1940, pp. 1–6.

———, *Chithipatra* (Letters), Vol. II (Kolkata: Visva-Bharati, rept. 2012).

———, *Chithipatra* (Letters), Vol. XI (Calcutta: Visva-Bharati, 1974).

———, *Creative Unity* (New York: Macmillan, 1922).

———, *The English Writings of Rabindranath Tagore*, Vol.III, ed. Sisir K. Das (New Delhi: Sahitya Akademi, 1996, rept. 2002).

———, *Ghare Bāire* (*Home and the World*), *RR*, Vol IV, 1987.
———, 'Greater India' in *The Visva-Bharati Quarterly*, Vol. ,IX, NS 1943–1944, pp. 1–7.
———, 'Hindu Brāhmo' in *RR*, Vol IX, 1988, pp. 724–730.
———, 'Hindu Visvavidyālaya' (Hindu University) in *RR*, Vol.IX, 1988, pp. 603–612.
———, 'The Ideal of Visva-Bharati' in *Proceedings of the Bengal Education Week*, Vol.I, 1936 (Calcutta: Working Committee of the Bengal Education Week, 1936), pp. 73–81.
———, 'Jāvā jātrir patra' (Letters of a Traveller to Java) in *RR*, Vol. X, 1989, pp. 499–550.
———, *Letters from Abroad* (Madras: S Ganesan, 1924).
———, 'My Educational Mission' in *Modern Review*, Vol. XLIX, No. 6, June 1931, pp. 621–623.
———, 'The Nation' in *Modern Review*, Vol. XXII, Nos. 1–6, July–December 1917, pp. 1–3.
———, *Nationalism* (New York: Macmillan, 1917).
———, *Palli Prakriti* [The Nature/Characteristics of the Village] (Calcutta: Visva-Bharati, 1962).
———, *Patradhārā*, Vols. I–III (Santiniketan: Santiniketan Press, 1938).
———, *Personality* (New York: Macmillan, 1918).
———, *The Religion of Man* (London: George Allen & Unwin, 1931).
———, *The Spirit of Japan* (Tokyo: Indo-Japanese Association, 1916).
———, *Talks in China* (Calcutta: Visva-Bharati, 1925).
———, 'The Visva-Bharati Ideal' in *Visva-Bharati Ideal*, eds. Rabindranath Tagore and C F Andrews (Madras: GA Natesan & Co, 1923, pp. 1–23.
———, 'Viswabodh' (Universal Consciousness) in *RR*, Vol. VII, 1988, pp. 721–728.

Collection of Letters edited by others

Bhattacharya, Sabyasachi, ed, *The Mahatma and the Poet: Letters and Debates between Gandhi and Tagore 1915–1941* (New Delhi: National Book Trust, 1997).
Dasgupta, Uma, ed, *A Difficult Friendship: Letters of Edward Thompson and Rabindranath Tagore 1913–1940* (Delhi: Oxford University Press, 2003).
Dasgupta, Uma, ed, *Friendships of 'Largeness and Freedom': Andrews, Tagore, and Gandhi: An Epistolary Account 1912–1940* (Delhi: Oxford University Press, 2018).
Dutta, Krishna, and Andrew Robinson, eds, *Selected Letters of Rabindranath Tagore* (New Delhi: Cambridge University Press, South Asian Edition, 2005).
Guha, Chinmoy, ed and French letters translated, *Bridging East and West: Rabindranath Tagore and Romain Rolland Correspondence (1919–1940)*(Delhi: Oxford University Press, 2018).
Lago, Mary, ed, *Imperfect Encounter: The Letters of William Rothenstein and Rabindranath Tagore 1911–1941* (Cambridge, MA: Harvard University Press, 1972).

James Henry Cousins and Margaret E. Cousins's Works

Cousins, James H, 'Art and Education' in *Visva-Bharati Quarterly*, Vol.I Part 1, NS, May–July 1935, pp. 11–16.
———, 'The Choice' in *The Golden Book of Tagore*, ed., Ramananda Chatterjee (Calcutta: The Golden Book Committee, 1931), p. 61.
———, *The Cultural Unity of Asia* (Madras: Theosophical Publishing House, 1922).

———, 'Dublin: The City of Revolutions' in *The Modern Review*, Vol. XX, July–December1916, pp. 450–454.
———, *Faith of the Artist: Essays* (Madras: Kalakshetra, 1941).
———, 'First Impressions of Tagore in Europe' in *The Modern Review*, Vol. XIX, No.110, August 1916, pp. 175–179.
———, *Footsteps of Freedom: Essays* (Madras: Ganesh & Co, 1919).
———, 'Introduction' in Abinash Ch Bose, *Three Mystic Poets: A Study of WB Yeats, AE and Rabindranath Tagore* (Kolhapur: School and College Bookstore, 1946), pp. i–vi.
———, *Modern English Poetry: Its Characteristics and Tendencies* (Madras: Ganesh & Co, 1921).
———, *New Ways in English Literature* (Madras: Ganesh & Co, 1917, revised edn, 1919).
———, *Renaissance in India* (Madras: Ganesh & Co, 1918).
———, and Margaret E. Cousins, *We Two Together* (Madras: Ganesh &Co, 1950).
Cousins, Margaret E., *The Music of Orient and Occident: Essays towards Mutual Understanding* (Madras: BG Paul & Co, 1935).

Secondary Works

The Aberdeen Daily Journal, January 13, 1906.
Anderson, Amanda, *The Way We Argue Now: A Study in the Cultures of Theory* (Princeton, NJ and Oxford: Princeton University Press, 2006).
Andrews, CF, 'My Life Story' in *Visva-Bharati Quarterly*, Vol. VI, Part I, NS, May–July 1940, pp. 9–19.
Aronson, Alex, *Romain Rolland: The Story of a Conscience* (Bombay: Padma Publishing House, 1946).
———, 'Tagore's Educational Ideas' in *International Review of Education*, Vol. VII, No. 4, 1961, pp. 385–383.
Ashcraft, W Michael, *The Dawn of a New Cycle: Point Loma Theosophists and American Culture* (Knoxville, TN: University of Tennessee Press, 2002).
Benet, William Rose, *Saturday Review of Literature*, 8 (4 June 1932).
Bevir, Mark, 'Theosophy as a Political Movement' in *Gurus and Their Followers: New Religious Reform Movements in Colonial India*, ed., Anthony Coupley (New Delhi: Oxford University Press, 2000), pp. 159–179.
Blavatsky, H P, *An Abridgement of the Secret Doctrine*, eds Elizabeth Preston and Christmas Humphreys (London: Theosophical Publishing House, 1966).
Bose, Abinash Chandra, *Three Mystic Poets: A Study of WB Yeats, AE and Rabindranath Tagore* (Kolhapur: School and College Bookstore, 1946).
Bose, Sugata, *A Hundred Horizons: The Indian Ocean in the Age of Global Empire* (Cambridge, MA and London: Harvard University Press, 2006).
Breckenridge, Carol L et al, eds, *Cosmopolitanism* (London and Durham, NC: Duke University Press, 2002).
Buber, Martin, *Between Man and Man* (London: Routledge & Kegan Paul, 1947).
Carey, Daniel, and Lynn Festa, eds., *The Post-colonial Enlightenment: Eighteenth-Century Enlightenment and Postcolonialism* (Oxford: Oxford University Press, 2009).
Chatterjee, Dilip K, *James Henry Cousins: A Study of His Works in the Light of the Theosophical Movement in India and the West* (Delhi: Sarada Publishing House, 1994).
Chatterjee, Ramananda, ed., *The Golden Book of Tagore* (Calcutta: Golden Book Committee, 1931).
Chakravarty, Bikash, ed., *Poets to a Poet 1912–1940: Letters from Bridges, Rhys, Yeats, Sturge Moore, Travelyan and Pound* (Calcutta: Visva-Bharati, 1998).

Clarke, Austin, 'An Irish Poet in India' in *The Irish Times*, 22 May 1943, p. 10.

Cohen, Joshua, ed., *For Love of Country?* Martha Nussbaum et al (Boston, MA: Beacon Press, 1996).

Coomaraswamy, Ananda Kentish, *Essays in National Idealism* (Colombo: Colombo Apothecaries Co, 1910).

Coupley, Anthony, ed., *Gurus and Their Followers: New Religious Reform Movements in Colonial India* (New Delhi: Oxford University Press, 2000).

Denson, Alan, *James H. Cousins and Margaret E. Cousins: A Bio-Biographical Survey* (Kendal: Alan Denson, 1967).

Devi, Maitreyi, *Tagore by Fireside* (Calcutta: Rupa, 1961).

Dumbleton, William A, *James Cousins* (Boston, MA: Twayne Publishers, 1980).

Dutta, Krishna, and Andrew Robinson, *Rabindranath Tagore: The Myriad-Minded Man* (1995; New Delhi: Rupa, 2005).

Farrell, Michael, *Collaborative Circles: Friendship Dynamics and Circles & Creative Work* (Chicago, IL and London: University of Chicago Press, 2001).

Foley, Tadhg, and Maureen O'Connor, eds,. *Ireland and India: Colonies, Culture and Empire* (Dublin and Portland, OR: Irish Academic Press, 2006).

Friedman, Susan Stanford, *Planetary Modernisms: Provocations on Modernity across Time* (New York: Columbia University Press, 2015).

Gandhi, Leela, *Affective Communities: Anticolonial Thought and the Politics of Friendship* (Delhi: Permanent Black, 1997).

Gandhi, MK, *Hind Swaraj*, ed., AnthonyParel (1909; New Delhi: Cambridge University Press,2004).

Ghosh, Santidev, *Nrityakalā o Rabindranāth* [Dance and Tagore] (Calcutta: Ananda Publishers, 1999).

Greater India Society Bulletin No.1, November 1926.

Guha-Thakurta, Tapati, *The Making of a New 'Indian' Art: Artists, Aesthetics and Nationalism, c.1850–1920* (Cambridge: Cambridge University Press, South Asian Edn., 2007).

Guiness, Selina, 'James Cousins and His Nation of Free Slaves', in *Ireland and India: Colonies, Culture and Empire*, eds., Tadhg Foley and Maureen O'Connor (Dublin and Portland, OR: Irish Academic Press, 2006), pp. 68–80.

Home, Amal, ed., *The Calcutta Municipal Gazette: Tagore Supplement* (Calcutta: Calcutta Municipality, 1941).

TheIrishStatesman, August 23, 1924.

TheIrishStatesman, October 4, 1924.

The Irish Statesman, August 29, 1925.

The Irish Times, 24 May 1913.

The Irish Times, 22 May 1943.

Israel, Jonathan, *Radical Enlightenment: Philosophy and the Making of Modernity1650–1750* (Oxford: Oxford University Press, 2001).

Joyce, James, *A Portrait of the Artist as a Young Man*, ed., Seamus Deane (London: Penguin, 1992).

Keown, Edwina, and Carol Taaffe, eds, *Irish Modernism: Origins, Contexts, Publics* (Oxford and New York: Peter Lang, 2010).

Kiberd, Declan, and PJ Mathews, eds, *Handbook of the Irish Revival: An Anthology of Cultural and Political Writings, 1891–1922* (Dublin: Abbey Theatre Press, 2015).

Kopf, David, *The Brahmo Samaj and the Shaping of the Modern Indian Mind* (New Delhi: Archives Publishers, 1988).

Lennon, Joseph, *Irish Orientalism: A Literary and Cultural History* (Syracuse: Syracuse University Press, 2004).

———, '"Where the East and the West Are One": James Cousins and Postcolonial Aesthetics' in *Ireland and India: Colonies, Culture and Empire*, eds., Tadhg Foley and Maureen O'Connor (Dublin and Portland, OR: Irish Academic Press, 2006), pp. 81–96.

Mahalanobis, Prasanta Chandra, 'The Visva-Bharati' in *The Calcutta Municipal Gazette: Tagore Supplement*, ed., Amal Home (Calcutta: Calcutta Municipality, 1941), pp. 1–5.

Majumdar, Sirshendu, *Yeats and Tagore: A Comparative Study of Cross-cultural Poetry, Nationalist Politics, Hyphenated Margins and the Ascendancy of the Mind* (Bethesda: Academica Press, 2013).

McCabe, Colin, 'Finnegans Wake at Fifty' in *Critical Quarterly*, Vol. XXXI, No. 4 (Winter 1989), pp. 2–14.

Mehta, Uday Chand, *Liberalism and Empire: India in British Liberal Thought* (New Delhi: Oxford University Press, 1999).

Mercer, Kobena, ed., *Cosmopolitan Modernisms* (Cambridge, MA and London: MIT Press, 2005).

Mitter, Partha, *Art and Nationalism in Colonial India, 1890–1922: Occidental Orientations* (Cambridge: Cambridge University Press, 1998).

———, *Indian Art* (Oxford: Oxford University Press, 2000).

———, 'Reflections on Modern Art and National Identity in Colonial India: An Interview' in *Cosmopolitan Modernisms*, ed., Kobena Mercer (Cambridge, MA and London: MIT Press, 2005), pp. 24–49.

The Modern Review, Vol. XIX, No.110, July–December 1916.

The Modern Review, Vol. XXII, Nos. 1–6, July–December 1917.

The Modern Review, Vol. XXVI, Nos. 1–6, July–December 1919.

The Modern Review, Vol. LXII, Nos 1–6, July–December 1937.

The Modern Review, Vol. XCIV, Nos. 1–6, January–March 1956.

Mohanty, Sachidananda, *Cosmopolitan Modernity in Early 20thCentury India* (2015; London and New York: Routledge, 2018).

Mukherjee, Himangshu Bhushan, *Education for Fullness: A Study of the Educational Thought and Experiment of Rabindranath Tagore* (1962; London and New York: Routledge, 2013).

Mukherjee, Sujit, *Passage to America: The Reception of Rabindranath Tagore in the United States* (Calcutta, Allahabad, Patna: Bookland, 1964).

Nag, Kalidas, 'Greater India: A Study in Indian Internationalism' in *Greater India Society Bulletin*1, November 1926, pp. 1–61.

Nandy, Ashis, *The Intimate Enemy: Loss and Recovery of Self under Colonialism* (Delhi: Oxford University Press, 1983).

Nash, Catherine, 'Geo-Centric Education and Anti-imperialism: Theosophy, Geography, and Citizenship in the Writings of J.H. Cousins', in *Journal of Historical Geography*, Vol. XXII, No. 4, 1996, pp. 399–411.

Nussbaum, Martha C., *Not for Profit: Why Democracy Needs the Humanities* (Princeton & Oxford: Princeton University Press, 2012).

O'Connell, Kathleen M., *Rabindranath Tagore: The Poet as Educator* (Kolkata: Visva-Bharati, 2012).

Oppenheim, Janet, *The Other World: Spiritualism and Psychical Research in England 1850–1914* (Cambridge: Cambridge University Press, 1985).

Pal, Prasantakumar, *Rabijibani* (Tagore's Life) Vol. VII: 1914–1920 (Calcutta: Ananda Publishers, 1997).

Proceedings of the Bengal Education Week, Vol. I, 1936 (Calcutta: Working Committee of the Education Week, 1936).

Rao, Rahul, *Third World Protest: Between Home and the World* (Oxford: Oxford University Press, 2010).

Robb, Peter, *Useful Friendship: Europeans and Indians in Early Calcutta* (Delhi: Oxford University Press, 2014).

Robbins, Bruce and Paulo Lemos Horta, eds, *Cosmopolitanisms* (New York: New York University Press, 2017).

Russell, George (AE), 'Literature and Life: The Wisdom of the East' in *The Irish Statesman*, August 23, 1924, pp. 758–759.

———, 'Literature and Life: The Leaders of Indian Nationalism' in *The Irish Statesman*, October 4, 1924, pp. 111–112.

———, Review of Tagore's *Talks in India* in *The Irish Statesman*, August 29, 1925, pp. 792–794.

Said, Edward, *Orientalism* (1978; London: Penguin, 1995).

Schuchard, Ronald, *The Last Minstrels: Yeats and the Revival of the Bardic Arts* (Oxford: Oxford University Press, 2008).

Sen, Probodhchandra, *India's National Anthem* (Calcutta: Visva-Bharati, 1949).

Spencer, Robert, *Cosmopolitan Criticism and Postcolonial Literature* (Basingstoke: Palgrave, 2011).

Spivak, Gayatri Chakravorty, *A Critique of Postcolonial Reason: Towards a History of the Vanishing Present* (Cambridge, MA: Harvard University Press, 1999).

Tattwabodhini Patrika, No. 466, Saka1804 [1882].

Taylor, Kathleen, *Sir John Woodroffe, Tantrā and Bengal: 'An Indian Soul in a European Body?'* (London and New York: Routledge Curzon, 2001).

The Times, 13 July 1912.

van der Linden, Bob, *Music and Empire in Britain and India: Identity, Internationalism and Cross-Cultural Communication* (New York: Palgrave Macmillan, 2013).

Visva-Bharati Patrika (Shravan-Ashwin), 1362 BS.

The Visva-Bharati Quarterly, Vol. I Part 1, NS, May–July, 1935.

TheVisva-Bharati Quarterly, Vol. VI, Part j, NS, May–July 1940.

TheVisva-Bharati Quarterly, Vol. IX, NS 1943–44.

Viswanathan, Gauri, 'India, Ireland and the Poetics of Internationalism' in *Journal of World History*, Vol. XIV(1), March 2004, pp. 7–30.

Weir, David, *American Orient: Imagining the East from the Colonial Era through the Twentieth Century* (Amherst and Boston, MA: University of Massachusetts Press, 2011).

Yeats, WB, *The Collected Letters of WB Yeats 1865–1895*, Vol. I, eds., John Kelly and Eric Domville (Oxford: Clarendon Press, 1986).

———, *The Collected Works of WB Yeats, Vol. V, Later Essays*, ed., William H. O'Donnell (New York: Charles Scribner's Son, 1994).

———, *The InteLex Electronic Edition of the Collected Letters of WB Yeats* (Oxford: Oxford University Press, 2002).

Websites

The Internet Archive: https://archive.org/

Overman Foundation: https://overmanfoundation.wordpress.com/2013/08/10/a-rare-interview-of-paul-richard/

APPENDIX

The Appendix presents a selection of poems, translations, letters, essays, interviews, and lectures to offer an insight into the collaborative ideas, mutual admiration, and camaraderie between Tagore and Cousins. These representative pieces highlight various facets of the affinities between them and are meant to show how Cousins viewed Tagore, and vice-versa.

The Appendix has five sections: in the first section, readers will find the English translation of Tagore's poem on Shahjahan, the Mughal Emperor from *Lover's Gift*, and Cousins's poem, 'The Taj Mahal'. Cousins claims in Letter 15 that his poem has similarities with Tagore's. Hence, the two poems have been placed together here. The second section of the Appendix contains Tagore's letter to the Nobel Committee recommending Cousins for the Nobel Prize in Literature for 1934. The letter is significant as Tagore not only underlines the universalist ideas in Cousins's writing, but also states that the award would be utilised for education in India. The third section has one of the two drafts of a poem by Tagore, the second draft being a revision following Cousins's suggestions. This is an indication of how Tagore valued Cousins as a poet in the English language. The fourth section contains an essay and a letter of Tagore. The essay on the ideal of Visva-Bharati, not included in any of the prose collections of Tagore, can be considered as one of the most precise statements of Tagore on the ideals of his university. The letter to Andrews demonstrates Tagore's assertion to retain the autonomy of Visva-Bharati and determined refusal to bow down to any power. The fifth section contains two of Cousins's representative essays and one interview. The first essay is on Tagore's first reception in Europe which is actually his own response to the English *Gitanjali*. It is a 'brother-poet' applauding the 'literary democracy' that he finds in Tagore's poetry. In a sense, Cousins, more than Yeats, places Tagore in a more extensive poetic tradition of the West. In the interview, Cousins extols the virtues of the Bengal School of Art over western art by relating the former to Indian classical tradition. The Interview also gives us an impression of Cousins's understanding of Indian classical tradition. The other essay is a review of Tagore's *Creative Unity*, a book that Cousins prized very highly. The essay is also probably the only extensive appreciation of Tagore's book in the light of the latter's ideas of nationalism and internationalism. Since Cousins's works are long out of print and difficult to obtain, and since Cousins has now nearly passed into oblivion, these representative pieces are meant to give readers some idea of how Cousins saw Tagore and his deep engagement with India's classical tradition.

Appendix I

A

Tagore's translation of poem no. 7 in *Balākā* which appears as the opening poem of his volume *Lovers' Gift*

> You allowed your kingly power to vanish, Shajahan, but your wish was to
>   make imperishable a tear-drop of love.
> Time has no pity for the human heart, he laughs at its sad struggle
>   to remember.
> You allured him with beauty, made him captive, and crowned the
>   formless death with fadeless form.
> The secret whispered in the hush of night to the ear of your love
>   is wrought in the perpetual silence of stone.
> Though empires crumble to dust, and centuries are lost in shadows,
>   the marble still sighs to the stars, 'I remember.'
> 'I remember.'— But life forgets, for she has her call to the Endless:
>   and she goes on her voyage unburdened, leaving her memories to the
> forlorn forms of beauty.

Source: *Lover's Gift* (New York: Macmillan & Co, 1918), p.7.

B

James Cousins's poem 'The Taj Mahal'

1. *The Paradox*

> What love exhaled what beauty! What desire
> Broke whitely past the flesh, and in dumb stone
> Found silence louder than the heart's wild tone
> That for vast sorrow raised this moonlit pyre!

Fame to white flame, minar and slender spire
He bade arise, consuming his deep moan.
Vain! vain! His grief for us to bliss has grown
Through beauty's quenchless and preserving fire.
Canst Thou not leave us to our little ends,
Allah? Nor our dear purposes annoy
With something deeper than the eye can see,
As here, where, more than stricken love intends,
Sorrow is throned on everlasting joy,
And death is crowned with immortality.

2. *The Forgotten Workers*

Ten thousand and ten thousand came and went,
Forgotten builders of one lasting name;
Even as fuel perishes to flame,
Grapes to new wine, their strength for others spent.
Yet here they have enduring monument,
One with the master's whom our lips proclaim
Beyond the loud irrelevance of fame,
The worker lost, in his great work content.
Ah! Smile on us who build Thy House of Life,
Allah! that we, though nameless, have the grace
To perish greatly, in Thy rising fame,
Where beauty wields pains hammer, death's keen knife.
Grant us oblivion in Thy shining Face!
All else forgotten! Thou alone remain!

3. *The Murmurs in the Dome*

Sunrise. The servant makes his morning round,
And on the tombs his duster flicks and swings
With a soft swish. A raucous beggar sings.
High in the dome, caught swiftly from the ground,
Murmur and murmur echo and rebound,
Transfiguring those abject common things
To heavenly presences on rustling wings
Joined in a conclave of celestial sound.
Had we but ears made pure that we might hear,
Allah! beyond this flying dust of speech,
The authentic Voice that our vain words eclipse;
Ah! then, the Infinite low-murmuring near,
We might outsing our beggar whine, and reach
A godlike utterance on human lips.

4. *The Builder's Rest*

For her alone, love's queen, this queenly tomb
He planned; and for himself in thought essayed
On Jamuna's thither margin to be laid
In a severer pomp of kingly gloom.
Ah! vainly men to fashion fate presume!
Steadfast through passing empires, her arrayed
In deathless beauty he himself had made,
Dust by her dust, he finds his perfect doom.
Open our eyes, and unto them display,
Allah! the hidden Taj that through our strife
Invisibly we build with passion's fire
And thought's high sculpturing. Grant us each day
Beautiful burial, sweet death I life,
And peace at last, beside the heart's desire!

Poet's note: *The Taj Mahal at Agra, in North India, was built by the Mohammedan Emperor Sha Jehan, over the body of his wife, Mumtaz Mahal. It was begun in 1630 and finished in twenty years by twenty thousand workmen.*

Source: *Collected Poems, 1894–1940* (Madras: Kalakshetra, 1940), pp. 193–196. The poem was first published in *The Modern Review*, August 1918.

Appendix II

Tagore's Letter to the Nobel Committee Secretary proposing Cousins for the Nobel Prize in Literature

December 27, 1934

To

Nobelstiftelsen
Sturegatan, Stockholm 14
Sweden

Dear Sirs,
I, the undersigned, being a 'representative of the domain of literature' (item 7), hereby propose Dr. James H. Cousins, Principal of Madanapalle College, Madanapalle, Madras Presidency, India, an author worthy of receiving the Nobel Prize in Literature.

This proposal is based on the high quality and idealistic influence of his poetry and prose, which have won warm appreciation by competent critics in Europe, Asia and America.

A copy of each of six out of his twenty books of prose and twenty of poetry is being sent to you. In all of them will be found the expression of some aspect of his philosophy which visualises humanity as one family, and sees a fully rounded-out education, including aspiration and creative expression in the arts, as the way towards the mutual appreciation that will evoke the peacewill in humanity.

I can assure you that, should Dr. Cousins be fortunate enough to win the Prize, it would be put to good use in his work for education in India.

Yours faithfully,
Rabindranath Tagore
Recipient of Nobel Prize for Literature, 1913

Source: Rabindra Bhavana, Visva-Bharati, West Bengal, India

Appendix III

The first draft of the poem 'Darkly rollest thou on ...' which was received by Cousins in March 1918

Darkly rollest thou on, thou unseen water of Existence,
at the shock of whose bodiless rush the infinite space shivers and frets
into ferment of things and eddying bubbles of suns.
Hast thou utterly lost thy heart, Eternal Wanderer, to the lovely lover of the Ever-away
calling to thee, asking for thy all?

And is it for the hurry of thine eagerness that thy unbound tresses
break into stormy riot
and from thy heaving breast the stars are flung in the sky
from the torn necklace of the mist?
Never for once thou dost look behind nor linger to gather what is dropped
speeding on without care or regret in thy panting pursuit of the Reachless.

Pure thou art in thy radiance sheathed in the sacred dark,
For nothing clings to thee who pourest out thy fullness every moment.
At the touch of thy steps the dust of the world is made sweet
and the shower of dance rhythms shaken from thy limbs
freshens life in the sacred bath of death.

If in sudden weariness thou didst stop for a moment
the world would start up in a scream into a hideous heap of wrecks
growing into its own self an absolute deaf, blind black and grossly frightful,
and the smallest speck of dust would pierce the sky through its infinity
with its unbearable weight of pause.

Ah, it has quickened my poet's thought
this dance of the unseen feet shaking their anklets of light.
for their steps are echoing in my heartbeats
and in my blood swells the psalms of the ancient sea.

I seem to remember my course of forgotten ages
ever tumbling from life to life and form to form
scattering my being in endless gifts, in sorrowings and songs.

The tide runs high, the wind blows, thy boat flutters like thy own desire, my heart.
Leave behind the boarding of the shore,
and sail forth on thy voyage over the unfathomed dark
towards the light without limit

The second draft of the poem sent by Tagore to Cousins on 6 March 1918

Darkly you sway on unseen, Eternal Runaway,
the shock of whose bodiless rush frets the stagnant space into froth of things
and eddying bubbles of suns.
Is your heart utterly lost to your Lover, ever calling you across his immeasurable loneliness?
And it is for the aching urge of your hurry that your tangled tresses break into stormy riot
and fire pearls are flung in your path from your
torn necklace of the mist?
You never care to look behind, nor linger to gather what is dropped in your panting pursuit of the reachless
The splendour of your purity shines unsullied sheathed in the dark,
for nothing pollutes you who pour out your fullness every moment.

At the touch of your fleeting steps the dust of the world is made sweet
and the dance-storm shaken from your limbs freshens life with the sacred shower of death
If in sudden weariness you stopped for a moment the world would howl
into a hideous heap of encumbrance
growing to its own self a barrier gross, blind and frightful,
and the smallest speck of dust would pierce the sky through its infinity
with its unbearable weight of pause.

Ah, it has quickened my poet's thought this rhythm of the unseen feet
shaking their anklets of light.
For their steps are echoing in my heartbeats, and in my blood swells
the psalms of the ancient sea.

I seem to scan across ages my life tumbling from world to world
    and form to form,
scattering my being in endless gifts, in sorrowings and songs.

The tide runs high, the wind blows, thy boat dances like thy own desire,
my heart.
Leave behind the boarding of the shore, and sail on thy voyage over the
    unfathomed dark
towards the light without limit.

Source: Rabindra-Bhavana Archive, File No. 72. The original Bengali poem is poem no. 8 in the volume *Balākā.* A revised version of the translation was published as the opening poem in the volume *The Fugitive* (1921).

Appendix IV

A

The Ideal of Visva-Bharati

Address by Rabindranath Tagore

My friends have often puzzled themselves with the question as to what it was that led a poet like me to organise for myself a variety of responsibilities that has assumed the name of Visva-Bharati.

My answer would be, that the idea had its nebulous beginning in my subconscious mind in an atmosphere of literature in which my young spirit first became aware of the magical touch of West mostly through its poetical creations. It was at the time when in our country an age-long cultural segregation had given way to the knocking of the western humanity at our gate, and the fact that its urging had a profound truth was proved by the response it met in our own creative outburst. It spoke of a human universe which, though variedly enriched by the products of different climates in its different latitudes, has an unbounded sky over it bared in all directions to the meteorological communication of mind. We became conscious for the first time of the universal Man marching across all physical boundaries and must have vaguely felt its imperative claim for a great spiritual fulfilment.

Nations are kept apart not merely by international jealousy but also by their own past, handicapped by the burden of the dead and decaying, the breeding ground of diseases that attack the spiritual man. I could not believe that generations of peoples, century after century, must have their birth chamber in a moral and intellectual coffin which has its restricted space-regulation for a body that has lost its movements. Civilisation, as it becomes tired, has its inevitable tendency to accumulate dead materials and to make elaborate adjustment for their accommodation, leaving less and less room for life with its claim to grow in freedom. There are signs of that in India, and I know to-day that it is more or less true in all races, for our mind has its inclination to grow lazy as it grows old and to shirk its duty to make changes in the rhythm of the changing times. India should never passively accept her doom of obscurity which is not merely external but belonging to a mental perspective obstinately provincial. We have to know that in the modern age, the problems of each country are parts of the world problem. We must develop a mentality that intelligently recognises truth in its universal aspects both in our dealings with the physical world, as well as, the moral world of man. I know that the practical difficulties in the way of our countrymen in actively responding to the message of world unity are very great. But what counts is not the difficulty but lack of faith in the ideal and diffidence in its expression. I do recognise that the pitiful meagreness of our education and a number of extraneous causes, have all contributed to our degeneracy contaminating our spiritual standard of life with superstitious corruption which belongs to the sub-human.

What has been the most effective means of dragging our minds down to a materialistic cult of piety is the complex social organism which came by its existence purely as a device to regulate the inter-relationship of different groups of our people at varying stages of development. Our real difficulty arises owing to the mixing up of the fact of our social barriers with the religious conception that they represent an eternal truth. I cannot think of a greater anachronism than the belief, deliberately cultivated in the name of religion, that, from the beginnings of beginnings, the lord of all creations has instituted our unfortunate differences which no course of evolution can change or curses of adverse history demolish.

This handicap is peculiar to our country. But through the very tremendousness of the difficulty we must realise that this problem has been given to us by our providence on the solution of which depends our salvation. We have the incubus of caste difference, we have scriptural injunctions that aggravate its mischief, we have traditional beliefs that obstruct the freedom of social communication and being mostly irrational: divide us from the rest of the world, confining us in a dim-lighted isolation of our own make and choice. These are the impediments that stand in the way of our national self-realisation and thwart us in our self-revelation to the great universe of man. No amount of the caricature of the political pose of fortunate races can help us to avert the humiliation of a barren history whose source of futility lies deep in our own nature and mental and social habits. Let the politicians struggle in their characteristic way trying to win opportunities which are necessarily external and yet valuable within their limits. But Visva-Bharati if it ever can be fortunate in its resources, in its men and materials, hopes to exercise its influence through education in an extensive field of life which comprehends the living springs of creative forces and the freedom of mind directing those forces to great purpose.

For all civilisations are creations. They do not merely offer us information about themselves; but give outer expression to some inner ideals which are creative. Therefore we judge each of them not by how much it has produced, but by the truth of its aspiration expressed in its activities. When, in things which are a creation the structure gets the better of the spirit, then it is condemned. When a civilisation merely gives a large stock of facts about its own productions, its mechanical parts, its outward successes, then we know that there must be anarchy in its world of idea, that some living organ is lacking, that it will be torn with conflicts and will not be able to hold together human society in the spirit of Truth.

It is the mission of man to build up his own age with his own resources of intellect and sacrifice of love, to create circumstances where he could have his perfect freedom. It is only the barbarian who passively accepts his shelter and sustenance from indulgent Nature of foreign charity or an instinct which blindly goes on weaving webs in an unchanging pattern fashioning cocoons within which darkly live imperfectly formed beings, the enclosures which have restricted room only for their solitary tenants.

In the modern days our mind in India is brought up as an indigent tenant on the basement floor of an alien culture where it can have only a meagre accommodation and not sufficient scope for hospitality. It is the sign of abject poverty when we may have barely enough for our own feeding and no surplus left for others. We have been reduced to such a scantiness of intellectual living because through long disuse we have lost the courage of faith in our power to create. What is worse there are a considerable number of deluded mortals among us who believe themselves superbly admirable only because they can imitate, ludicrously unconscious of the incongruity of the misfit. Our true claim to be proud depends upon our capacity to give and not in any display of foreign feathers however gorgeous they may be.

All that is true in humanity is ever waiting at our gate to be invited. It is not for us to question it about the country to which it belongs, but to receive it in our home and bring before it the best that we have. The truth of all civilisations has to be judged not by their success in pilfering or begging, but by their hospitality the offerings of which remain inexhausted even when the hosts themselves take their departure from the arena of history. That India after long ages of her spiritual and intellectual magnanimity should be allowed to carry on a penurious existence eking out her living by gleaning grains in foreign fields of harvest is an insult to our ancestors. It comes from utter forgetfulness whose origin is in our persistently turning our face away from our own inheritance.

I have felt the meeting of the East and the West in my own individual life. I belong to the latter end of the nineteenth century. And to our remote country in Bengal, when I was a boy, there came a voice from across the sea. I listened to it. It would be difficult to imagine what it meant for me in those. I was deeply stirred and felt as if I had discovered a new planet on the horizon where a paradise waits for our exploration.

It was the last vanishing twilight of the Romantic West. We had been living in the atmosphere of the lyrical literature of poets like Shelley, Keats, Wordsworth, and in a boundless perspective of idealism. In Europe, the afterglow of the French Revolution had not died out, and people were dreaming of freedom, of the brotherhood of man. They still believed in the human ideals that have their permanent and ultimate value in themselves. I cannot express how it did move my soul. It was that atmosphere, that great human appeal of the Western civilisation which won our hearts and made us glad and proud of the fact that we had the opportunity and power to receive it.

The West at that time believed in the freedom of personality. We heard about Garibaldi, about Mazzini, and their history revealed to us an aspect of humanity with which we were imperfectly familiar – the great ideal of the freedom of self-expression for all races and for all countries. We felt great admiration for the people who were dedicated to that dream, through their literature, and also through their practical endeavours.

There are times when some particular people play the part of messengers of humanity. They come to rescue human relations from all kinds of fetters of ignorance or moral degeneracy, despair and weakness of will. We thought the present age belonged to the West, that they had come to save the world from all forms of feebleness and ineptitude. We knew what India herself had done in olden times. We knew what Greece had offered to humanity and which still remains inexhaustible. All these great civilisations had the effect of redeeming the minds of men from fetters of insult, from sluggishness and stupidity. And we imagined that the West had come to us with a message of life which was universal, which had nothing provincial or exclusively national in it.

And I say as an individual that the West and the East did meet in India in my younger days. But how short-lived was that white flame of promise that was brought to us, which lost its radiance growing redder and redder through a few centuries of an indecent success in a material bloatedness, the success which seems like a greedy balloon exultantly loading itself to a bursting point with an inflammatory gas. All the great countries of the West and their infatuated disciples in the East are busily carrying on some diabolical conspiracy of desolation. The poison is deep within their own selves. They try, and try to find some solution, but they do not succeed, because they have lost their faith in the universal personality of man.

While the dark crater of their inner being is vomiting forth mutual suspicion, hatred and anger, they furiously try to invent some outer machinery which they think will solve their difficulties. It does not work, it fails at critical times, because man is human, while machinery is impersonal. Men of power have efficiency in outward things; but their humanity is dishonoured. They do not trust the divine in man, the harvester, the music-maker, the dreamer of the dream of creation.

West fights against physical evil, and that is a great thing. I often think she should come to help us, fight our material adversity, which has its source in our ignorance. We are unfortunate. We had formerly our own system of education – that has vanished. We had our industries to help us to fill up – the deficiencies of an unreliable agriculture, but all those industries have perished. And we pray that the West would come to us as a member of a common humanity. We claim it from them who have wealth which is over-flowing, and we are in the direst and deepest shadow of poverty and distress on our side of the world.

We have been waiting for the Person. Such a personality as we see in Mahatma Gandhi. It is only possible in the East for such a man to find recognition. This man has neither physical nor material power, but his humanity reveals itself in its simple majesty and invokes within us a strong assurance of Man the indomitable; and the people downtrodden for centuries, their backs bent down under loads of indignity suddenly stand up ready to suffer, and through suffering, conquer. And our women – who only the other day were secluded behind walls and enveloped in a dusk of helplessness, have come out to follow this man. Not an association, not an organisation, not a politician, but a Man! And his message goes deep into our veins. He attacks the enemies that are within us. Not like the political machinery of the West that tries to work through the external. But he touches the inner spirit. The people believe in him, in this man who is not a Brahmin, but belonging to a class of money-makers who have been despised for centuries.

When times were dark, there came a Man in other days to people who needed salvation, emancipation from the fetters of materialism. He came to their door. The babe born in obscurity, brought exaltation to man. Not machinery, not association, not organisations, but an immense future taken birth in a child. And when all the machinery will be rusted, he will live.

I have felt that the civilisation of the West to-day has its law and order, but no personality. It has come to the perfection of a mechanical order but what is there to humanise it? It is the Person who is in the heart of all beings. We have seen, we have known him within us, in the depth of our consciousness. Only when West comes to Him will there be peace. And I who belong to an unrecognised corner of the world, have been cherishing the hope for long years that Visva-Bharati will find voice to proclaim that peace is not waiting to be concocted out of their cleverness by men who do not believe in it, to be constructed through political manoeuvring performed by nations boasting of their power, but peace can only be realised in the spiritual revelation of Man whose inexhaustible wealth is in his own fulfilment.

Source: *Proceedings of the Bengal Education Week, Vol. I, 1936*, ed. Md Qudrat I-Khuda, pp. 78–83.

B

(Tagore's letter to CF Andrews)

AUTOUR DU MONDE, PARIS
April 24, 1921

When I sent my appeal for an International Institution to the western people I made use of the word 'University' for the sake of convenience. But that word has not only an inner meaning, but also an outer association in the minds of those who use it; and that fact tortures my idea into its own rigid shape. It is unfortunate.

I shall not allow my life to be pinned to a word for a foreign museum, like a dead butterfly. It must be known, not by a deposition, but by its own life growth.

I saved my Santiniketan School from being trampled into smoothness by the steam roller of the Education Department. My school is poor in resources and equipment, but it has the wealth of truth in it, which no money can ever buy; and I am proud of the fact that it is not a machine-made article perfectly modelled in a work-shop – it is our very own.

If we must have a University, it should spring from our own life and be maintained by our own life. Someone may say that such freedom is dangerous, and that a machine will help to lessen our personal responsibility and make things easy for us. Yes! Life has its risks, and freedom has its responsibility; and yet they are preferable on account of their own immense value, and not for any other ulterior results.

So long, I have been able to retain my perfect independence and self-respect because I had faith in my own resources and proudly worked within their sovereign limits. My bird must still retain its freedom of wings and not be tamed into a sumptuous nonentity by any controlling agency outside its own living organism. I know that the idea of an International University is complex, but I must make it simple in my own way. I shall be content if it attracts round it men who have neither name nor fame nor worldly means, but who have the mind and the faith; who are to create a great future with their dreams.

Very likely, I shall never be able to work with a Board of Trustees, influential and highly respectable – for I am vagabond at heart. But the powerful people of the world, the lords of the earth, make it difficult for me to carry out my work. I know it, and I have had experiences of it in connexion with Santiniketan. But I am not afraid of failure. I am only afraid of being tempted away from truth in pursuit of success. The temptation assaults me occasionally; but it comes from the outside atmosphere. My own abiding faith is in life and light and freedom, and my prayer is:

> 'Lead me from the unreal to Truth'

This letter of mine is to let you know that I free myself from the bondage of help, and go back to join the great 'Brotherhood of the Tramps', who seem helpless, but are recruited by God for His own army.

Source: Rabindranath Tagore, *Letters from Abroad* (Madras: S Ganesan, 1924), pp. 111–113.

Appendix V

A

First Impression of Tagore in Europe

James H. Cousins

In the month of August 1912, I indulged in my first 'continental' holiday. A long and stiff session in school-teaching terminating in annual examinations had been followed by an unexpected appointment to a summer course. The appointment carried with it remuneration which, being equally unexpected, could only fitly find an expected outlet. Nothing short of Paris could meet the requirements of the occasion.

But Paris has a trick of 'extras'. The closet calculation of conducted tours, all-found, could not provide an arithmetical mesh sufficiently fine to meet all possibilities of little fish escaping in the deep waters of explorations which, even in the virtuous light of day, transformed themselves into francs and centimes. It therefore became necessary to find a less leaky habitat for the tail-end of the month, and fate, and the worst railway system I had till then known, landed me in the historical and quaint city of William the Conqueror, Bayeux, in Normandy. In its neighbourhood I found the little town of Balleroy, with its exquisite church designed by the architect of the Louvre, and a comfortable hotel managed by a stout widow with the largest smile and the smallest quantity of English possible, that is, none.

That year made a record in rainfall in Western Europe. Fortunate individuals who wandered as far eastward as Copenhagen smiled pitifully on those of us who dwelt under the Atlantic cloud: but there were compensations. Mine announced itself in a note from a friend who happened to be staying at her seaside house on the coast of Normandy, to the effect that as we were all evidently destined to be drowned, we might as well perish together. The note added: 'Mr Yeats is here.' I thanked God for the deluge that floated us (there were two of *us*, of course) into the more immediate precinct of one of the world's master singers than was possible on lecture platforms, or in drawing-rooms sacred to the gods and half-gods of the Irish Literary Revival, or in the crush-room of the Abbey Theatre in Dublin.

Our luck turned out to be greater than our dreams of it. Instead of one poet, we had two: one in the flesh, the tall, dark, ever distinguished leader of the Irish literary and dramatic movement; one in the spirit, almost, as it were, in a pre-natal state awaiting birth into the English language, but living royally, vitally, in the splendid imagination and enkindled joy of another: one was Yeats, the other Tagore. I have often wondered if the immortal singer of the songs of the Spirit in the Fast has come near a realisation of the place that his songs occupied in the mind of the immortal singers of the songs of the Spirit in the West before fame had ratified them. When I had the privilege four years later of coming face to face with Rabindranath in his Calcutta home, I had a mind to clear up my wonder, but it was as difficult to break through his interest in the work of Yeats and his fellow-singers, and to get him to talk of his own work, as it had been in Normandy to get Yeats to talk of anything but Tagore. After all, I suppose, it does not matter much to the individuals whether or not they realise in what relationship they stand to one another. They cannot add an inch to their stature, for each is supreme in his place; nevertheless, to others not at their height, there must be something stirring in the spectacle of a poet of transcendent genius standing on the house-top of enthusiasm, proclaiming, on the slightest provocation, the splendours of the genius of a brother-poet.

At that time, Rabindranath was a name unknown in English letters, but a few at the heart of things literary were in the secret of a coming revelation. Yeats carried with him in Normandy a manuscript book containing the poems of Tagore which he was then prefacing for the India Society's edition of 'Gitanjali'. He read – or, rather, chanted as only he could – every one of the poems, adding to. Their inherent quality – a glory of music and interpretation. Time has blurred the ear's memory of those after-dinner recitals, but it has not falsified the first conviction that those little mouthfuls of lyrical prose were among the abiding things of the Soul, and that they would work a beneficent revolution in English literature, since they entered it at its highest – in the purest of musical speech, full of the authenticity of creation, rather than the adumbrations of translation, and glowing with a spirit that was new to the West, yet essentially in affinity with the spirit of the seers of all time, who are also the utterers.

My first impression of Tagore's poetry, made through ear-gate, was that it was of the nature of direct statement of subjective experience kin to that of Maeterlinck and Emerson, but differing from Maeterlinck in its wonderful clarity and certainty, and from Emerson in its equally wonderful simplicity and *finesse*. It seemed to move at an altitude far above all derivation, and with a sense of finding in the history of religion, philosophy and literature a gratifying, but hardly essential, corroboration, not a source or a justification. This was not, of course, felt as a pose or a conscious quality, but rather as the concomitant of spiritual authenticity that is at home in all lands and new in all ages.

I did not see 'Gitanjali' in print until Macmillan's edition came out. Then it came upon me in a crowded tramcar in one of the dirtiest and most odoriferous' districts of Liverpool. I had put the book in my pocket to while away a forty-five minutes' tram journey by mean streets among a crowd consisting of tired women and squirming babies interspersed with the silk hat of suburban respectability going to evening church and the sharp odour of alcohol from labour off duty and having 'a good time'. I had to hang on to a strap by one hand – my seat having gone to a lady – but I had taken the precaution to cut my 'Gitanjali', and so it was not difficult to hold it and turn the pages when required.

I learned then the meaning of a 'joy-ride', and I fancy my fellow-passengers felt something of its radiation, for I *had* to pass the book to my companion to share the glow of re-discovery which showed itself in brightened eyes and heightened colour as France and a chanting poet's voice built themselves in the midst of the drabness and repulsiveness of our physical environment, and the eye gave confirmation to the ear in hailing the wonderful new thing in poetry – a voice that had no need to speak of truth or of beauty, since it was itself beauty and truth.

One might, I suppose, rest satisfied with the exalted pleasure of such experiences, but after all, they are somewhat of the nature of refined sensuality unless they evoke a response in some deeper degree of one's being than the exclusively aesthetic in thought or feeling. Their influence must be ephemeral unless one's own consciousness supplies the medium of fixation, and this can only be done by thinking around the aesthetic impacts, finding their inter-relationships, and their relationships with the great facts and intuitions of life. It is quite certain that Tagore would resist any attempt to systematise him, and rightly so, for he is not a system but a life. At the same time, since he is a life, an organism for the expression of a hidden spiritual life, he must preserve a symmetry and coherence in his parts. Every line, every thought in his writings, hangs upon every other, and it is through the discovery of their coherence that those outside himself can put their image of him in their shrine, the *Bhoga murti* to which they can present the offerings of thought that would wither under the eye of the very-God. The mind is, as a scripture says, the slayer of the real, but it is also the path to the real for those on the hither side of inspiration. In creation, the artist may, nay must, overleap the mind; in understanding, we cannot.

That is my excuse, if not my justification, for having found in 'Gitanjali' a series of poems which organically, though not in their printed order, present a coherent view of the life of humanity and its relationship with the universe, and which may, I think, be regarded as Tagore's message to the world.

In reading any new poet, I instinctively search for his *greatest* 'word', that is, a declaration that has springing out of it the greatest range of branches and twigs of vision and thought. That attained, the rest of the poet's utterances put on an illuminating perspective.

Tagore's greatest thought is, I believe, his enunciation of the fundamental perfection within all things.

> Only in the deepest silence of night the stars
> smile and whisper among themselves – 'Vain is
> this seeking! Unbroken perfection is over all!'
> One life works through all degree of life.
> The same stream of life that runs through my

> veins night and day runs through the world and
> dances in rhythmic measures.

Thus, the visible creation is not merely symbolised as, but actually is, the Body of God. The poet, therefore, always sees the Divine working through the human.

> When I bring to you coloured toys, my child. I
> understand why there is such a play of colours
> on cloud, on water, and why flowers are painted
> in tints.

He sets up a personal relationship between himself and the Divine.

> Thou settest a barrier in thine own being and
> then callest thy severed self in myriad notes.
> This thy self-separation has taken body in me.
> The great pageant of thee and me has overspread
> the sky. With the tune of thee and me all the
> air is vibrant, and all ages pass with the hiding
> and seeking of thee and me.

He conducts his life through reliance on the Great Life of which his own is a part.

> My poet's vanity dies in shame before thy sight.
> O master poet, I have sat down at thy feet.
> Only let me make my life simple and straight,
> like a flute of reed for thee to fill with music.

That Great Life is within conscious reach of everyone; the fulfilment of its law is love:

> They come with their laws and their codes to
> bind me fast; but I evade them ever, for I am
> only waiting for love to give myself up at last
> into his hands.

In this love there is no impoverishment:

> Deliverance is not for me in renunciation. I feel
> the embrace of freedom in a thousand bends of
> delight.
> No, I will never shut the doors of my senses,
> The delights of sight and hearing and touch will
> bear thy delight.

> Yes, all my illusions will burn into illumination
> of joy, and all my desires ripen into fruits of
> love.

Rather does such a love lead to purification of its members for sheer joy of making them fitter instruments to express the Great Life:

> Life of my life, I shall ever try to keep my body
> pure, knowing that thy living touch is upon all
> my limbs …
> And it shall be my endeavour to reveal thee in
> my actions, knowing it is thy power gives me
> strength to act.

What distinguishes Tagore's expression of his vision from the expression of western poets is that his religion and philosophy are not departments of his work, but its 'fundamental ether', its vital substance. His religion is without theology, though not without personality: his philosophy is without argument, though not without rationale. The outstanding quality that shows in every line of his poetry is *life*, but not the little span of sensation and lower thought that is the western connotation of the word amongst Minor poets and minor critics. His affinities in English literature are Herbert and Vaughan, and Crashaw, and among living poets the seer-singer of the Irish renaissance, AE, and the highland and mystic singer, James L. MacBeth Bain. But while these are Tagore's spiritual kindred, he has as comrades the whole hierarchy of immortal song; and one of the most fascinating speculations as to the future is the influence that Tagore will exert on English literature. He comes to it, not simply as a translation, but as a powerful original, post-Whitman in technique, that is, uniting the freedom of *vers libre* to literary craftsmanship. He has bettered the mechanics of the younger English poets, but he has done more; he has let loose a spirit of eclecticism in thought and phrase that will put an end to the fallacy of equating vulgarity with literary democracy, and that will materially help towards the accomplishment of the much-needed poetical Restoration.

Source: *New Ways in English Literature* (1917: Ganesh & Co, 1919), pp. 16–26.

B

Exhibition of Indian Arts and Crafts

Interview with Mr. Cousins
(Special Interview – 'The Chronicle')

THE Exhibition of Indian Arts and Crafts, under the auspices of The 1921 Club, Art Section, Madras, was opened on the 1st of March in the YMIA Buildings, Georges Town, by Lady Emily Lutyens, wife of Sir Edwin Lutyens, the well-known architect, and the sister of Lord Lytton. The chief interests in the

Exhibition were the examples of the work of the Modern Bengal School of painting, though the Moghul and Medieval paintings were also among the exhibits on view. The collection includes specimens of painting of nearly 30 Indian artists. Babu Asit Kumar Haldar, whose drawing shows a unique power that is full of very great promise for the future even more than what it has achieved already, had come here to assist Mr. James H. Cousins who was in charge of the exhibits in painting, the handicrafts section being in charge of Mrs. Adzdr. Mr. Cousins is an enthusiastic admirer of the Bengal School (as you will doubt – less infer from the following interview I had with him) and he is one of the pillars of support which it has been the good fortune of the Neo-Bengal School to secure from this good friend of India. The present exhibition of Indian paintings is the fifth of its kind that has been organised through the zeal and initiative of Mr. Cousins, who is now the Secretary of the Art Section of the 1921 Club. I may perhaps add that the Art Section itself is free from politics, though the Club is a distinct political organisation.

The Exhibition rooms were very plainly and tastefully set out. A white background shows up the seventy and odd representative pictures which are mounted on simple white or coloured cardboard as the artistic necessities of the picture may demand. The pictures in groups (as in the case of the sketches by Mr Haldar) were pinned on wooden screens. The exhibition gave one the impression of simplicity, humility, and repose.

Mr Cousins, to whom I wrote for an interview, kindly received me at the Exhibition rooms, and I give below the full report of the interview which will throw a flood of light on the art that is unfortunately little understood by Indians themselves.

Question – What is the fundamental difference between the art of the West and of the Neo-Bengal School?

Answer – The answer to this question was, I think, unconsciously given by two visitors to the gallery, both Europeans. One dismissed the entire collection as being stiff and uninteresting, with the possible exception of one picture – that of a man shooting an arrow at a pair of doves on a tree. The other, evidently moved by something in the collection, passed slowly from picture to picture. I hazarded the question as to whether he cared for them. He replied: 'They fascinate me.' 'Why?' 1 asked. 'Because', said he, 'every one of them expresses soul.' I think that is just the difference. Western art has been given the *Dharma* of expressing the muscularity, vigour and emotion of life. The Bengal artists (indeed, one might say, all true Indian artists) are the natural expressors of the higher mental and spiritual aspects of humanity and nature. Western art represents things as they are viewed from the outside. Eastern art interprets things from the inside.

Question – To a Western art-critic the characteristics of the Bengal School appear to be its gloominess, its lack of courage and humour, and a very imperfect knowledge of drawing except in one or two isolated cases. Have these charges any basis?

Answer – The 'gloominess' is a matter of taste – or, perhaps, I should rather say habit which has become prejudice. Painting may be the direct expression of the artist's genius and environment, but it may also be the expression of some counter-balancing need. Western artists seek the short summer light because for eight months in the year they live in semi-darkness. Indian artists seek for relief from the constant superfluity of light and heat in the short but magical morning and evening hours, just after dawn and before sunset. I do not understand the charge of 'lack of courage' though, I think, I understand the mental limitations which see courage only in physical action, and fail to see it in the exquisite calm expression of mental and spiritual vision. Humour of the comic paper variety is certainly not present to any extent in these pictures, save perhaps in the case of Mr. G. N. Tagore's somewhat keen-edged satires. But it appears to me that humour is valuable in the West as a set-off to the tragic element which is inherent in the Western conception of Life and Death. Whereas in India, the idea of Life as a continuous succession, of which the present life is only one phase, takes the tragedy out of things. The Sanskrit drama, for example, for the reason I have stated, has no tragedies. Tragedy and comedy belong to the lower slopes of the hill of life: the Bengal artists paint from the summit. As to bad drawing, I remember hearing this charge levelled against AE in Ireland long ago. Yet, people used to come from America to attend his exhibitions and carry his paintings home as trophies. The pictures of the Bengal School are not to be classified as 'drawings.' They are visual expressions of moods and visions of the soul, in which there is a higher accuracy than that of the inch-tape. Many of the paintings are anatomically normal, and indicate purpose in other pictures which do not agree with the conventional habit of the eye.

Question – Then, again, there is the charge that the artists of the Bengal School ignore the rules of proportion in their drawing of the limbs and of the hands. What is your own view regarding this?

Answer – My view is that a little more observation and thought would put this charge out of court, as happened in my own case. I resented the elongated eyes and snaky fingers of the Bengal pictures when I first saw them. But afterwards, when I saw these same features on visiting Bengal, I realised that I had been labouring under the same mental disability as most Europeans and many Indians, in assuming that what I was familiar with was the normal and accurate, and that naturally any variation from it was abnormal and inaccurate. There is this also to be remembered – that when the artists are depicting Divinity and Super-humanity they revert to the ancient Shastric rules for such depiction. Two excellent examples of the difference between these methods were upon the walls of the Exhibition, Dr AN Tagore's 'Buddha' and his 'Divine Craftsman: Viswakarman' which was exhibited for the first time this year in Calcutta. The first is a supremely beautiful expression of the calm of illumination. The proportions are perfectly normal. The second is built entirely on the so-called 'false anatomy.' But this anatomy is that of the Shastras which provide conventional idealistic form and measurement for the expression of that which is beyond form and measurement. When one accepts this convention, as one accepts the convention of singing in drama, one is then free to comprehend the vast conception which the artist has succeeded in giving visual expression to in the space of fifty square inches.

Question – What do you think of the charge of imitation that is levelled against the younger members of the Bengal School?

Answer – I don't think very much of it. All young artists, in any art, imitate one another. But if they have the full vision and expression, they disclose something of their own, which makes even a repetition of the subject already done valuable to the art-lover. There are several pictures in the Exhibition dealing with 'Radha and Krishna,' and some Indian visitors have complained that they are all different from one another! There is more danger in an artist's imitation of himself than of others, for repetition is a sign of decay of power.

Question – Do you hold that the Bengal School of painting is truly expressive of the Indian genius?

Answer – I hold that the Bengal School is one true expression of the Indian genius, but I look for other equally true expressions arising in other parts of the country. The object of bringing this collection of Bengal paintings to Madras is not to turn Madras art students into copyists of the Bengal School. Rather do we hope that these pictures will act (to use a homely figure of speech) as a bucket of water put down a dry pump in order to provoke it to send its own water to the surface.

Question – Has it the stamp of what one might call the national characteristic?

Answer – It depends on what you mean by 'national!' There is a tendency in times of national emotion to regard as unnational anything that does not agree with the enthusiasms of the day, and from this point of view it might be possible to find persons who would regard the pictures of the Bengal School as unnational, seeing that there is not a single spinning wheel in the whole collection! But taking the permanent things of India, so far as I can comprehend them, as a standard – spiritual idealism, gentleness, simplicity, beauty, delicacy – I certainly think that the work of the Bengal School is truly national.

Question – Will the Neo-Bengal School exert any considerable influence on the art or the world? If so, in what direction?

Answer — Yes, it not only will exert a considerable influence on the art of the world, but has already done so. Some years ago, an Exhibition of the paintings of the School in Paris and London attracted a great amount of attention and the works exhibited in December and January last at the home Exhibition of the Indian Society of Oriental Art in Calcutta are to be sent to Europe. I myself exhibited a set of the pictures in Japan three years ago, have received invitations to show similar pictures in America if at any time my fate takes me to that country. The direction in which these pictures will influence the art of the world will be upwards, by which 1 mean that it will have the tendency to direct Western art towards the finer impulses and suggestions of the Spirit. The present confusion in art outside India arises from the exhaustion of the eye and the lower emotions. This exhaustion cannot be relieved through fantastic variations of things seen and felt, such as have been attempted by the Cubists, Futurists and similar groups of revolutionaries in art: it can only be relieved by a raising of the consciousness of the artist to a higher level, the level of the Spirit. This, the work of the Bengal School is helping to do.

Source: *Rupam: A Journal of Oriental Art, Chiefly Indian*, edited by Ordhendra Coomar Gangoly, No. 11, July 1922, pp. 99–104.

C

Tagore's Message to the World

(As proclaimed in his latest book "Creative Unity")

James H. Cousins

In his latest book "Creative Unity" (Macmillan, New York), Rabindranath Tagore throws a gulf across the gulf that Western criticism has set between the function of thought and the function of expression, between philosophy and literature. He has given to the world a volume which, by virtue of its transcendent qualities of its utterance, takes rank among the masterpieces of world-literature; a volume, which at the same time sets, the profoundest thought close to the world's vast problem of disease and agony today, and out of the unflinching but passionate diagnosis, prescribes for temporal ills, the heroic but only availing remedies of pharmacopeia of eternal Truth. He has thus rendered a signal and far-reaching service to both literature and philosophy by giving his unique gifts of brilliance and astonishment of idea, of splendour and vividness, of figure and phraseology, to the expression of an urgent, moving and world-bracing purpose; and by releasing philosophy from the bare prison of textualism and scholastic history, and setting it to the testing of the activities of life with the warning, pleading, counselling with the trumpet of high literature at its lips. He has made it impossible for any who has ears to hear the resonant and shining message of this book to acquiesce any longer in the indolent and uncritical acceptance of literature as the polite mental libertinism of humanity, and humanity as its medicine and penance.

Before a book such as this, criticism of the negative order lays aside his microscope and scalpel—or expends itself to a feeble reference to the merely external fact that the essays included in "Creative Unity" were written under a variety of circumstances and without immediate organic relationship to a single central theme. What is vital to the world is not the question of the mechanism of these essays or the connections with the former presentations of their substance in their author's books on Personality and Nationalism. But the fact that they present adequately and maturely their writer's plea for the establishment in human relationships of a unity, which, by participation in the Divine function of Creation, attains peace and joy; a creative unity in contradistinction to the present world-wide religious, racial and social disunity which, because it is essentially uncreative, and merely productive and destructive, is vowed to spiritual abasement, intellectual poverty, and physical misery.

Such is, in brief, the message of "Creative Unity" and of Tagore to the world. To realise its full significance, it is necessary to understand the implications which the author puts on the worlds "creative" and "unity" and on the words 'nationalism' and 'internationalism' which, to Tagore, stand for the organised expression in human society of the opposed forces of destruction and creation.

There is a rough and ready idea in the popular mind of the West that 'creation' means the making of something out of nothing. The subtler mind of the East postulates a Creative Power, and a substance, which, in being capable of response, to the Creative Power, has within itself the principle of creation. All activity of a creative kind is seen as the making (Sanskrit *kit*, to make) of new combinations within limited are as of the (to us) unlimited sphere of possible variation in life, substance, and form. Creation, therefore, in this sense, is not simple reproduction or multiplicity, but the setting up of a process which draws around a special centre of energy certain related expressions in substance and quality, and by 'making' some new object of art, thrills the maker and the beholder with joy in the disclosure through the finite of the wonder and beauty of the Infinite. Artistic creation is possible only through acts of unification in materials and qualities; social creation (instead of the vast proliferation of today) is possible only though acts of unification in the thoughts and feelings, the aims and movements of human beings. Says Rabindranath,

"We feel that the world is a creation" (in the sense that has just been set forth); 'that in its centre there is a living idea which reveals itself in an eternal symphony played on innumerable instruments all keeping perfect time. We know that this world-verse, that runs from sky to sky, is not made for the mere enumeration of facts; it has direct revelation in our delight. The delight gives us the key to the truth of existence; it is personality acting upon personalities through incessant manifestations.'

When a great seer and sayer points his finger towards "the truth of existence," it behoves those who have set out with open eyes on the Great Exploration for that very Truth, to pay heed to all that is involved in the crucial statement that "the truth of existence" is "personality acting on personalities"… this full-minded attention is all the more necessary here because it happens that, through the exigencies of a language in which the mental and material solidity of the Greek genius is predominant the only word personality that Tagore could find for the full expression of that ultimate Being, or Life, or Consciousness, within which 'our little systems' and the incalculable universes revolve, is commonly regarded as meaning just the reverse. And this work-a-day reading of the word has come down through two thousand years of verbal custom from the days of the theatre of Greece and Rome, when, (as in Japan today) the actor hid himself behind a *persona*, or mask, the thing through which he spoke (Latin *per* through, *sono* to speak). In the vocabulary of "Creative Unity", the derivation of 'personality' is taken further back, from the thing spoken through, to the living speaker;

and this deepening of meaning refers not only to the personalities that are cells in the body of the Great Personality, but also to the Great Personality Itself. Within the totality of existence, and within its details, there is consciousness, feeling and activity. No one in these terms gives full expression to the Entity in whom three functions are co-ordinated and given unity of life. The word 'personality' is taken as coming (despite its limitations) nearest to adequacy of meaning.

In the exercise of consciousness, feeling and activity there arises a sense of satisfaction beyond the pleasures of thought, of sensation, or of movement. This deeper pleasure is the ananda (bliss) of eastern thought that is the response between one person and another and between the nominally separated personalities and the Personality of the whole. "The spirit itself beareth witness with one spirit," as the Christian scripture has it: "and that immediacy of intercommunication arises out of the simple inescapable fact that there is no getting beyond that totality; that there is nothing but that Being, that Life, that Divine Personality." This according to Tagore is 'the truth of existence.' It is also the justification of all those efforts to express in terms of race and place some apprehension of the Divine Personality which have been called anthropomorphism and idolatry.

It is obvious that a mind to which this 'truth of existence' (the Divine personality acting on human personalities) is not merely a literary idea but the very breath of its nostrils cannot but look with disapproval on any human activity whose tendency is towards exclusiveness or the building of barriers against the flow of the Universal Life. There is within each human being the impulse to creative unity. Says Rabindranath,

"It is the object of this Oneness within us to realise its infinity by perfect union of love with others. All obstacles to this union create misery, giving rise to the baser passions that are expression of finitude and of that separateness which is negative and therefore *maya*."

Now the word 'love' used in the foregoing paragraph is not a mere evaporation from the surface of a fluid sentimentality. It is the poet's expression of the truth that in the Universal Life there is a principle of cohesion through which it maintains its identity and continues its activity. Separate any branch absolutely from the tree of life and it will die – but the assumption of such separation is an impossibility; were it possible, the world would collapse. Take away the cohesive principle ('love') from the Universal Being, and it would disintegrate into nothingness – but the notion is absurd, for Life and Love are instrumental; you cannot get around them, or behind them, or through them, or beyond them. For which reason Rabindranath says,

"In love we find a joy which is ultimate because it is the ultimate truth."

Love too was the ultimate in the great seer-poet, Shelley. It was love that released the chained Prometheus, and with him set free the suppressed powers of nature and humanity. It is characteristic of the different approach of West and East to 'ultimate truth' that to Shelley love was the key of liberation while to Tagore it is the chord of binding. Yet, both are, in the end, the same. The freedom that Shelley dreamed of was freedom for love to find its full expression and voluntarily to seek its affiliation: the binding that Tagore affirms is the voluntary merging of the self of illuminated human beings with others in love. The one dreamed of love attainable; the other asserts love present and invincible if put into action. The Western poet from the side of humanity capable of Divinity, says: 'We must love in order to be free.' It is characteristic also of the contrasted but complementary points of view of West and East, that, while both poets regard human unity as the essential condition of true creation in the arts and sciences (Shelley is the great chant of English at the end of 'Prometheus Unbound,' Tagore in 'Creative Unity')the Western poet sees the attainment of world-comradeship as an event beyond the chained Titan over the tyrant Jove: and the eastern poet affirms the essential unity of humanity as existence here and now, and its recognition as the measure and test of all movements that take to themselves the sacred name of Freedom.

We have said 'the measure and test' – not the denial. It is just here that the contact of the message of Rabindranath Tagore with the national movements of the present day has been subject to misinterpretation. Years ago, when the writer of this article was doing his share of work on the literary side of the national revival in Ireland, the word 'international' was as a red rag to a bull; it drew upon it a fierce opposition with lowered horns and dilated nostrils. There are those in India today who, in their zeal for their country's welfare, set themselves against the world-wide appeal of Tagore. To his 'internationalism' they oppose their 'nationalism,' and do not realise (as the writer failed to realise years ago) that they are setting the part against the whole: asserting the fallacy that the interests of a constellation are opposed to the interests of any of the stars which compose it, lifting a rebellious heart to do hurt to the body of which it is a member.

The real enemy of nationalism is itself, in its imposition of narrowness and exclusiveness on its own aims and methods: for these cut it off from the flux of the Divine Life, turn creative energy into destructive fever, and set up antagonisms which breed antagonisms. The enemy of Indian nationalism is not internationalism but an alien nationalism. The "plantations" of English settlers in Ireland and the coming of the "John Company" to India were not international movements but predatory excursions from the lair of nationalism which intend to bring back to the lair as much and as good prey as might be snared or pounced upon.

Against the whole spirit and operation of burglarious nationalism, Rabindranath sets his condemnation and prophecy in speech that is kindred to the lightening which, (as Paul Richard puts it in "The Scourge of Christ"), if it does not illuminate, slays. "The wriggling tentacles of a cold-blooded utilitarianism," says Rabindranath, "with which the West has grasped all the easily yielding and succulent portions of the East, are causing pain and indignation throughout – the Eastern countries" — and causing it nowhere more strongly than in the heart of the great patriot who flung away title in rebuke of sin against the spirit of internationalism in the barbarities inflicted by the agents of one nation on another. One feels the flame of noble scorn in his condemnation of foreign rule that holds itself aloof from the people it rules. He says,

"You must now that red tape can never be a common human bond: that official sealing-wax can never provide means of human attachment, that it is a painted ordeal for human beings to have to receive favour from animated pigeon-holes, and condescension from printed notice but never speak."

But this condemnation strikes no more strongly at a foreign bureaucracy that at an Indian bureaucracy if it assumes the method of the machine. Organisation, Tagore admits, is necessary. It is when the spirit of the machine assumes ascendancy that it becomes not only obnoxious to the elastic and expansive spirit of humanity, but dangerous to the machine itself: for "the repressed personality of man generates an inflammable moral gas deadly in its explosive force."

Here we are at the central point of Tagore's message to the world in its application to the world-struggle now going on: the point which, if deeply pondered, would banish from the criticism of his utterances the false antithesis of nationalism and internationalism. The real struggle at every stage of human history, whether between or within nations, has been, he tells us, "between the living spirit of the people and the methods of nation-organising"; between the expanding soul of humanity (Indian or English) and mechanical limitations that refuse to adapt themselves to that expansion. We must take care, however, not to look upon the protagonists of this struggle as external enemies, one of whom must achieve victory by the annihilation of the other. The spirit of expansion and the spirit of organisation are not foes, but partners in one operation, and each achieves victory by making sufficient concession to the other to permit the expression of the Divine Personality. There must be growth, says Rabindranath, but "growth is not that enlargement which is merely adding to the dimensions of incompleteness", it is "the movement of a whole to a yet fuller wholeness" which implies flexible organisation at every stage of the process; and there must be the shaping service of a limitation that is yet free from rigidity, "some spiritual design of life" which curbs the activities of the peoples into an 'organic whole'. The symbol for 'nation-organising' should not be red-tape, which must be cut or loosed, but an elastic band capable of infinite expansion.

In this co-operative struggle the human spirit has the force of evolution with it, driving it forward by necessity, calling it onward by idealism, towards the ideal of voluntary association. When its demands and methods are in line with the spirit of harmony, it succeeds but if its demands and methods are set towards power, it suffers frustration until it learns the better way. Harmony is the condition in which man's true nature, which is spiritual, finds adequate and appropriate expression, for harmony is the medium whereby personality communicates fully and joyfully with personality and ends the high way and communication with the Divine Personality — which is "the truth of existence." But power, personal or national can only be generated through restriction and suppression which, carried beyond a certain point, brings about its own destruction. The living air is universal, harmonious, beneficent; but capture a portion of it in a receptacle and subject it to the pressure, and you produce an elastic, expulsive force which will submit to the pressure just to a point of balance between its own resistance and the resisting power of the agent of pressure. If and when explosion comes, it is not the air that is shattered, but the things that compress it. The yielding air, that the bird of gentle wing hardly ruffles in its passage through it, becomes the ruin of that which presses it beyond endurance.

There is safety only in harmony. The political leaders of the great nations see this truth, but only give it half allegiance. Today they are seeking safety in a *harmony* artificially produced in a balance of *power.* They might as well try to simulate the harmony of the world-encircling ocean by making an alliance of icebergs. They will only sink with their own weight, collide with their own mass-attraction. If they want real harmony they must melt – melt out of "the exclusive advantage which they have unjustly acquired" through the exercise of frigid power. Instead of this "they are concentrating their forces for mutual security:" and in this concentration Tagore sees trouble, for the strong think only of the strong, and ignore the weak, wherein, he says, lies the peril of their losing their harmony at which they aim, and collapsing in a welter of still greater destruction than that from which they are blindly trying to extricate themselves. Tagore throws his conviction on this matter into a figure of speech which is supremely Indian, intensely vivid, and conclusive.

"The weak are as great a danger for the strong, as quicksand, for an elephant. They do not assist progress because they do not resist. They only drag down."

The League of European Elephants is on the edge of Asian Quicksand – "Yet in the psychology of the strong no account is taken of "terribleness of the weak." The 'powers' on both sides of the Pacific have made a pact safeguarding them from one another: but Japan has under her feet the dangerous weakness of Korea.

This is the perilous position in which humanity stands today. It is summed up in a passage in "Creative Unity" which is not only literature at its highest (feeling and thinking with intensity), but is an admonition carried to highest of prophecy that cries on behalf of the repressed of all lands and ages, the doom, sooner or later, of one enemy of the human spirit, the spirit of greed which incarnates in the rapacious nations:

"Politicians calculate upon the number of nailed hands that are kept on the sword-hilts; they do not possess the third eye to see the great invisible hand that clasps in silence the hand of the helpless and waits its time. The strong form a league by a combination of powers, driving the weak to form their own league alone with their God. I know I am crying in the wilderness, when I raise the voice of warning; and while the West is busy with its organization of a machine-made peace, it will continue to nourish by its iniquities the underground forces of earthquake in the eastern continent. The West seems unconscious that Science, by providing it with more and more power, is tempting it to suicide and encouraging it to accept the challenge of the disarmed; it does not know that the challenge comes from a higher source."

What is the way of escape from the universal catastrophe that is inherent in these circumstances? It has moved by implication parallel with the foregoing considerations. The solid clear-edged path of constructive idealism is under every step of the poet's criticism – though with the sensitiveness of the artist, he refrains from the didactic summarisation of the obvious. He says,

"I have often been blamed for merely giving warning, and offering no alternative. When we suffer as a result of a particular system, we believe that some other system would bring us better luck. We are apt to forget that all systems produce evil sooner or later, when the psychology which is at the root of them is wrong ... And because we are trained to confound efficient system with moral goodness itself, every ruined system makes us more and more distrustful of moral law. Therefore, I do not put my faith in any new institution, but in the individuals all over the world who think clearly, feel nobly and act rightly, thus becoming the channels of moral truth."

Tagore's message, therefore, as summed up in this book, is addressed neither to thought which stultifies itself in systems nor to feeling which circumscribes and artificially intensifies itself in exclusive movements, but to that share of the Divine Being which every man or woman possesses in his and her personality. But the ends of personality are not fulfilled in appropriation and accumulation: these frustrate the purpose of life, the interplay of Personality on personalities.

"For us the highest purpose of this world is not merely living in it, knowing it and making use of it, but realising our own selves in it through expansion of sympathy: not alienating ourselves from it and dominating it but comprehending and uniting it ourselves with perfect union."

Two means at hand to this end are education and art; in the first, but in a different form and spirit from that obtainable in India today can be found a meeting ground between persons and groups of persons "where there can be no questions of conflicting interests," but only a common pursuit of truth and a common sharing of the world's sharing of culture: in the second is the means of attainment of expression, which is fulfillment.

"In everyday life our personality moves in narrow circle of immediate self-interest, and therefore our feelings and events, within that short range, become prominent subjects for ourselves. In their vehement self-assertion they ignore their unity with the All. But art gives our personality the disinterested freedom of the eternal, there to find it in its rue perspective."

Source: *The Modern Review*, Vol. XXXII, Nos 1–6, July to December 1922, pp. 66–70.

INDEX

Page numbers followed with "n" refer to footnotes.

For Product Safety Concerns and Information please contact our EU representative GPSR@taylorandfrancis.com
Taylor & Francis Verlag GmbH, Kaufingerstraße 24, 80331 München, Germany

www.ingramcontent.com/pod-product-compliance
Lightning Source LLC
Chambersburg PA
CBHW071118100726
47908CB00008B/2419

* 9 7 8 0 3 6 7 7 1 1 1 4 6 *